KT-592-249

TRUDI TATE

# Modernism, history
# and the First World War

MANCHESTER
UNIVERSITY PRESS

MANCHESTER AND NEW YORK

distributed exclusively in the USA by St. Martin's Press

Copyright © Trudi Tate 1998

The right of Trudi Tate to be identified as the author of this work has been asserted by her in accordance with the Copyright, Designs and Patents Act 1988.

*Published by* Manchester University Press
Oxford Road, Manchester M13 9NR, UK
*and* Room 400, 175 Fifth Avenue, New York, NY 10010, USA

*Distributed exclusively in the USA by*
St. Martin's Press, Inc., 175 Fifth Avenue, New York,
NY 10010, USA

*Distributed exclusively in Canada by*
UBC Press, University of British Columbia, 6344 Memorial Road,
Vancouver, BC, Canada V6T 1Z2

*British Library Cataloguing-in-Publication Data*
A catalogue record for this book is available from the British Library

*Library of Congress Cataloging-in-Publication Data applied for*

ISBN   0 7190 4999 7 *hardback*
       0 7190 5000 6 *paperback*

First published 1998

02   01   00   99   98        10   9   8   7   6   5   4   3   2   1

Typeset
by Northern Phototypesetting Co. Ltd, Bolton

Printed in Great Britain
by Bell & Bain Ltd, Glasgow

# CONTENTS

CONTENTS

## III  WAR AND POLITICS

# ACKNOWLEDGEMENTS

Many people have assisted me in the writing of this book. I am particularly grateful to Gillian Beer for her generous advice throughout the project and to Maud Ellmann for her encouragement and support. Thanks are due to Sue Cheshire, David Dickinson, Ian Donaldson, David Glover, Mike Hammond, Mary Jacobus, John Kerrigan, Vasant Kumar, Sarah Meer, Rod Mengham, Mark Micale, Peter Middleton, Ian Patterson, Lawrence Rainey, Suzanne Raitt, Karen Seymour, Helen Small, Hugh Stevens, Toni Tate, John Tate, Gill Thomas, Pam Thurschwell, David Trotter, Stephen Wall, and Jay Winter. The Modernism Seminar at the Centre for English Studies, London, has been a constant source of inspiration and debate; thanks to Claire Buck, Carolyn Burdett, Rebecca Dawson, Geoffrey Gilbert, and Lyndsey Stonebridge. The book could not have been completed without the intellectual generosity and warm support of Con Coroneos.

The staff of the University Library and English Faculty Library, Cambridge; the National Library of Scotland, Edinburgh; the Hartley Library, University of Southampton, and the Imperial War Museum photographic department have been unfailingly courteous and helpful. Darwin College, Cambridge, and the universities of Edinburgh and Southampton provided financial help with my research, and Clare Hall, Cambridge provided me with a Visiting Fellowship and a lively environment in which to complete the writing.

Portions of Chapter 1 were published in Sarah Sceats and Gail Cunningham, eds, *Image and Power* (London, Longman, 1996) and in Raitt and Tate, eds, *Women's Fiction of the Great War* (Oxford, Clarendon, 1997); a version of Chapter 2 was published in *Essays in Criticism* (1997); versions of Chapter 5 were published in *Modernism/Modernity* (1997) and *Women: A Cultural Review* (1997); a version of Chapter 6 was published in *Textual Practice* (1994). Permission to reproduce the plates in Chapter 5 was kindly granted by the Trustees of the Imperial War Museum, London.

# INTRODUCTION

In a scene excised from *The Years* (1937), Virginia Woolf describes a group of passengers sitting on the London Tube in 1914, desperate for news of the war.[1] 'Three British Cruisers Sunk', they read, and they scramble through the newspaper, looking for more information. But there is no more news, only 'items': triplets born, strawberries picked, 'that was all' (418). Twenty years after the event, Woolf remembers the First World War as a time of darkness and silence in which no one, including the combatants, knew what was going on nor why they were involved.[2] Whole nations found themselves bearing witness to events they did not understand and, by and large, could not see. Writing in 1915, Freud remarked that he was standing too close to the war to see it properly.[3] As time passed, many writers struggled to express what they had seen – or not seen – in the event that was to shape the history of the entire twentieth century.

This is a study of the relationship between modernist fiction, the First World War, and cultural history. It explores the ways in which writing attempted to bear witness to the trauma of the war and its consequences. All the works I will discuss are concerned with the distinction between witnessing and seeing, and they worry about how one is placed in relation to a history one has lived through but not seen, or seen only partially, through a fog of ignorance, fear, confusion, and lies.[4] This question troubled combatants as well as civilians,

---

1  Woolf, material excised from the galley proofs of *The Years* (1937), rpt in the appendix to *The Years*, ed. Hermione Lee (Oxford University Press, 1992), 414–66.
2  Woolf, *The Years*, 266.
3  Freud, 'Thoughts for the Time on War and Death' (1915), Pelican Freud Library 12, *Civilization, Society and Religion* (Harmondsworth, Penguin, 1985), 61.
4  Referring to the trauma of Nazism, Shoshana Felman argues that 'our era [is] an *age of testimony*, an age in which witnessing itself has undergone a major trauma'. Attempts to memorialise and document the events of the Shoah involved bearing witness without necessarily seeing; Felman also identifies the problem of people who saw but refused to bear witness. This seems right, but the problem had begun to emerge some twenty years earlier, in the First World War. Felman, 'In an Era of Testimony: Claude Lanzmann's *Shoah*', *Yale French Studies*, 79, *Literature and the Ethical Question* (1991), 41, 45.

and the chapters of this book read across a range of writings: by soldiers and nurses (Barbusse, Blunden, Remarque, Borden, Manning, and others) and civilians such as Woolf, HD, Lawrence, Kipling, and Faulkner. While the discussion focuses on literature produced in Britain during and after the war, it also looks at fiction from other countries which was influential in Britain: the best-selling soldiers' narratives of Barbusse (*Under Fire*, 1916) and Remarque (*All Quiet on the Western Front*, 1929), and *Soldiers' Pay* (1926), William Faulkner's first novel which appeared in Britain in 1930 and was championed as a war novel by Arnold Bennett. I am interested in the ways in which the different writings interact, and how they take up ideas which circulated in other, non-literary writings – in politics, medicine, psychoanalysis, propaganda, and in the newspapers.

One aim of this study is to rethink the ways we read modernism. The term itself is imprecise and much contested, yet it remains a useful description of writings which were self-consciously avant-garde or attempting to extend the possibilities of literary form in the late nineteenth and early twentieth centuries.[5] The formal and theoretical aspects of modernism have been closely analysed, but its place in the history of its own time has received surprisingly little attention.[6] Rarely is the fiction of Woolf or Lawrence read alongside the war memoirs of returned soldiers such as Blunden or Graves.[7] Yet modernists and war writers reviewed one another's books, and war writings were discussed in avant-garde journals such as the

---

5 Stan Smith, *The Origins of Modernism: Eliot, Pound, Yeats and the Rhetorics of Renewal* (Hemel Hempstead, Harvester, 1994); Peter Nicholls, *Modernisms: A Literary Guide* (Basingstoke, Macmillan, 1995); Michael Levenson, *A Genealogy of Modernism: A Study of English Literary Doctrine 1908–1922* (Cambridge University Press, 1984).

6 One recent phase of criticism effaces history altogether and reads modernism as a version of post-structuralism, producing some startling anachronisms. To take just one of many examples, Marianne DeKoven writes of 'Irigaray's Platonic paradigm' in Forster's Malabar caves, and 'Conrad's representation of the Irigarayan vaginal passage' in *Heart of Darkness. Rich and Strange: Gender, History, Modernism* (Princeton University Press, 1991), 185, 95. Despite its subtitle, this study has more to say about recent critical theory than about the history of modernism, including the First World War.

7 For detailed overviews of First World War writing in Britain, see Samuel Hynes, *A War Imagined: The First World War and English Culture* (London, The Bodley Head, 1990); Claire Tylee, *The Great War and Women's Consciousness: Images of Militarism and Womanhood in Women's Writings, 1914–64* (Basingstoke, Macmillan, 1990); Bernard Bergonzi, *Heroes' Twilight: A Study of the*

*Little Review* and the *Egoist*. Reading them together, the distinction between 'modernism' and 'war writing' starts to dissolve – and was by no means clear at the time – and modernism after 1914 begins to look like a peculiar but significant form of war writing.

Eric Hobsbawm argues that we cannot understand the events at the end of the twentieth century unless we know about its beginnings. This applies to literary history as well as to politics and international relations. The literature of the early twentieth century, both modernist and non-modernist, helps us to think about how cultures imagined themselves in this period of specific crisis.[8] Gillian Beer has shown that Woolf's modernism does not efface her predecessors so much as argue with them; this book seeks to show that Woolf and other modernists were arguing with their own present, too.[9] Modernist fiction often engages in lively debate with ideas and arguments taking place elsewhere in society, including in the newspapers. As Stan Smith has pointed out, even a writer as supposedly conservative and backward-looking as T. S. Eliot was responding to the political events around him. Smith demonstrates that *The Waste Land* has a good deal to say about the peace settlements and revolutions of 1919–21.[10]

---

*Literature of the Great War* (London, Constable, 1965). On the soldiers' narratives, see George Parfitt, *Fiction of the First World War* (London, Faber and Faber, 1988); Hugh Cecil, *The Flower of Battle: British Fiction Writers of the First World War* (London, Secker and Warburg, 1995).

8   J. M. Winter rightly points out that the war was commemorated in many different ways, some of which were looking back to nineteenth-century social conventions and not forwards or sideways to 'modernism'. Yet there is perhaps more dialogue between modernism and other cultural activities – including spiritualism – than Winter allows for in his argument. What interests me are the ways in which the literature, including modernism, actively engages with other acts of commemoration, memory, and analysis of the war. Winter, *Sites of Memory, Sites of Mourning*; Adrian Gregory, *The Silence of Memory: Armistice Day 1919–1946* (Oxford, Berg, 1994).

9   Beer, *Arguing with the Past: Essays in Narrative from Woolf to Sidney* (London, Routledge, 1989), 139–40, 156.

10  Smith, *The Origins of Modernism*, 128, 144–51; see also Maud Ellmann, *The Poetics of Impersonality: T. S Eliot and Ezra Pound* (Brighton, Harvester, 1987); Peter Middleton, 'The Academic Development of the Waste Land', *Glyph Textual Studies*, 1 (1986), 153–80; David Roessel, '"Mr. Eugenides, the Smyrna Merchant" and Post-War Politics in *The Waste Land*', *Journal of Modern Literature*, 16, 1 (1989), 171–6.

War, like writing, shapes perception. For Gertrude Stein, the Great War made modernism readable; it 'created the completed recognition of the contemporary composition'.[11] Modernism, like other writings of the period, attempts to make the war 'readable' and to write it into history. The First World War is often perceived as a complete break with the past. Yet it also represented a kind of imaginative continuity. Stein believed she had been conscious of war all her life. From the age of six to sixteen, this consciousness came not from experience, but from reading. 'During these years there was no war and if there was it was not any war of mine. But of course there was history, and there were novels historical novels and so there was in a way war all the time.'[12] Reading about war brought Stein a lot of pleasure, and in *Wars I Have Seen* (1945) she meditates on the place of war in the fantasy lives of civilians. Throughout her childhood and adolescence, she writes, there was no war 'outside of me', but it existed powerfully in her imagination. 'What is there inside in one that makes one know all about war' (9), she wonders. The answer, perhaps, is literature: 'as an omnivorous reader naturally there was a great deal of war'; reading brought 'romantic war', 'not to believe in but to dream' (9, 15).

How did people imagine themselves as subjects in a period of 'total war'? Did gender make a difference, or was gender itself perceived differently? This topic has been addressed by a number of studies of women's writings of the First World War.[13] But gender is only one aspect of subjectivity and of writing, and this book tries to develop a broader view. As I have argued elsewhere, we should perhaps be concerned that gender has, paradoxically, become rather a

11  Stein, 'Composition as Explanation' (1926), rpt in *Look At Me Now and Here I Am: Writings and Lectures 1909–45*, ed. Patricia Meyerowitz (Harmondsworth, Penguin, 1984), 28.

12  Stein, *Wars I Have Seen* (1945; London, Brilliance Books, 1984), 7.

13  Tylee, *The Great War and Women's Consciousness*; Sharon Ouditt, *Fighting Forces, Writing Women: Identity and Ideology in the First World War* (London, Routledge, 1994); Margaret Randolph Higonnet *et al.*, eds, *Behind the Lines: Gender and the Two World Wars* (New Haven, Yale University Press, 1987); Helen M. Cooper *et al.*, eds, *Arms and the Woman* (Chapel Hill, University of North Carolina Press, 1989); Lynne Hanley, *Writing War: Fiction, Gender and *mory* (Amherst, University of Massachusetts Press, 1991); Sandra Gilbert *usan Gubar, *No Man's Land*, vol. 2 (New Haven, Yale University Press, *orothy Goldman, ed., *Women and World War I: The Written Response *, Macmillan, 1993).

depoliticised focus for reading our culture and its history. It does not seem helpful to treat gender as the final point of inquiry, as if it provided the answers to questions about the war. We might also ask ourselves what we do not see when we focus upon gender and whether we need to question our critical assumptions rather more rigorously.[14] This study reads writings by women and men; pro- and anti-war writers; civilians, combatants, and a civilian who pretended to have been in combat. I am not trying to produce a taxonomy of war writings, nor to make a case for 'women's writing' or 'men's writing'; I am increasingly convinced that this kind of categorising obscures more than it illuminates. The works I discuss are preoccupied with questions of who has seen what, and how one is positioned in relation to war's trauma. Who is witness, and what is it that has been witnessed? Who has the right to speak, to oppose the war or to support it? How does the war affect the ways people think about their bodies, fragile in the face of modern weaponry? These concerns often far outweigh questions of gender or sexual difference.

This book focuses on narratives of the First World War and asks what happens to narrative when people find themselves surrounded by propaganda, bogus statistics, inaccurate news stories. This was a condition experienced by all writers of the period, many of whom were also propagandists.[15] The writings show signs of anxiety as writers face the fact that stories have been mobilised by all sides for the war effort; narrative, along with other forms of representation, is enlisted to prolong and justify mass slaughter. This is true of all wars, of course, but it reached a new level of intensity in the First World War when propaganda was organised 'scientifically' for the first time, especially in Britain. Widespread literacy made it easier to spread lies. This was a matter for concern during and after the First World War and remains a problem in wartime right up to the present day. It also raised serious questions about democracy, account-

14 Tate, introduction to *Women, Men and the Great War: An Anthology of Stories* (Manchester University Press, 1995); Suzanne Raitt and Trudi Tate, introduction to *Women's Fiction and the Great War* (Oxford, Clarendon, 1997).

15 Peter Buitenhuis, *The Great War of Words: Literature as Propaganda 1914–18 and After* (London, Batsford, 1989); Hynes, *A War Imagined*, ch. 2; Mariel Grant, *Propaganda and the Role of the State in Inter-War Britain* (Oxford, Clarendon, 1994); Helen Small, 'Mrs Humphry Ward and the First Casualty of War', in Raitt and Tate, eds, *Women's Fiction and the Great War*.

ability, and the possibility of rational decision-making. Modernism was never simply a celebration of the technologies of representation; nor of other technologies, notwithstanding the enthusiasms of the Futurists. The writings are often anxious about the uses to which representation and its technologies are put, from the newspapers which lie about the war to a vast readership to the development of new weapons technology – poison gas, aerial bombing, the tank.

Literary history, perhaps understandably, has never shown much interest in military hardware. But such objects sometimes occupy an important place in politics and culture. Like narratives, they can turn into cultural artefacts which, as Fredric Jameson points out, are always 'socially symbolic acts'.[16] Chapter 5 tries to understand what happened when a major new weapon was invented during the First World War, taking as its example the tank. How was it presented to the civilian public? What cultural significance did it have? The chapter provides a short cultural history of the tank, a highly visible new military object which was one of the few inventions of the war to be developed first in Britain. Its military value at the time was rather doubtful, but its cultural significance was immense. The tank was mobilised in a vigorous propaganda campaign in Britain in the latter part of the war, and the chapter traces the astonishing variety of representations and stories which surrounded it. The campaigns around the tank raised troubling questions about technology, democracy, and human agency; this too was part of the political and cultural context in which the writers were working, and to which their writing responds.

The book is in three parts. Part I examines the problem of bearing witness to the war which emerges in the writing of HD, Kipling, and Ford Madox Ford. All three writers were concerned, in different ways, with the trauma of war, and with how they were placed in relation to its events. HD and Kipling were civilians with relatives at the front;[17] Ford was a soldier. The war continued to be a source of anguish long after it had ended, and all three writers tried to

---

16 Jameson, *The Political Unconscious: Narrative as a Socially Symbolic Act* (London, Methuen, 1981), 20.
17 HD's husband, Richard Aldington, went to the war, as did her brother, who was killed in 1918. Kipling's son was killed at Loos in 1915.

express the mental suffering it caused for civilians as well as for soldiers. This took some strange forms, most notoriously in Kipling's 'Mary Postgate' (1915), the story of a woman who seems to take sadistic pleasure in witnessing the death of an airman. As the man dies, Mary feels 'an increasing rapture'. 'She ceased to think. She gave herself up to feel. [...] She leaned forward and listened, smiling. There could be no mistake. She closed her eyes and drank it in'.[18] The story has been interpreted in many ways and has even been treated as sociological evidence that women took pleasure in men's suffering.[19] But 'Mary Postgate' is not about a real event; Kipling made it up. The story is interesting precisely because it is not true. It indicates some of the ways in which the war was imagined in 1915, and hints at the perverse fantasies which might circulate among civilians. This part of the book also looks at two acute problems which developed during the war: the emergence of war neurosis (popularly known as shell shock) and the widespread use of propaganda, reading the literature against the medical, political, and journalistic writings which addressed these matters at the time.

Part II examines the ways in which bodies are figured in writings of the First World War, looking at narratives of soldiers and nurses alongside the work of two non-combatants, Lawrence and Faulkner. Like every war, the First World War produced specific kinds of physical injury, and Chapter 3 traces how these are represented by writers who saw and imagined the terrible sights produced by the new technologies of war. The combatants' narratives attempt to write a kind of history of the war, but what also emerges is their interest in the war as a place of fantasy. History and fantasy meet in highly unsettling ways around the image of the injured soldier, and Chapter 4 examines representations of soldiers who return from the war with visible injuries – figures which are used in the writings to rethink the meaning of bodily difference. These are analysed alongside Freud's theorising of sexual difference from the same period, and the chapter argues that we need to pay closer attention to the historical context in which Freud was writing.

Part III is concerned with the political consequences of the war, and traces the anxieties which arise around agency, responsibility,

18  Kipling, 'Mary Posgate', in *A Diversity of Creatures* (1917; Harmondsworth, Penguin, 1987), 355.
19  Gilbert, 'Soldier's Heart', in Gilbert and Gubar, *No Man's Land*, vol. 2, 288–9.

and notions of citizenship in Britain during and after the war. Chapter 5 examines these matters in the writings and representations which surrounded the tank. Chapter 6 takes Woolf's *Mrs Dalloway*, one of the most 'aesthetic' of modernist novels, and asks what it has to say about its historical moment. The chapter argues that the novel is partly a satire on certain aspects of the postwar settlements and on British domestic politics in the early 1920s. The book also raises questions about what is remembered, and what forgotten, both at the time and in subsequent readings. Our inability to see the history and politics at work in much modernist writing is itself a perplexing question for our own time.

# I

# Witness to war

# 1

# War neurotics

I N AUGUST 1914, the expatriate modernist poet HD learned that she was pregnant.[1] In May 1915, the baby was stillborn – killed, HD believed, by the Great War. Shortly before the birth, HD had been shocked by the news that the passenger ship *Lusitania* had been sunk with 1200 civilian casualties. Whether medically true or not, HD's view that the war indirectly killed her child is a significant and by no means unusual response. It suggests a direct relationship between violent public events and the private lives of civilians during wartime; for HD, civilians, like soldiers, could suffer from crippling war neuroses – an idea which recurs throughout her war writing. Her fiction raises compelling questions about how civilians are placed as witnesses to, or victims of, war's trauma. Similar questions arise in the writing of Rudyard Kipling, and I will discuss 'Mary Postgate' at the end of the chapter.

Is HD's view of her lost child specifically a woman's response to the Great War, or a feminist protest that the violence of war has permeated even the most private of spaces, the unborn child in the womb? Perhaps, yet HD's work resists precisely this kind of rigid gendering. Rather, she explores the peculiar effects of trauma on both women and men, and the uneven ways in which the war penetrates civilian society. She does this through her representations of

1 For biographical information on HD, see Barbara Guest, *Herself Defined: The Poet H.D. and her World* (London, Collins, 1985); Susan Stanford Friedman, *Psyche Reborn: The Emergence of H.D.* (Bloomington, Indiana University Press, 1987); Friedman, *Penelope's Web: Gender, Modernity, H.D.'s Fiction* (Cambridge University Press, 1990); Rachel Blau duPlessis, *H.D.: The Career of that Struggle* (Brighton, Harvester, 1986); Friedman and duPlessis, eds, *Signets: Reading H.D.* (Madison, University of Wisconsin Press, 1990). On HD's writing of the Second World War, see Susan Edmunds, *Out of Line: History, Psychoanalysis, and Montage in H.D.'s Long Poems* (Stanford University Press, 1994).

war neurosis: a disorder usually associated with soldiers, and commonly, if inaccurately, known as 'shell shock'.[2]

## Civilian war neuroses

*Did* civilians suffer from war neuroses during the Great War? The medical journal *The Lancet* did not think so at the beginning of the war. As late as September 1915, it was arguing that no one, whether soldier or civilian, would suffer any long-term mental problems as a result of the conflict. Indeed, it claimed, because civilian neuroses were caused largely by boredom, the excitement of the war ought to make them diminish, if anything. For civilians, *The Lancet* argued, 'the spectacle of millions of men abandoning home, family, ambition, money, and laying down their lives for a principle is so glorious as to transfigure "the pictures of mangled bodies and human beings gasping in their dark struggle against death"'.[3] (The quotation comes from the superintendent of a lunatic asylum.) The term 'spectacle' is striking here. Soldiers – men – are seen to have a symbolic function; their bodies form a grotesque 'picture' whose meaning transcends and redeems its own horror. Civilians do not see this 'picture', of course: they imagine it. And when civilians actually did imagine some of the horrible sights of the Great War, they became susceptible to war neuroses, as *The Lancet* found itself reporting only a few weeks later. A woman was admitted into Leicester Mental Hospital as a direct result of war news: five of her seven sons at the front had been wounded. The Dorset County Asylum reported that 'stress was frequently a well-recognised cause of

2 For the history of the term 'shell shock', see for example Harold Merskey, 'Combat Hysteria', in *The Analysis of Hysteria* (London, Baillière Tindall, 1979), 37–9; Merskey, 'Shell Shock', in G. E. Berrios and H. Freeman, eds, *150 Years of British Psychiatry, 1841–1991* (London, Gaskell, 1991), 248–55.

3 'Insanity and the War', *The Lancet*, 4 September 1915, 553. Hysterical breakdown among soldiers was in fact documented as early as December 1914; recognition of the condition was uneven in the profession, and there was considerable debate as to whether war neuroses were primarily physical or psychological in origin. See Chris Feudtner, '"Minds the Dead Have Ravished": Shell Shock, History, and the Ecology of Disease-Systems', *History of Science*, 31, 4 (1993), 377–420, 384. F. W. Mott argued as late as 1919 that the war created no new neuroses; it simply exposed the existing weaknesses. Mott also believed that heredity was an important factor in soldiers' war neuroses. Mott, *War Neuroses and Shell Shock* (London, Hodder and Stoughton, 1919), 111–12, 30.

mental breakdown, and that not a few cases were associated with the war, both among the wives of soldiers and young recruits'.[4] By March 1916, *The Lancet* had come to accept the reality of civilian war neuroses, arguing: 'While the stress of war on the soldier is discussed, it should not be forgotten that the nervous strain to which the civilian is exposed may require consideration and appropriate treatment.'[5] Even in Britain, symptoms of war shock among civilians were 'by no means uncommon'.

Eventually the idea of non-combatant war neurosis was commonplace enough to be the subject of a mild joke; in February 1918, *The Lancet* drew attention to a court case about the sale of some dubious milk: 'The defendant claimed that the milk reached the consumer exactly as it came from the cows, but it was drawn at a time when there was an air raid and the animals were suffering from shell shock.' The defence was unsuccessful, and the dealer was fined. None the less, *The Lancet* declared, 'there can be little doubt that such a defence might well be valid', for, like humans, cows are susceptible to stress or fright, which can impair the quality of their milk.[6]

Civilian war neuroses appeared in other medical writings during and after the war. In *Shell Shock and its Aftermath* (1926), Norman Fenton argues:

> The nervous effects of war strain on civilians is brought out by Redlick [in a 1915 article], who, studying them during the war, frequently found insomnia among peasants, who had never before known anything of sleeplessness, dreams about war disturbing their sleep. Variations in body temperature and modifications in heart action without

---

4 'Incidence of Mental Disease Directly Due to War', *The Lancet*, 23 October 1915, 931. See also Eric Leed, *No Man's Land: Combat and Identity in World War I* (Cambridge University Press, 1979). Feudtner notes that C. Stanford Read's study, *Military Psychiatry in Peace and War* (London, H. K. Lewis, 1920) found that nearly 25 per cent of war-neurotic soldiers in one hospital had not been to the front line. Feudtner also points out that this kind of breakdown became more common as the war progressed. '"Minds the Dead Have Ravished"', 386, 412 n. 20, 413 n. 35. See also Ruth Leys' fascinating work on psychoanalysis and war neuroses, 'Traumatic Cures: Shell Shock, Janet, and the Question of Memory', *Critical Inquiry*, 20, 4 (1994), 623–62; 'Death Masks: Kardiner and Ferenczi on Psychic Trauma', *Representations*, 53 (1996), 44–73.
5 'War Shock in the Civilian', *The Lancet*, 4 March 1916, 522.
6 'Shell Shock in Cows', *The Lancet*, 2 February 1918, 187–8.

apparent adequate cause were also common occurrences among the civilians Redlick studied.[7]

Clearly, British civilians suffered much less direct violence than French civilians in the battle zones. But they were subject to trauma none the less. Edwin Ash's propagandistic book, *The Problem of Nervous Breakdown* (1919), argues that British civilians showed tremendous stability of nerve during the war; the terror of attack served to strengthen the 'national nerve'; like steel, it has been tempered by the 'experiences of red-hot war in our midst'. Even as Ash invokes an unshakeable 'British nerve' (the opposite, it seems, of British 'nerves'), he acknowledges that civilians were susceptible to neurotic symptoms. He goes on to claim that, while civilian neuroses existed during the war, they were generally similar to the neuroses of peacetime. None the less, there were cases in which 'complete mental imbalance occurred, and stricken persons became deluded into the false belief that they were pursued by spies, or suspected of spying, or being persecuted by the Government in various mysterious ways'.[8] In other words, war neuroses were *not* always the same as peacetime neuroses: some were specific to the experience of the war, whether real or fantasised. It is also worth noting that a sense of being mysteriously persecuted was not always a delusion. As Phillip Knightley points out, many people were wrongly arrested and persecuted as spies during the First World War.[9] Finally, Ash admits that civilians subjected to mechanical violence, such as bombing raids, often exhibited symptoms like those of 'shell-shock of the battlefield' – 'loss of voice, paralysis, [...] sleeplessness, terrifying dreams' and so forth.

We find, then, that the idea of civilians suffering from war neuroses was by no means unknown during the Great War, and it turns up in a number of works of fiction, such as Rebecca West's *The Return of the Soldier* (1918), in which the civilian narrator suffers from war-neurotic dreams about the trenches. In Rose Macaulay's

---

7 Norman Fenton, *Shell Shock and its Aftermath* (London, Henry Kimpton, 1926), 149.

8 Edwin Ash, *The Problem of Nervous Breakdown* (London, Mills and Boon Ltd, 1919), 274–5.

9 Phillip Knightley, *The First Casualty: The War Correspondent as Hero, Propagandist, and Myth Maker from the Crimea to Vietnam* (London, Andre Deutsch, 1975).

*Non-Combatants and Others* (1916), a returned soldier talks in his sleep 'like a little child, like a man on the rack' about the horrible sights of war. His sister hears him and begins to suffer from hallucinations, 'seeing her friends in scattered bits, seeing worse than that, seeing what John had seen'.[10] A Canadian woman in Ford's *Parade's End* is 'bedridden at the news' that two of her sons have been killed in the war.[11] F. Scott Fitzgerald refers bluntly to 'non-combatant war neuroses' in *Tender is the Night* (1934). In *The Three Hostages* (1924), John Buchan suggests that shell shock is in fact more prevalent among civilians than among soldiers; a doctor in the novel makes the bizarre claim that 'in spite of parrot talk about shell shock, the men who fought suffer less from it on the whole than other people. The classes that shirked the war are the worst.'[12] In Arnold Bennett's *Lord Raingo* (1926), two civilian women are driven mad by air raids. Bennett himself became extremely ill and depressed after he visited the front in June 1915; Buitenhuis argues that his symptoms were partly a psychic response to the war.[13]

Later work on what is now called 'post-traumatic stress disorder'[14] draws explicit parallels between civilian disaster survivors and combat veterans: their symptoms, it is argued, are often remarkably similar. Survivors of war, floods, earthquakes, rape, the atomic bombs, and the Nazi concentration camps often exhibit similar traumatic symptoms.[15] In *Beyond the Pleasure Principle*, published not long after the end of the war, Freud noted the similarities between civilian survivors of railway disasters and shell-shocked

10 Rose Macaulay, *Non-Combatants and Others* (1916; London, Methuen, 1986), 18, 21.
11 Ford Madox Ford, *Parade's End* (1924–8; Harmondsworth, Penguin, 1982), 336.
12 John Buchan, *The Three Hostages* (1924; Harmondsworth, Penguin, 1953), 13.
13 Peter Buitenhuis, *The Great War of Words: Literature as Propaganda 1914–18 and After* (London, Batsford, 1989), 80.
14 This term emerged after the Vietnam War. Harvey Schwartz, ed., *Psychotherapy of the Combat Veteran* (Lancaster, MTP Press Ltd, 1984), xi; Cathy Caruth, introduction to *Trauma: Explorations in Memory* (Baltimore, Johns Hopkins University Press, 1995), 3–5.
15 Bruce I. Goderez, 'The Survivor Syndrome: Massive Psychic Trauma and Post-traumatic Stress Disorder', *Bulletin of the Menninger Clinic* (Kansas), 51, 1 (1987), 97.

soldiers.[16] Civilians exposed to violence and terror, whether public and shared (railway accidents, floods, war) or individual and private (rape), can suffer from serious traumatic symptoms. Direct experience of pain, loss of autonomy, and fear of mutilation or death can produce mental disturbance, often expressed in the body, for many years afterwards.

Does this help us to understand HD's view that her child was killed by the trauma of war? If the shock had been caused by the air raids on London, for example, then the models of war neuroses or post-traumatic stress disorder might readily be applied. But HD's case is striking precisely because it is *not* a response to direct violence. 'I had lost the first [child] in 1915', she remembered many years later, 'from shock and repercussions of war news broken to me in a rather brutal fashion.'[17] It was a story which did the damage. The death of her brother at the war in 1918 contributed to HD's anxieties; the bereavement was thought to have contributed to the death of her father shortly afterwards.[18] Similarly, Katherine Mansfield was haunted by the news of her brother's death, and found she could not stop herself imagining the sights of war. 'I keep seeing all these horrors', she wrote in 1918, 'bathing in them again and again (God knows I don't want to) and then my mind fills with the wretched little picture I have of my brother's grave. What is the meaning of it all?'[19]

HD wrote about her memories of the Great War and the death of her first child many times throughout her life.[20] In *Asphodel*, an early memoir of the war years, she states bluntly of the protagonist's stillborn child: 'Khaki killed it.'[21] In a letter to Norman Holmes

16  Freud, *Beyond the Pleasure Principle* (1920), Pelican Freud Library 11 (Harmondsworth, Penguin, 1984), 281; Merskey, 'Shell Shock', 246–7.
17  HD, *Tribute to Freud*, rev. edn (Manchester, Carcanet, 1985), 40.
18  Susan Stanford Friedman, *Penelope's Web: Gender, Modernity, H.D.'s Fiction* (Cambridge University Press, 1990), 63.
19  Katherine Mansfield, letter to Ottoline Morrell, November 1918, rpt in *The Critical Writings of Katherine Mansfield*, ed. Clare Hanson (Macmillan, Basingstoke, 1987), 32.
20  See Gary Burnett, *H.D. Between Image and Epic: The Mysteries of her Poetics* (Ann Arbor, UMI Research Press, 1990); Burnett, 'A Poetics out of War: H.D.'s Responses to the First World War', *Agenda*, 25, 3–4 (1988), 54–63.
21  HD, *Asphodel*, ed. Robert Spoo (Durham NC, Duke University Press, 1992), 108.

Pearson in 1937, she wrote: 'In order to speak adequately of my poetry and its aims, I must you see, drag in a whole deracinated epoch. Perhaps specifically, I might say that the house next door was struck another night. We came home and simply waded through glass, while wind from now unshuttered windows, made the house a barn, an unprotected dug-out.'[22] This might be the 'carnage on Queen's Square' imagined in *Bid Me to Live*. Though the damage to London was minor compared with the devastation of the battle-fields, it had a profound effect on those who lived through the aerial bombardments – the first of their kind in Britain.[23] 'What does that sort of shock do to the mind, the imagination', HD wrote to Pearson, '– not solely of myself, but of an epoch?' (72). Her analysis with Freud, she wrote some years later, was partly to gain skills which might help 'war-shocked and war-shattered people' from the Great War in the period leading up to the next war.[24]

In 'Magic Mirror', an unpublished memoir written in the 1950s, HD remembers receiving the news of the *Lusitania*, recounting the memory through the characters of Rafe and Julia in *Bid Me to Live* (originally entitled 'Madrigal'): 'Rafe Ashton (though not so stated in Madrigal) destroyed the unborn, the child Amor, when a few days before it was due, he burst in upon Julia of that story, with "don't you realize what this means? Don't you feel anything? *The Lusitania has gone down.*"'[25] We should be cautious about accepting this at face value, however, as Friedman notes: 'Here and later in a repetition of this memory, H.D. added to the typed manuscript the pencilled words: "(But this never happened. Surely this was fantasy.)"'[26] HD's memories of the war were written and rewritten over a period of more than forty years, the act of writing itself compounding them with fantasy. Fantasy might be constituted differently from the memory of real events, but it can be equally

22  HD, letter to Norman Holmes Pearson, ed. Diana Collecott, *Agenda*, 25, 3–4 (1988), 72.

23  These are described in a strange, uneasy scene in Woolf's *The Years* (1937). See Gillian Beer's discussion of aeroplanes and air raids in Woolf's writings: 'The Island and the Aeroplane: The Case of Virginia Woolf', in Homi Bhabha, ed., *Nation and Narration* (London, Routledge, 1990), 265–90.

24  HD, *Tribute to Freud*, 93. See also Claire Buck, *HD and Freud: Bisexuality and A Feminine Discourse* (Hemel Hempstead, Harvester, 1991).

25  HD, 'Magic Mirror' (1955), quoted in Susan Stanford Friedman, *Psyche Reborn*, 29.

26  *Psyche Reborn*, 301 n. 20.

disturbing. As time passes, the distinction between real and fantasised memories can become blurred. But whatever its source, HD's
response to the news of the *Lusitania* provides some useful insights
into her thinking about the war. The sinking of the *Lusitania*
became one of the great scandals of the war, forcing civilians in
Britain (and to some extent in the United States) to realise that they
too were serious targets.

## The sinking of the *Lusitania*

In February 1915, Germany established a submarine blockade
around the entire United Kingdom, which then included all of Ireland.[27] Any vessel in this zone was declared to be a legitimate target,
subject to attack without warning. A major imperial struggle took
place at sea, as each nation attempted to cripple the other's economy and to starve out its civilians. This was a significant factor, it is
argued, in Britain's eventual victory.[28]

On 1 May 1915, the *Lusitania* departed from New York, carrying nearly two thousand passengers and a secret cargo of war munitions for Britain. A number of passengers had received letters and
telegrams, warning that the ship was likely to be attacked. The
morning that it sailed, the *New York Tribune* published a notice
from the Imperial German Embassy in Washington, warning that all
ships entering the war zone were at risk of being destroyed. These
warnings were ignored, however, and the ship sailed. At about 2
p.m. on 7 May, a German U-boat torpedoed the *Lusitania* as it
passed by the south coast of Ireland. A second explosion, caused
either by the munitions cargo or by one of the ship's engines, fol-

---

27 For this discussion, I have drawn upon the following historical accounts:
Thomas A. Bailey and Paul B. Ryan, *The Lusitania Disaster: An Episode in Mod-
ern Warfare and Diplomacy* (New York, The Free Press, 1975); Des Hickey and
Gus Smith, *Seven Days to Disaster: The Sinking of the Lusitania* (London,
Collins, 1981); Edwyn A. Gray, *The Killing Time: The U-Boat War 1914–18*
(London, Seeley, Service and Co., 1972); C. L. Droste, *The Lusitania Case*, ed.
W. H. Tantum (1916; London, Patrick Stephens Ltd, 1972); Colin Simpson,
*Lusitania* (London, Longman, 1972), as well as reports from *The Times* and the
*Manchester Guardian*, 8–15 May 1915. The newspaper reports are not at all
reliable, however, and I have not used these for factual information.
28 Civilian morale is considered to have been an essential factor in the outcome of
the war. See for example John Turner, ed., *Britain and the First World War*
(London, Unwin Hyman, 1988), 5.

lowed a few seconds later. The attack was not planned, as it happens, but this was not known at the time. Within twenty minutes, the ship, which was 790 feet long, had completely sunk. Incompetence, confusion, and cost-cutting by the shipping company meant that crew did not know how to use the life-boats properly. The *Lusitania* was sinking rapidly at an angle, which made their task even more difficult. Passengers were crushed by falling life-boats and killed trying to get off the ship; others were drowned. Bodies were washed up on the Irish coast for several days afterwards. Some were buried in mass graves; others were returned to the United States. (The corpses of the first-class passengers were embalmed before being sent back.) The newspapers printed pictures related to the disaster every day for about a week afterwards. In all, nearly 1200 passengers and crew died; all of them civilians. Around 198 of the dead were American citizens – neutrals at this stage of the war. One passenger went into labour when the ship began to sink; both she and the baby were drowned.

Though the event had little military significance, the sinking of the *Lusitania* became a key symbol in the British propaganda campaign to bring the United States into the war. It was widely reported in all the British papers, with outraged commentary about German barbarism. *The Times* for example called it an outrage, a crime, a wholesale massacre, and an action of diabolic character,[29] and devoted several pages to the story every day for about a week (running alongside its rather positive reports of the disastrous Gallipoli campaign). The British papers reported that the sinking of the *Lusitania* was crassly celebrated in Germany: a story which was generally untrue, but which was used by propagandists to revive civilian support for the war.[30] It was an important issue within the United States, too, and was frequently cited during the presidential campaign of 1916. When the US entered the war on Britain's side in April 1917, the *Lusitania* was seen by many people as a key factor in this decision. (In Willa Cather's war novel, *One of Ours*, one of

29  *The Times*, 10 May 1915, 5.
30  For details of the propaganda campaigns around the *Lusitania*, see Arthur Ponsonby, *Falsehood in War-Time* (London, George Allen and Unwin, 1928); H. C. Peterson, *Propaganda for War: The Campaign Against American Neutrality, 1914–1917* (Princeton University Press, 1939), ch. 5; Trevor Wilson, *The Myriad Faces of War* (Cambridge, Polity, 1986), 735.

the American characters cites three reasons for enlisting: 'Belgium, the Lusitania, Edith Cavell'[31] – all represented in newspapers and propaganda as cases of violated 'femininity'.) However, the *Lusitania* was less the *cause* than the *justification* of the American entry into the war: its function was imaginary or ideological.

But this is precisely its importance in our understanding of HD's response it. As I have already argued, it is well established that civilians, like soldiers, will suffer from war neuroses if they are subjected to violence. HD takes this point further, however, to suggest that violent events can cause physical or psychic shock *even to people who are not present*. Witnessing such events at a distance, or being exposed to them indirectly, discursively, through stories, can cause war neuroses, just as some soldiers suffered from shell shock without ever going into battle. In other words, HD's response to the sinking of the *Lusitania*, like her writings about the First World War, suggest that the stories which circulate in a society can damage people's bodies, or send them mad.

It is this imaginary effect of war that HD addresses in her war fiction. I want to look at two of her prose works about the Great War: 'Kora and Ka', a short story about a man who is still suffering from the war in the late 1920s, and *Bid Me to Live*, a novel about a woman's war experiences during 1917. Both stories deal with the problem of being a witness – indirectly – to the violence of the war,[32] and both ask how this interacts with structures of gender. But neither work posits a simple parallel between gender and violence; nor does it suggest that 'the war at home is also a war in the home'.[33] We need to resist the urge to find simple parallels or causal relationships between gender conflict and military conflict.[34] Nor am I

---

31  Willa Cather, *One of Ours* (1922; London, Virago, 1987), 236. See also Wilson, *Myriad Faces of War*, 190.

32  Questions about the difference between witnessing and seeing arise even more intensely in the Nazi holocaust: see Shoshana Felman, 'In an Era of Testimony: Claude Lanzmann's *Shoah*', *Yale French Studies*, 79, *Literature and the Ethical Question* (1991), 39–81; Shoshana Felman and Dori Laub, *Testimony: Crises of Witnessing in Literature, Psychoanalysis, and History* (London, Routledge, 1992).

33  Friedman, *Penelope's Web*, 139.

34  Here, my argument is directly opposed to Sandra Gilbert's reading of the war as a metaphorical 'battle of the sexes'. 'Soldier's Heart', in Sandra Gilbert and Susan Gubar, *No Man's Land: The Place of the Woman Writer in the Twentieth Century*, vol. 2 (New Haven, Yale University Press, 1989).

LIVERPOOL JOHN MOORES UNIVERSITY
LEARNING SERVICES

convinced that HD is trying to define 'women's experience' or 'women's consciousness' of the Great War. Rather, her works explore how femininity is constituted in relation to the war. Furthermore, HD's writing also recognises masculinity as a tenuous and contested construction; here her war fiction can productively be read alongside the soldiers' narratives by Aldington, Barbusse, Blunden, Graves, Manning, and Remarque. (These works are discussed below in Chapter 3.) Neither femininity nor masculinity emerges as a single, unproblematic structure in her fiction; nor does she set up masculinity as the 'cause' of war, as some later critics have suggested.

'Kora and Ka' is a particularly interesting story in this context: a work written by a woman which explores a man's reactions to the Great War. Like *Bid Me to Live*, this story demonstrates that the collective trauma of war spreads far beyond its immediate time and place, and can have a profound effect on the lives of both women and men.

## HD's war fiction

'Kora and Ka' was completed in 1930 and published privately in 1934.[35] It is a strange, impenetrable piece of writing and a striking study of the effect of war neuroses in the decade following the war.[36] 'Kora and Ka' has two main characters: Kora, a woman who has left her husband and children, and John Helforth, the man she lives with now. (The name John Helforth was also one of HD's writing pseudonyms, under which she published a short novel entitled *Nights*, in 1935.) Helforth suffers from the delusion that his mind has been occupied by a 'Ka' – a spirit from Egyptian mythology

35  'Kora and Ka' and 'Mira-Mare' (Dijon, Darantière, 1934); rpt in Bronte Adams and Trudi Tate, eds, *That Kind of Woman: Stories from the Left Bank and Beyond* (London, Virago, 1991). Page numbers cited are from this edition.

36  For the history of war neuroses, see Martin Stone, 'Shellshock and the Psychologists', in W. F. Bynum, Roy Porter and Michael Shepherd, eds, *The Anatomy of Madness: Essays in the History of Psychiatry*, vol. 2 (London, Tavistock, 1985); Eric Leed, *No Man's Land*; Ted Bogacz, 'War Neurosis and Cultural Change in England, 1914–22: The Work of the War Office Committee of Enquiry into "Shell-Shock"', *Journal of Contemporary History*, 24, (1989), 227–56; Elaine Showalter, *The Female Malady: Women, Madness and English Culture, 1830–1980* (London, Virago, 1987).

which lives on after the body has died. The story is narrated by Helforth in two interwoven voices: his own, and the Ka's. This makes it difficult to follow, partly because it is a representation of a nervous breakdown, narrated from within.

The story opens with a struggle between Helforth and the imaginary spirit as it tries to take over his mind. The struggle is centred on the act of looking, an act which is mentioned many times in the first few pages of the story. 'Helforth must see everything', we are told, but his eyes trouble him. He suffers from hallucinations, some of them very like Septimus' visual delusions in *Mrs Dalloway*. At work he sees the undermanager 'as under layers of green water, violet-laced'; the figures in his ledger shine 'violet-laced, nine, six, up through transparent seaweed' (188). He decides to see a doctor, and hallucinates as the doctor tries to test his eyes. The doctor asks him to read from a printed chart:

> As the huge page loomed before Helforth, he felt himself grow smaller. Helforth felt himself draw away, back and back, the length of the doctor's room and out of the wall behind it. Helforth became Helforth, minute at the minimizing other-end of an opera-glass. [...]
>
> A globe rather like the shape of the Venetian glass that Kora had set on the table last night, again reminded Helforth that man was a microbe. He saw a world like a drop of water and himself enclosed in it. (189)

The doctor diagnoses 'nerves' and recommends that Helforth stop working. But work is not the cause of his nervous disorders, though this does not become clear until half-way through the story. Helforth's illness dates from the war, some ten years earlier, and its symptoms are uncannily similar to war neuroses: hallucinations, a sense of dissociation, loss of certainty about his sexual identity. What is so striking about this, however, is that Helforth has not in fact been a soldier; his distress arises not from battle experience, but from the lack of it.

Out of the confusing chronology of the story and Helforth's disordered mind, one thread clearly emerges: his memory of the war. Both of his older brothers went to the front and both have been killed. Helforth was meant to avenge them, but the war ended before he was old enough to enlist. He blames their mother. 'Mother could have kept Larry at home,' he says:

I was too young. Larry was of course vicious to have told me, in precise detail, all that he did. It was a perverse sort of sadism. I loved
Larry. I would have gone on, loving men and women if it hadn't been
for Larry. How could I love anyone after Larry? My mother used to
say, 'Bob would have been too noble-minded to have regretted Larry.'
Bob? But Bob went that first year, dead or alive he was equally obnox-
ious. He was the young 'father', mother's favourite. I was sixteen. By
the time I was ready, the war actually was over. Mother reiterated on
every conceivable occasion, 'Larry is only waiting to get out there.' I
don't know what mother thought 'there' was. It was so near. It was
'here' all the time with me. Larry was sent to avenge Bob, I was to be
sent to avenge Larry. It was already written in Hans Anderson [sic], a
moron virgin and a pitcher. We were all virgin, moron. We were virgin, though Larry saw to it that I was not. Larry. (197)

Larry has initiated Helforth into various kinds of adult experiences,
providing him with an identity as a bisexual man – an identity he
values, and wants to maintain.[37] But when Larry is killed, war stories and sex stories become confused, and Helforth regresses into an
angry, infantile state, raging against his dead brothers, his mother,
Kora's children.

War-neurotic soldiers often suffered from regression. In an
essay published in 1920, Maurice Nicoll described a number of case
studies; one soldier regressed to the age of twelve, and then to the
age of five, then relived his own life up to his departure for the war.
Another regressed into very young infancy, becoming 'as much a
tyrant as a baby', and demanding to be fed every two hours.
Responding to the war through regression, wrote Nicoll, 'is the
exact opposite of adaptation by progression, the psychic movement
being inwards, away from the level of reality-consciousness,
towards a level of phantasy-consciousness. The movement may be
slow or sudden; it may be arrested early or it may go so far that the
patient becomes blind, deaf, dumb, and quadriplegic or psychically

---

37  HD was very interested in the possibilities of bisexual identities around the
    time that she was writing 'Kora and Ka'. Her male lover of that period was
    Kenneth Macpherson, a bisexual whom HD's lesbian companion, Bryher, had
    married in 1927. When HD consulted with Freud, around the time that the
    story was published, she reported to Bryher that Freud described her as the
    'perfect bi–'. See duPlessis, H.D., 83, 144 n. 20; Friedman and duPlessis,
    Signets, 227.

infantile, or both.'[38] The war neurotic is trying to run away from the war, not physically, '*but psychically*', writes Nicoll; one way of doing this is to relive his '*ontogenetic development*'.[39]

Where combatants often tried, unconsciously, to escape the war through illness, HD suggests that civilian men might flee into illness for the opposite reason – to enter the war and share its suffering. Helforth also tries to assert an unambiguous masculinity within the household, but it rapidly fragments into hallucination and despair:

> I will to be John Helforth, an Englishman and a normal brutal one. I will strength into my body, into my loins. [...] I insist on masculinity and my brutality. (194–5)

> I have meant to be robust; I have meant to smash furniture. I find myself seated on the low rush-bottomed arm-chair. I beat my hands on its sides [...] I say 'when are we going back? I can't stay here forever.' It is her [Kora's] turn, at this moment, to retaliate, she does not. Then I sway. Ka is coming [...]. I hear a voice, it is only Kora but still I say, 'Ka shan't get me.' [...] I go on, I say, 'cow', I say, 'mother, mother, mother.' Then I fling myself down, anywhere, head on the table, or head that would beat through the wooden floor to the rooms that lie beneath it, 'Larry'. (195–6)

Helforth is dangerous and self-destructive, like a severely disturbed child. He is undergoing psychoanalysis for his problems, and he is encouraged to speak about them with Kora. He blames his mother for the death of his brother Larry (199). 'Kora says my attitude is fantastic' – that is, a product of fantasy – 'and linked up with mother-complex' – another symptom found among war-neurotic soldiers.[40] Helforth disagrees:

> I say I do not think so. I explain it lucidly, as if she herself were a complete outsider, and herself had never heard of that war. I demonstrate

---

38  Nicoll, 'Regression', in H. Crichton Miller, ed., *Functional Nerve Disease* (London, Henry Frowde, 1920), 102–5; Leys, 'Traumatic Cures', 633. W. H. R. Rivers argues that some war neurotics, like children, cannot distinguish between real and fantasised experiences. *Instinct and the Unconscious*, 2nd edn (Cambridge University Press, 1922), 151.

39  Nicoll, 'Regression', 102; italics in original.

40  H. Crichton Miller described twenty-eight examples of combatant 'mother-complexes', speculating that it might be a factor in more than 20 per cent of war-neurotic cases. Miller, 'The Mother Complex', in *Functional Nerve Disease*, 115–28.

how, systematically, we were trained to blood-lust and hatred. We were sent out, iron-shod to quell an enemy who had made life horrible. That enemy roasted children, boiled down the fat of pregnant women to grease cannon wheels. He wore a spiked hat and carried, in one hand, a tin thunder-bolt and, in the other, a specialised warrant for burning down cathedrals. He was ignorant and we were sent out, Galahad on Galahad, to quell him. His men raped nuns, cut off the hands of children, boiled down the entrails of old men, nailed Canadians against barn doors ... and all this we heard mornings with the Daily Newsgraph and evenings with the Evening Warscript. The Newsgraph and the Warscript fed [our] belching mothers, who belched out in return, fire and carnage in the name of Rule Britannia. (199)[41]

Helforth speaks as if he were an ex-soldier, explaining the war to a civilian. He tells Kora horrible tales from the war, but they are instantly recognisable not as real atrocities, but as famous (and untrue) propaganda stories from the newspapers: raped nuns, mutilated children, crucified Canadians.[42] Atrocity propaganda aimed to produce support for the war, as I will discuss in Chapter 2. British propaganda was extremely successful, generating the 'right' kind of disgust and hatred, and rekindling civilian interest in the war. Yet HD suggests it might also have another effect, producing a profound kind of sickness – a war-neurotic response to stories which were simply unbearable to imagine, and which displaced stories of real suffering. More than this: 'Kora and Ka' raises questions about true and false stories of the war, exploring the ways in which civilians are placed, distant from the actual events, and unable to tell the difference.

As a young man, Helforth equates manhood with soldiering. But the war ends before he is old enough to go, locking him into a state of eternal childhood – 'a small lout in my mother's drawing-room' (195) – struggling against a sense of guilt and the imaginary power of his now-absent mother, for whom Kora is partly a substitute. Helforth's war fantasies lead him into a war-neurotic 'mother-complex'. He sees the newspaper stories as feeding monstrous

41 Robert Spoo corrects 'out' to 'our' here in his recent edition of 'Kora and Ka' (New York, New Directions, 1995). The original published version has 'out'.
42 Peter Buitenhuis, *The Great War of Words: Literature as Propaganda 1914–18 and After* (London, Batsford, 1989); Ponsonby, *Falsehood in War-Time*; Arthur Marwick, *The Deluge: British Society and the First World War*, 2nd edn (Basingstoke, Macmillan, 1991); Philip M. Taylor, *Munitions of the Mind*, rev. edn (Manchester University Press, 1995), ch. 21.

women ('belching mothers') who in turn produce more propaganda ('fire and carnage') to keep the war going. 'I did not realise,' he says later, 'that *nothing* depended on me, that a row of aunts was choros out of Hades, that the "family" was only another name for warfare and sacrifice of the young' (200) – an idea which also animates Mary Butts' story of young men damaged by the war, 'The Golden Bough' (1923). Some of Helforth's hatred is directed towards Kora, too, a mother who has left her husband and children to be with him. Kora misses her children, which makes Helforth jealous and resentful.

Perhaps the most striking aspect of this passage is Helforth's use of 'we'. If he is a man, he must have experienced the war; if not in reality, then in fantasy. For the war isn't just 'out there', but is '"here" all the time', in Helforth's head. His identity keeps merging with the dead men he has loved, to the point that he feels he really has shared their war experiences. He fantasises about his own body in pieces, his feet as amputated lumps (185), his face seared away. These fantasies challenge familiar representations of war as a shared masculine 'truth' – an idea satirised, particularly, through the use of images from propaganda. It also reminds us that there was no single masculine experience of war. Despite the vast mobilisation, the majority of British men were actually civilians, and found themselves located in an odd position in relation to the discourses of soldiering and masculinity.[43] In 'Kora and Ka', HD suggests that some men enacted a masquerade of masculinity, imitating the illnesses of men at war.

*Bid Me to Live* was written and revised during the late 1930s and 1940s, but not published until 1960, shortly before HD died.[44] It is

43  Approximately six million British men (12.5 per cent of the male population) served in the war. This includes mechanics, cooks, medical workers, and many other non-fighting members of the armed forces. J. M. Winter, *The Experience of World War I* (Oxford, Equinox, 1988) 119; Eric Hobsbawm, *Age of Extremes: The Short Twentieth Century, 1914–1991* (1994; London, Abacus, 1995), 44.

44  Friedman, *Penelope's Web*, 364. The introduction to the 1984 Virago edition dates the writing of the novel incorrectly. For a detailed discussion of *Bid Me to Live* as a war novel see Claire Tylee, *The Great War and Women's Consciousness: Images of Militarism and Womanhood in Women's Writings, 1914–64* (Basingstoke, Macmillan, 1990).

a survivor's account of the First World War, written and revised in the years surrounding the Second. The novel focuses on one character: a civilian woman named Julia who suffers from war neuroses. The novel also traces specific ways in which the war permeated civilian lives during 1917, from the direct experience of the Zeppelin raids on London,[45] to the indirect and imaginary effects of battles taking place out of sight – in the sea off Cornwall, for example, or in France, where Julia's husband Rafe is a soldier. (The central characters are based closely on HD and her husband Richard Aldington, from whom she became estranged during the war.[46]) The war is also felt through the presence of a 'multitude' of soldiers in London: 'heroic angels' who are really doomed men, waiting to face injury, madness, and death.[47]

The war transforms the city of London, both physically and imaginatively. Zeppelins, frightening figures out of science fiction, appear like whales in the sky:

> Superficially entrenched, they were routed out by the sound of aircraft; she stumbled down the iron stairs (that was the Hampstead flat) and bruised her knee. Just in time to see the tip-tilted object in a dim near sky that even then was sliding sideways and even then was about to drop. Such a long way to come. It drifted from their sight and the small collection of gaping individuals dispersed. Leviathan, a whale swam in city dusk, above suburban forests. (11)

At this stage of the novel, Julia and Rafe are both living as civilians

---

45 The early Zeppelins were extremely vulnerable, but by 1917 the Germans had developed an improved airship which flew at high altitudes and was difficult to shoot down, 'rendering obsolete the entire British air defence system'. Guy Hartcup, *The War of Invention: Scientific Developments, 1914–18* (London, Brassey's Defence Publishers, 1988), 158–60. Compared with attacks on civilians during the Second World War, the air raids during the Great War killed a very small number of people. But we should not underestimate their imaginary effects; for the first time, British civilians found themselves targets of a war which was actually being fought elsewhere. It was also the first time that civilians came under attack from the air, and was much more terrifying than the low casualty figures might suggest. See also Wilson, *Myriad Faces*, 509–10.

46 *Richard Aldington and HD: The Early Years in Letters*, ed. Caroline Zilboorg (Bloomington, Indiana University Press, 1992); *Richard Aldington and HD: The Later Years in Letters*, ed. Caroline Zilboorg (Manchester University Press, 1995).

47 HD, *Bid Me to Live* (1960; London, Virago, 1984), 123, 126. Subsequent references are to this edition.

in London, reading, writing, working on their Greek translations. Their similar occupations suggest equality and perhaps harmony between a woman and a man,[48] but the city they inhabit has become unsettled and is threatening violence. The war will transform London into a place of dread and emptiness:

> City of dreadful night, city of dreadful night. She saw the railed-in square, the desolation of the empty street. It was a city of the dead. There were no lights visible in the blocks of walls that surrounded them, iron balconies gave on to the square and the plane-trees stood stark metal. They lifted metallic branches to a near sky that loomed now with a sudden spit of fire. A volcano was erupting. Along streets empty of life, there were pathetic evidences of life that had once been, an ash-tin, a fluttering scrap of newspaper, a cat creeping stealthily, seeking for stray provender. Ashes and death; it was the city of dreadful night, it was a dead city. (109)

There are obvious echoes of T. S. Eliot in this passage – another non-combatant whose work is complexly engaged with the effects of the First World War[49] – as well as direct references to James Thomson's poem, 'The City of Dreadful Night' (1874). The city is represented as stark, dry, and empty – unlike the war zone, which we know to be muddy and full of bodies, both dead and alive.

In *Paint it Today*, the city at war is depicted as a sinking ship (in another echo of the *Lusitania*, perhaps): 'Small city railings splintered and city parks infested with a black trail of livid, wretched creatures who shivered against each other as the crash came nearer. Who woke as from a dream when distant rumblings died away, and scurried like black rats fleeing the sinking wreck, washing up on the pavements.'[50]

When the Zeppelin ('Leviathan') in *Bid Me to Live* attacks the city, Julia receives a minor injury as she runs for shelter. The very insignificance of the injury directs us towards a more important

---

48  This works against Gilbert's claim that women inevitably felt liberated by the war, and is closer to the lament, found in much writing of the period, that the war destroyed culture and civilisation, for women as well as for men. .

49  Stan Smith, *The Origins of Modernism* (Hemel Hempstead, Harvester, 1994), ch. 7.

50   HD, *Paint it Today*, ed. Cassandra Laity (New York University Press, 1992), 45. The narrator of this strange and awkward novel says that the post-war 'convalescence' is 'even more painful' than the war itself (67). *Paint it Today* was written in 1921. Friedman, *Penelope's Web*, 141, 362.

aspect of the passage, in which Julia imagines such a fall with a child in her arms. 'Suddenly, [...] her mind, which did not really think in canalized precise images, realized or might have realized that if she had had the child in her arms at that moment, stumbling as she had stumbled, she might have ... No. She did not think this. She had lost the child only a short time before' (11–12). Like HD, Julia has lost a newborn child during the war, and she has the peculiar sense that the war will kill the child for a second time.

At the end of this scene, Rafe decides to enlist. This decision takes Rafe and Julia into separate worlds, where gender difference and the distinction between combatant and civilian seem to be identical. When Rafe returns later, now an officer on leave, Julia realises that they have both been completely changed by their separate war experiences. He is no longer the same person she married (16); he is a stranger, 'not-Rafe' (45), an uncanny presence who looks like her husband but is somehow not the same. Rafe has been altered by his experience of being a soldier, while Julia has been changed by the loss of her child. At the beginning of the book, Julia sees the experiences as parallel, and resents being told about the men's suffering. 'I spared you what I went through,' she thinks, but 'you did not spare me. I did not tell you; my agony in the Garden had no words' (46). Such a loss, she argues, is specific to women, kept in the private sphere, with no shared language to express it – unlike the suffering of war, which Rafe has tried to describe to her.

Is this an example of the 'battle of the sexes' which critics such as Sandra Gilbert find running as a counter-narrative to the war?[51] Is Julia cast as Rafe's victim; is this a novel about women's suffering at the hands of men? It seems to me that from the very first paragraph, *Bid Me to Live* problematises precisely these issues:

> Oh, the times, oh the customs! Oh, indeed, the times! The customs! Their own, specifically, but part and parcel of the cosmic, comic, crucifying times of history. Times liberated, set whirling out-moded romanticism; Punch and Judy danced with Jocasta and Philoctetes, while wrestlers, sprawling in an Uffizi or a Pitti, flung garish horizon-blue across gallant and idiotic Sir Philip Sidney-isms. It was a time of isms. And the Ballet.

51 Gilbert, 'Soldier's Heart'. For a detailed critique of Gilbert's argument, see Claire Tylee, '"Maleness Run Riot": The Great War and Women's Resistance to Militarism', *Women's Studies International Forum*, 11, 3 (1988), 199–210.

They did not march in classic precision, they were a mixed bag. Victims, victimised and victimising. Perhaps the victims came out, by a long shot, ahead of the steady self-determined victimisers. (7)

Out of a nightmarish vision of history, flung out of chronology into an anachronistic, violent dance (Punch and Judy, Jocasta and Philoctetes), the relationship between victim and victimiser is rendered uncertain. Who is the victim, who the oppressor, in this scene? It is by no means clear, and remains ambiguous, despite the sympathetic focus on Julia, throughout the novel. Julia and Rafe – woman and man; civilian and soldier – are simultaneously victim and victimiser, in their marriage, in the war, and in their relationships with others. To complicate matters further, Rafe has volunteered for the war; is he simply its victim?[52] Rather than reading *Bid Me to Live* as an expression of sex warfare, or as a competition in suffering, I would argue that the novel shows how the war, as both experience and discourse, interpellates women and men differently, constructing them differently as gendered subjects.

But the difference is endlessly modified by other structures of power and difference. When Rafe comes home on leave, for example, he dreams about the war and mutters about ghastly sights in his sleep.[53] Rafe is suffering from a mild form of war neurosis, an illness which makes him seem even more of a stranger to Julia. The difference between woman and man, soldier and civilian, seems to extend even into the unconscious. But this structure is disrupted only a few pages later, when Julia wakes from a brief sleep with a 'muddle of poisonous gas and flayed carcasses' in her head (39). These are Rafe's nightmares which have spilled into her unconscious, just as traces of poisonous gas are transferred from his body into hers when they kiss (39). Rigid distinctions between woman and man, civilian

---

52  Richard Aldington enlisted because he feared – with good reason – that he would soon be conscripted. Conscription was introduced for single men in January 1916 and for married men in May 1916. Zilboorg, *Richard Aldington and H.D.*, 21; John Gooch, 'The Armed Services', in Stephen Constantine, Maurice Kirby and Mary Rose, eds, *The First World War in British History* (London, Edward Arnold, 1995), 189.

53  Horrible sights were recognised as early as 1916 as a cause of war neuroses among soldiers, as Harold Wiltshire argued in the *Lancet*, citing examples of men suffering from shell shock when they witnessed 'fellows in pieces' or a trench 'like a butcher's shop'. Wiltshire, 'A Contribution to the Etiology of Shell Shock', *Lancet*, 17 June 1916, 1208.

and soldier, are broken down even as they are invoked. Traces of the horror faced by soldiers overflow into civilian lives, just as HD believed that the distant suffering of the *Lusitania* victims had a concrete effect upon her body, and killed her child.

As the war progresses, Julia too begins to suffer from war-neurotic symptoms, dissociated from her surroundings, at times on the verge of madness. She is most disturbed by big groups of soldiers in London, men 'who might be ghosts to-morrow, the latest vintage (1917) grapes to be crushed' (119). She goes to the cinema and is surrounded by soldiers. The narrative interweaves images from the film with Julia's vision of the crowd of doomed men. Fragments of the soldiers' song 'Tipperary' are scattered throughout the scene as Julia alternates between seeing the men as objects – spectacles – and identifying with them.

The film they are watching involves a long and rapid car journey down a mountain:

> She was part of this. She swerved and veered with a thousand men in khaki, toward destruction, *to the sweetest girl I know*. But no. A swift turn, a sudden slide of scenery, a landslide of scenery projected the car, its unknown mysterious driver onto a smooth road. He was rushing along a level road, such a road as lines the waterways outside Venice, on the way to Ravenna. Was he rushing to Ravenna? Where was this? It was outside, anyway. *Good-bye Piccadilly, good-bye Leicester Square*. They were all rushing toward some known goal. (123–4)

Watching the soldiers from above, Julia feels she is 'gazing into a charnel-house, into the pit of inferno', as the men sing with the 'voices of heroic angels, surging on toward their destruction, *pack all your troubles in your old kit bag and smile, smile, smile*' (126).

Like 'Kora and Ka' and HD's memory of the sinking of the *Lusitania*, *Bid Me to Live* is concerned with the problem of being a witness to the slaughter of war – but a witness who does not actually *see* the worst of what happens. As a witness, Julia can only imagine what the soldiers have to face. She is exposed to the war discursively, through stories and fantasies of the men's suffering. How can the trauma of war be represented? Does HD, a woman, civilian, and survivor, have the right to write of such things? Her war writings are troubled by these questions, torn between guilt and self-righteousness; staking a civilian claim to war experience – and suffering – yet helplessly aware of the greater suffering of the combatants. Powerlessness in the face of others' suffering – whether witnessed or imagined – was a significant cause of war neuroses in both civilians and soldiers during the Great War.

Yet *Bid Me to Live* also contains some remarkably callous moments. When Rafe and Julia remember seeing and touching a Michelangelo statue before the war, Julia thinks: 'Yes – that was it, the very touch of the fingers of Michelangelo had been transferred to theirs. Their feet, their hands were instilled with living beauty, with things that were not dead. Other cities had been buried. Other people had been shot to death and something had gone on. There was something left between them.' (72) Julia wavers between compassion and indifference – or even, as here, a perverse kind of pleasure – in the distant suffering of others.

Julia is a civilian war neurotic. Like Helforth, she suffers from dissociation, unsure of the limits and function of her own body, and struggling to place her life story within the larger narratives of history. Yet at times the experience of dissociation is strangely pleasurable, as she sees the world as 'magic lantern slides' (174), and wishes she could live in two dimensions (175). Where Helforth regresses into infancy and 'mother-complex', Julia meditates on her own maternity, both lost and potential, retreating (in a striking echo of Lawrence) into an imaginary space which she calls the *gloire*. 'I want to explain', she writes to Rico (the Lawrence figure in the novel),[54] 'how it is that the rose is neither red nor white, but a pale *gloire*':

> Perhaps you would say I was trespassing, couldn't see both sides, as you said of my Orpheus. I could be Eurydice in character, you said, but woman-is-woman and I couldn't be both. The *gloire* is both.

54 On HD's relationship with Lawrence see Carol Siegel, *Lawrence Among the Women: Wavering Boundaries in Women's Literary Traditions* (Charlottesville, University of Virginia Press, 1991); Helen Sword, 'Orpheus and Eurydice in the Twentieth Century: Lawrence, H.D., and the Poetics of the Turn', *Twentieth Century Literature*, 35, 4 (1989), 407–28; Peter E. Firchow, 'Rico and Julia: The Hilda Doolittle–D. H. Lawrence Affair Reconsidered', *Journal of Modern Literature*, 8, 1 (1980), 51–76; Jane Gledhill, 'Impersonality and Amnesia', 178–82; see also Paul Delany, *D. H. Lawrence's Nightmare: The Writer and his Circle in the Years of the Great War* (Hassocks, Harvester, 1979).

No, that spoils it; it is both and neither. [...]
The child is the *gloire* before it is born. The circle of the candle on my notebook is the *gloire*, the story isn't born yet.
While I live in the unborn story, I am in the gloire.
I must keep it alive, myself living with it. (176–7)

This is a profoundly unsettling moment in the novel, as Julia imagines escaping from the war into a utopian, maternal space. The scene could perhaps be read as an attempt to offer another kind of cultural imaginary – a feminine (or feminist) alternative to the culture which produced the trauma of the Great War. But I find this interpretation unconvincing. While Julia mediates privately on the *gloire*, the war continues; millions more will suffer and die before it is over. Her mediation cannot change this; nor will it help to prevent another, larger war which was to prove much more disastrous for civilians – as HD knows very well when she completes the novel in the late 1940s. If anything this scene functions as a challenge to theories which seek to analyse war simply in terms of gender.

Throughout her writings, HD explores and often dissolves the boundaries of subjectivity. At the same time, her war fiction represents subjects (Julia, Helforth) who are threatened to the point of severe neurosis by the war's reshaping of subjectivity. Not all transgressions of boundaries are liberating, for women or for men.

## Kipling, 'Mary Postgate'

One of the earliest works of fiction to allude to the idea of civilian war neuroses is Rudyard Kipling's story 'Mary Postgate', published in September 1915 and described at the time as 'the wickedest story ever written'.[55] Kipling was an active supporter of the war, mainly through his work as a propagandist. The precise nature and extent of his propaganda work is still uncertain, but, according to Buitenhuis, 'The evidence suggests that Kipling did write propaganda quite often at the request of various government departments'.[56] His son John went to the front with the Irish Guards and went missing

---

55 'Mary Postgate', published September 1915; rpt in *A Diversity of Creatures* (1917; Harmondsworth, Penguin, 1987). Page references are to this edition.
56 Buitenhuis, *The Great War of Words*, 184 n. 4.

in action on his first day of battle. His body was never found.[57] Kipling's attitude towards the war changed profoundly and he spent the rest of his life commemorating and making reparation to the dead.[58] A number of his later stories look sympathetically at shell-shocked soldiers after the war: 'The Janeites', 'A Madonna of the Trenches', 'A Friend of the Family'.

'Mary Postgate' is considered by many critics to express Kipling's rabid loathing of the Germans at this stage of the war. Buitenhuis calls it 'the most vivid testament of hatred to come out of England in the Great War' (108); he also notes that the story was published not long after the notorious Bryce Report on German atrocities in Belgium – much of it 'a tissue of invention, unsubstantiated observations by unnamed witnesses, and second-hand eyewitness reports' (27). Trevor Wilson comments that 'The first half of 1915 was a special time of hate in Britain. For in this phase of the war atrocity-mongering reached its peak.'[59] The scandals of Edith Cavell and the *Lusitania* occurred in the same year. 'Mary Postgate' intervenes in the hysterical responses to these events, occupying an uneasy position somewhere between 'literature' and 'propaganda', and positing a violent and strangely sexualised civilian response to the war.

Mary Postgate is a lady's companion who has raised Wynn, her employer's nephew, from an unlovely boyhood. Wynn joins the Flying Corps and is killed in training. After his funeral, Mary destroys all his personal possessions in a fire which will 'burn her heart to ashes' (352). While she is doing this, she finds a German airman who seems to have fallen out of a plane into the garden. He is badly injured and begs for help, but Mary refuses, and watches him die. The most disturbing aspect of this story is the pleasure – a 'secret thrill' of sexual ecstasy – she takes in his suffering. What are we to

---

57  Harold Orel, *A Kipling Chronology* (Basingstoke, Macmillan, 1990), 59; Angus Wilson, *The Strange Ride of Rudyard Kipling* (London, Secker and Warburg, 1977), 303–4. Sandra Gilbert speculates that 'Mary Postgate' might be an expression of Kipling's 'guilt' over the death of his son; this seems unlikely since John died after the story was written. *No Man's Land*, vol. 2 (New Haven, Yale University Press, 1989), 289.

58  Buitenhuis, *The Great War of Words*, 169–71. Kipling was an Imperial War Graves Commissioner for eighteen years. He also researched and wrote *The Irish Guards in the Great War* (1923).

59  Wilson, *The Myriad Faces of War*, 182.

make of this? A number of critics have argued that Mary Postgate suffers from delusions. The airman, in this reading, is simply an hallucination – an interpretation which diminishes the story's horror and perhaps makes it more palatable to postwar readers.[60] This reading is oddly persuasive, even though the text provides no supporting evidence. It might be argued that Mary Postgate is suffering from civilian war neuroses, caused by her grief at the death of the boy she has loved. This would explain her strange behaviour. Yet it seems to me that, unlike HD's war writings, the story is not really interested in the clinical problem of civilian war neuroses, which were just becoming recognised at the time it was written. Rather, the depiction of Mary Postgate might be read as a complex act of displacement. Its representations of neurotic behaviour perhaps function in ways which were not possible in the years following the war, when civilian war trauma was taken much more seriously.[61] Mary Postgate might be a war neurotic, but the precise form and meaning of her neurosis remain ambiguous.

For Mary Postgate, 1914 brings a war which, 'unlike all wars that Mary could remember, did not stay decently outside England and in the newspapers, but intruded on the lives of people whom she knew' (342). When the war begins, Wynn joins the flying Corps and is killed in training. Mary is delegated to organise the funeral, and finds herself entering 'a world where bodies were in the habit of being despatched by all sorts of conveyances to all sorts of places' (346). There are strong hints that Mary is in love with her young

60  This is argued most forcefully by Norman Page in 'What Happens in "Mary Postgate"?', *English Literature in Transition*, 29, 1 (1986), 41–7. 'Mary is assuredly the victim of a hallucination'; 'the airman never existed outside her own mind'; her suspicion that she has heard a plane is 'unequivocally [...] without foundation' (44). It seems to me that the story is actually equivocal on all these matters. For a range of different readings of this story, see for example Peter E. Firchow, 'Kipling's "Mary Postgate": The Barbarians and the Critics', *Etudes Anglaises*, 29, 1 (1976), 27–39; Angus Wilson, *The Strange Ride of Rudyard Kipling*; Clare Hanson, 'Limits and Renewals', in Phillip Mallett, ed., *Kipling Reconsidered* (Basingstoke, Macmillan, 1989).

61  Sandra Kemp notes that Kipling's postwar stories represent a number of characters with war neuroses. *Kipling's Hidden Narratives* (Oxford, Blackwell, 1988), 72. Kemp argues that war neuroses are 'surprisingly similar to the nervous disorders of peacetime'; the medical history suggests that this is not quite correct.

charge, but she cannot cry over his death; instead, she feels 'angry with the Germans' (347), even though Wynn has been killed in England.

Miss Fowler decides to give away Wynn's clothes and asks Mary Postgate to burn all his personal possessions in the destructor. Before lighting the fire, Mary fetches some paraffin from the village. As she walks, she imagines she can 'almost' hear the noise of a plane (349). She stops to talk with the village nurse, 'when a gun, they fancied, was fired immediately behind the house' (the Royal Oak public bar), 'followed by a child's shriek dying into a wail'.

> 'Accident!' said Nurse Eden promptly, and dashed through the empty bar, followed by Mary. They found Mrs Gerritt, the publican's wife, who could only gasp and point to the yard, where a little cart-lodge was sliding sideways amid a clatter of tiles. Nurse Eden snatched up a sheet drying before the fire, ran out, lifted something from the ground, and flung the sheet round it. The sheet turned scarlet and half her uniform too, as she bore the load into the kitchen. It was little Edna Gerritt, aged nine, whom Mary had known since her perambulator days. (350)

Edna dies 'between Nurse Eden's dripping hands'. 'The sheet fell aside and for an instant, before she could shut her eyes, Mary saw the ripped and shredded body.' Edna is transformed from a child into 'it' – an object lifted from the ground, a 'load'. Three women witness the death: Mary, Nurse Eden, and Edna's mother, who immediately faints.

> 'What in God's name was it?' [asked Nurse Eden].
> 'A bomb,' said Mary.
> 'One o' the Zeppelins?'
> 'No. An aeroplane. I thought I heard it on the Heath, but I fancied it was one of ours.' (350)

Mary fetches the doctor, who instructs her not to tell anyone what she has seen 'till we're sure' (351). A short while later, he informs her that the accident has been caused not by a bomb, but by the stable falling down:

> 'It's been dangerous for a long time. It ought to have been condemned.'
> 'I thought I heard an explosion too, ' said Mary.

'You might have been misled by the beams snapping. I've been look-ing at 'em. They were dry-rotted through and through. Of course, as they broke, they would make a noise just like a gun.'

'Yes?' said Mary politely.

'Poor little Edna was playing underneath it,' he went on, still hold-ing her with his eyes, 'and that and the tiles cut her to pieces, you see?'

'I saw it,' said Mary, shaking her head. 'I heard it too.' (351)

Could a falling building cause such a violent assault on a child's body? And what has Mary seen and heard: a gun, a bomb, or an old stable collapsing? Dr Hennis insists that no bomb has fallen. But he is a special constable whose job it is to maintain civilian morale and to suppress stories of German attack; his view needs to be treated with some suspicion.

When Mary returns home, she does not tell Miss Fowler about Edna Gerritt's death. Unprompted, Miss Fowler remarks that she has heard two planes pass overhead (351) at about the time the sta-ble fell down. So perhaps there *was* a plane. Or perhaps it is mass hysteria – or civilian war neuroses – among the women of the vil-lage: Mary and Miss Fowler hearing phantom aeroplanes; Mary and Nurse Eden imagining the explosion of a gun or bomb. The coincidence of two sets of hysteria on the one day seems unlikely, but the story keeps open the possibility that the strange events are war-neurotic hallucinations. But then the fantasy of the aeroplane seems to be true after all, for, when Mary returns to continue her task of burning Wynn's possessions in the destructor, she finds an injured man sitting by a tree. He seems to have fallen from a plane:

By [the fire's] light she saw [...] a bareheaded man sitting very stiffly at the foot of one of the oaks. A broken branch lay across his lap – one booted leg protruding from beneath it. His head moved ceaselessly from side to side, but his body was as still as the tree's trunk. He was dressed – she moved sideways to look more closely – in a uniform something like Wynn's, with a flap buttoned across the chest. (352)

Who is he?

For an instant, she had some idea that it might be one of the young [English] flying men she had met at the funeral. But their heads were dark and glossy. This man's was as pale as a baby's, and so closely cropped that she could see the disgusting pinky skin beneath. His lips moved.

'What do you say?' Mary moved towards him and stooped.

'Laty! Laty! Laty!' he muttered, while his hands picked at the dead wet leaves.

Now: 'There was no doubt as to his nationality' (352). From his haircut and peculiar speech, Mary Postgate judges the man to be a German aviator and the person responsible for Edna Gerritt's death. The man is fatally injured. He never speaks German, but a combination of oddly spelt French and English ('Laty [...] Cassée. Tout cassée [...] Che me rends. Le médecin! Toctor!'). It is perhaps reasonable to interpret this as a German accent, but the text never actually confirms that his uniform, his haircut, his pink scalp, or his odd speech are in fact German – or even that he has fallen from a plane. This uncertainty makes what follows particularly disturbing.[62]

Mary threatens the man with a gun, 'a huge revolver with flat-nosed bullets, which latter, Wynn said, were forbidden by the rules of war to be used against civilised enemies'. The women have acquired this 'terrible machine' 'after reading certain Belgian reports' – propaganda about German atrocities in Belgium, such as the Bryce Report (353).[63] Though Mary knows how to use the gun, she makes no attempt to kill the man; indeed, she is bizarrely 'careful to keep her finger off the trigger for fear of accidents' (353). The man is badly injured, and asks for a doctor.

'Stop that!' said Mary, and stamped her foot. 'Stop that, you bloody pagan!'

The words came quite smoothly and naturally. They were Wynn's own words, and Wynn was a gentleman who for no consideration on earth would have torn little Edna into those vividly coloured strips and strings. But this thing hunched under the oak-tree had done that thing. It was no question of reading horrors out of newspapers to Miss Fowler. Mary had seen it with her own eyes on the 'Royal Oak' kitchen table. (354)

Whether the man under the tree is responsible for Edna's death is

---

62  David Trotter has argued that the story is organised around disgust – Mary Postgate's revulsion at a foreigner with 'pinky skin'. *The English Novel in History* (London, Routledge, 1993), 250. This seems right, but the story is even more disgusted, it seems to me, by Mary Postgate herself. See also Trotter's discussion of torture in Kipling.

63  When the story was published, most readers would not have known that the atrocity stories were largely untrue.

never proven, but Mary takes her revenge: she will not kill him, but neither will she fetch help. She simply waits and watches him die under the tree. She becomes more repulsive as the scene proceeds, 'her underlip caught up by one faded canine, brows knit and nostrils wide'. Physically, she begins to turn into an animal, baring a tooth like a dog; flaring her nostrils like a camel.[64] Psychically, she becomes a kind of man, holding the gun and identifying with Wynn; at the same time she becomes more of a woman, suddenly aligning herself with the idea of 'woman's work':

> She had never believed in all those advanced views – though Miss Fowler herself leaned a little that way – of woman's work in the world; but now she saw there was much to be said for them. This, for instance, was *her* work – work which no man, least of all Dr Hennis, would ever have done. A man, at such a crisis, would be what Wynn called a 'sportsman'; would leave everything to fetch help, and would certainly bring It [the man] into the house. Now a woman's business was to make a happy home for – for a husband and children. Failing these – it was not a thing one should allow one's mind to dwell upon – but –'
> (354–5)

As the man suffers, Mary feels 'an increasing rapture'. 'She ceased to think. She gave herself up to feel. [...] She leaned forward and listened, smiling. There could be no mistake. She closed her eyes and drank it in' (355). When the man finally dies, Mary Postgate 'drew her breath short between her teeth and shivered from head to foot' – an image interpreted by many readers as a moment of orgasm – followed by '"*That*'s all right," said she contentedly.' Her contentment is followed by more self-indulgence: she returns to the house, 'where she scandalized the whole routine by taking a luxurious hot bath before tea, and came down looking, as Miss Fowler said when she saw her lying all relaxed on the sofa, "quite handsome!"'.

The airman's death seems to have awakened Mary Postgate's dormant sexuality, an idea which the story finds fascinatingly disgusting. Mary Postgate could be read as a civilian war neurotic who takes obscene pleasure in the suffering of others. In allowing the man to die, she enters the war as a kind of combatant, telling herself that her own side – represented by Wynn – would never have

---

64 Mary Postgate is likened to animals several times in the the story. She looks like a camel; Wynn calls her 'you old beast', and 'you dowey old cassowary'.

committed the action which killed Edna Gerritt (quoted above). This is true in its most literal sense: Wynn is unlikely to kill a civilian on his own side (though this does happen in war, usually but not always by accident). But, as a member of the Flying Corps, his training is precisely for the purpose of turning people into 'vividly coloured strips and strings'. Mary's peculiar behaviour might be caused by the terrible sight of the injured child's body *and* by the unconscious recognition that British airmen are enacting similar violence on other bodies elsewhere. More than this: her encounter with Dr Hennis suggests that her own side might be lying or suppressing the truth. For many civilians, the realisation that one's nation might be immoral or duplicitous was profoundly disturbing, as Freud noted in 'Thoughts for the Time on War and Death', published in the same year as Kipling's story.[65] 'Mary Postgate' also raises doubts about the official stories of war – the propaganda aimed at civilians such as Mary Postgate which Kipling himself wrote.

The war has come out of the newspapers and into civilian lives. But it takes a very curious form: a single man under a tree who may or may not have dropped a bomb on their village. Even as 'the war' seems to take a tangible form for the civilians in the story, it becomes more ambiguous and unknowable. And the civilians are even less certain of their own position in the war; are they legitimate targets? What actions can they take? Are they entitled to accurate information, or should they be protected from the facts for their own good (as Dr Hennis seems to think)?

'Mary Postgate', like HD's war writing, explores the ways in which the Great War permeated civilian lives and generated civilian war neuroses. However, where HD explores the uneasy positioning of civilians as absent witnesses, Kipling's story brings the war into the centre of civilian lives, turning them into active participants. Witnessing in 'Mary Postgate' is transformed into sexual hysteria; an excess of 'femininity' irrupting in the body of an apparently sexless woman. Much of the visible violence of the story occurs on female bodies: Edna's violent death, Mary Postgate's sinisterly controlled 'orgasm'. What is unseen for women in HD's war writing is

65 'Thoughts for the Time on War and Death' (1915), *Civilization, Society and Religion*, Pelican Freud Library 12 (Harmondsworth, Penguin, 1985), 61–2, 66.

not only seen but enacted by the women in Kipling's story. Similarly, in 'Swept and Garnished' (1915), Kipling imagines German guilt over alleged war atrocities in Belgium through the fantasies of a civilian woman. Frau Ebermann is suffering from influenza and is visited by five Belgian children – dirty, bleeding – killed in the German invasion. Here, too, Kipling is ambiguous; the hallucinations might be caused by a fever rather than by war-neurotic guilt.

In 'Mary Postgate', women's patriotism is displaced into a form of perverse sexuality – dangerous, disgusting, yet compelling. The disturbing figure of Mary Postgate might also be read as a projection, allowing Kipling to explore some of the uncertainties surrounding the patriotic myths and propaganda of 1915. Mary Postgate's obscene pleasure seems to function as a metaphor for a number of profound anxieties of this phase of the war – about the effects of propaganda, the mounting casualty figures, the possibility that Britain might lose the war, the sense that the war will never end. It is also an oddly displaced work of grieving, lovingly documenting the dead Wynn's possessions as they are taken to the destructor. 'Mary Postgate' wonders where the war is located – in the newspapers, 'here', or elsewhere – and it tries to imagine the traumatic consequences of its violence, whether real or fantasised.

Both HD and Kipling identify the problem of civilian war neuroses and the peculiar fantasies these can generate. Their writings express the anxieties of their historical moment, from fear of attack to guilt about witnessing the trauma of war from a position of relative safety. 'Total war' begins to be felt at the level of the psychic, and it shapes the ways in which civilians imagine themselves: as distant witnesses but also, increasingly, as military targets.

## 2

# Propaganda lies

I SIMPLY DO NOT believe in atrocities,' says Gringoire, the central character of Ford's war memoir, *No Enemy* (1929). 'No, I don't believe in atrocities. Or at the most I half believe in one. It is asserted – the Huns asserted it themselves but I found it difficult to believe – that they filmed the *Lusitania* whilst she was sinking. That I find atrocious.' Why? because it seems to take pleasure in the spectacle: 'that you should take a cinema machine to represent, for the gloating of others, the ruin and disappearance of a tall ship – that seems to me the most horrible of crimes.' Then again, 'perhaps they never did it. Perhaps they only said that they did.'[1]

Gringoire's story is one of thousands of false rumours which circulated during and after the Great War. In this chapter, I will argue that rumour takes on a new meaning in this period, as a result of propaganda. Lying for the sake of war has a long history, of course, but the Great War was the first to organise propaganda in a 'scientific manner'.[2] If military force is based upon deception, the Great War found a new target. In Britain, especially, a vast amount of propaganda was aimed not at the enemy, but at its own citizens, through bogus statistics, inaccurate news reports, and, most contentiously, false atrocity stories. These were much criticised after the war. Whether Britain was the most successful, and the most duplicitous, manufacturer of propaganda was a powerfully argued question throughout the 1920s.

This chapter examines some of the debates about British pro-

1  Ford Madox Ford, *No Enemy*, (1929; New York, Ecco Press, 1984), 108–10.
2  James Morgan Read, *Atrocity Propaganda 1914–1919* (1941; New York, Arno, 1972), 1; Philip Knightley, *The First Casualty: The War Correspondent as Hero, Propagandist, and Myth Maker from the Crimea to Vietnam* (London, Andre Deutsch, 1975), 81.

paganda during and after the war, and offers a reading of *Parade's End* (1924–8) in this context. *Parade's End* is fascinated by the circulation of rumours and lies; indeed, gossip – some of it true, most of it false – is one of the organising principles of the novel. Ford's own life was plagued by gossip and he was frequently accused of lying, as many critics have noted.[3] He also quite enjoyed being lied to,[4] though he disliked being the subject of scandal, writing to Stella Bowen in 1919: 'It is fatal to have controversy about oneself; it is much better to to have the worst lies told, unrefuted. No one believes the lies, tho' they may repeat them for the fun of the thing'.[5] But this biographical interest should not obscure its larger historical context: *Parade's End* is part of a complicated and often fraught debate which took place after the war. Not only does its notorious ambivalence point towards contemporary concerns about propaganda but, as the quotation from *No Enemy* suggests, it also reflects Ford's interest in the relationship between representation and pleasure in stories which circulated during the war.

In Britain, propaganda was organised on an unprecedentedly large scale. It came from a number of sources, both governmental and private, and appeared in newspaper articles, pamphlets, posters, photographs, and verbal rumours. Some of the stories were true, or partly true, while many were pure invention. Perhaps the most successful propaganda campaigns were those based on fictions about German atrocities. Harold Lasswell commented in 1927: 'A handy rule for arousing hate is, if at first they do not enrage, use an

---

3 Arthur Mizener, *The Saddest Story: A Biography of Ford Madox Ford* (London, The Bodley Head, 1971); Alan Judd, *Ford Madox Ford* (1990; London, Flamingo, 1991); Max Saunders, *Ford Madox Ford: A Dual Life*, 2 vols (Oxford, Clarendon, 1996). On *Parade's End*, see also James Longenbach, 'Ford Madox Ford: The Novelist as Historian', *Princeton University Library Chronicle*, 45, 2 (1984), 150–66; Robert Green, *Ford Madox Ford: Prose and Politics* (Cambridge University Press, 1981); Robert Holton, *Jarring Witnesses: Modern Fiction and the Representation of History* (New York, Harvester Wheatsheaf, 1994); Thomas Moser, *The Life in the Fiction of Ford Madox Ford* (Princeton University Press, 1980); Eric Meyer, 'Ford's War and (Post)Modern Memory: *Parade's End* and National Allegory', *Criticism*, 32, 1 (1990), 81–99.
4 Ford, *It Was the Nightingale* (1933; New York, Ecco Press, 1984), 20.
5 Letter of 2 May 1919, *The Correspondence of Ford Madox Ford and Stella Bowen*, ed. Sondra J. Stang and Karen Cochran (Bloomington, Indiana University Press, 1993), 116.

atrocity.'[6] The effects of this deception continued into the Second World War; the success of British propaganda in the First World War made people very sceptical about news of real Nazi atrocities during the 1930s and 1940s.[7] In Britain, almost no one who was touched by the Great War had any reliable information about it. Casualty figures were misrepresented; defeats were presented as victories; atrocity stories were invented; accounts of real suffering were censored; opposition to the war was suppressed. These aspects of the war have been thoroughly documented by social and political historians,[8] but their significance for literary and cultural history requires further attention.

Fiction of this period is often troubled by the need to bear witness to the Great War. Many writers were aware that the stories they had read and heard during the war might be unreliable, misleading, or simply untrue. How can one bear witness when one's knowledge is so imperfect? How do people imagine themselves as subjects, or indeed as citizens, in a culture which is mobilised around rumours, lies, and official secrecy?

## Atrocity stories

One of the most famous atrocity lies appeared in *The Times* on 10 May 1915, in which it was claimed that a Canadian officer had been crucified by the Germans:

> He had been pinned to a wall by bayonets thrust through his hands and feet; another bayonet had then been driven through his throat, and, finally, he was riddled with bullets.
>
> The wounded Canadians said that the Dublin Fusiliers had seen this done with their own eyes, and that they had heard the officers of the Dublin Fusiliers talking about it.[9]

6  Harold Lasswell, *Propaganda Technique in the World War* (London, Kegan Paul etc., 1927), 81.
7  Michael Sanders and Philip Taylor, *British Propaganda During the First World War* (Basingstoke, Macmillan, 1982), 163.
8  Trevor Wilson, *The Myriad Faces of War: Britain and the Great War, 1914–1918* (Cambridge, Polity, 1986), ch. 66; Mariel Grant, *Propaganda and the Role of the State in Inter-War Britain* (Oxford, Clarendon, 1994), ch. 2; Philip Taylor, *Munitions of the Mind*, rev. edn (Manchester University Press, 1995), ch. 21; C. Haste, *Keep the Home Fires Burning: Propaganda in the First World War* (London, Allen Lane, 1977).
9  'Torture of a Canadian Officer', *The Times*, 10 May 1915, 7.

A few days later, *The Times* repeated the story, citing different sources.

> There is, unhappily, good reason to believe that the story related by your Paris Correspondent [on 10 May] of the crucifixion of a Canadian officer during the fighting at Ypres on April 22–23 is in substance true. The story was current here at the time, but, in the absence of direct evidence and absolute proof, men were unwilling to believe that a civilized foe could be guilty of an act so cruel and savage.

Much of the second report is devoted to the question of plausibility, citing 'written depositions' supposedly in possession of British Headquarters. 'I have not heard that any of our men actually saw the crime committed,' comments the reporter, going on to speculate that the Canadian officer may have been dead before 'the enemy in his insensate rage and hatred of the English wreaked his vengeance on the lifeless body of his foe'. Despite the lack of first-hand evidence, 'There is not a man in the ranks of the Canadians who fought at Ypres who is not firmly convinced that this vile thing has been done'.[10] The officer is said to have been pinned to a wooden fence by four bayonets, his body 'repeatedly stabbed with bayonets'. The previous report had five bayonets and the body 'riddled with bullets' – a strange excess of weaponry which makes the Germans look inefficient as well as barbaric.

Like much of *The Times*' reporting of the war, the sources are obscure and the details of the story don't quite add up, but the story is persuasive precisely because of its rough edges; readers are offered a many-layered rumour, supported by evidence which is at once vague (an anonymous written deposition) and highly specific (the exact number of bayonets). It is a rumour, presented as a fact, and seems to have been widely believed at the time; civilians, particularly, had no way of verifying what they read in the newspapers.[11] Crucifixion stories – whether of babies, children, or

10  'The Crucifixion of a Canadian: Insensate Act of Hate', *The Times*, 15 May 1915, 7.

11  Read argues that, although soldiers were less likely than civilians to believe propaganda stories, there were said to be cases of real atrocities committed in reprisals for invented ones. *Atrocity Propaganda*, 6–7, 52. However, Robert Graves claims that the soldiers he knew believed neither the original story nor the accounts of reprisals. *Goodbye to All That* (1929; rev. edn 1957; Harmondsworth, Penguin, 1988), 154.

Americans – reappeared throughout the war, but no verifiable cases of crucifixion were ever found.[12]

What made this a good propaganda story? Crucifixion is of course a highly charged image, especially as both sides made strong claims of righteousness in the name of Christianity. British MPs often used the story in public speeches. And, as George Parfitt argues, soldiers were often seen as Christ-like figures whose suffering was blamed variously on the enemy, on women, and on the General Staff.[13] But the story has an anthropological significance, too. Crucifixion is the wrong kind of death in this war; an inappropriate use of its technology. The event is contaminated – dirty – matter out of place. The possibility that the officer may have already been dead offers both comfort and renewed distress. The act becomes monstrous in a different way; mutilation of a dead body serves no practical military aim, but is simply an act of defilement, a purposeless horror. At the same time, the story is slightly ridiculous, as a number of writers after the war suggested.

Other famous lies included stories of babies without arms, mutilated nurses, raped nuns, soldiers with their faces tattooed with enemy insignia, a Germany factory for converting battlefield corpses into usable products. The many terrible and revolting acts which really did take place during the Great War were hardly ever used as propaganda; indeed, true stories were rigorously censored in Britain throughout the war. The most compelling and memorable stories to be taken up and circulated were almost always fictions, and they were fictions of a particular kind. Some were recycled atrocity stories from earlier wars;[14] others were drawn partly from popular horror stories and partly from the conventions of pornography. Atrocity pamphlets appeared with titles such as *The Horrors of Wittenburg* (1916) and *Microbe-Culture at Bukarest*

---

12 The Bryce Report cites a number of these stories, all of them hearsay. No evidence could be found for any of them. Read, *Atrocity Propaganda*, 40–1; Peter Buitenhuis, *The Great War of Words: Literature as Propaganda 1914–18 and After* (London, Batsford, 1989), 27–8; Arthur Ponsonby, *Falsehood in War-Time* (London, George Allen and Unwin, 1928), 91–3.

13 George Parfitt, *Fiction of the First World War: A Study* (London, Faber and Faber, 1988), 25–30.

14 Lasswell, *Propaganda Technique in the World War*, 82–3. Lasswell comments that 'all atrocity stories show a family resemblance', though they will also change according to the technology of the time.

(1917). Irene Cooper Willis noted that propaganda stories about sexual mutilation were reported in lurid detail in the newspapers, especially in the *Daily News*.[15] There was even a scatalogical sub-genre. J. H. Morgan's *German Atrocities: An Official Investigation* (1916) included a section entitled 'Bestiality of German Officers and Men' which claimed that 'chateaux or private houses used as the head-quarters of German officers were frequently found to have been left in a state of bestial pollution'. Even though 'to use the beds and the upholstery of private houses as a latrine is not an atrocity, it indicates a state of mind sufficiently depraved to commit one'. Morgan also wrote that many incidents witnessed by British officers 'are so disgusting that they are unfit for publication', adding that 'Some of the worst things have never been published.'[16]

## Propaganda exposed

Studies of propaganda appeared throughout the 1920s and 1930s.[17] Mariel Grant notes that the very term 'propaganda' changed its meaning during this period, taking on new, negative connotations 'in response to the success of British propaganda in the First World War'.[18] Writing in 1927, Irene Cooper Willis argued that 'war plays the devil not only with bodies but with minds, and the ensuing intellectual deterioration of the warring nations, being less obvious than

---

15  Irene Cooper Willis, *England's Holy War: A Study of English Liberal Idealism During the Great War* (New York, Knopf, 1928), 133.

16  J. H. Morgan, *German Atrocities: An Official Investigation* (London, T. Fisher Unwin, 1916), 61–2. This book was reprinted six times in 1916. See also Joseph Bédier, *German Atrocities from German Evidence*, trans. Bernhard Harrison (Paris, Librairie Armand Colin, 1915).

17  Well-known studies include: Lasswell, *Propaganda Technique*; Cooper Willis, *England's Holy War*; Ponsonby, *Falsehood in War-Time*; George Sylvester Viereck, *Spreading Germs of Hate* (London, Duckworth, 1931); Frederick Lumley, *The Propaganda Menace* (New York, The Century Co., 1933); J. D. Squires, *British Propaganda at Home and in the United States* (Cambridge MA, Harvard University Press, 1935). Some propaganda works themselves included a discussion of lies in propaganda, such as Edwyn Bevan, 'The Truth about Lies', *Nineteenth Century*, 80 (September 1916), 612–22; Augustin Hamon, *Lessons of the World-War*, trans. Bernard Miall (London, T. Fisher Unwin, 1918), ch. 1, 'Terrorism and Untruth'.

18  Grant, *Propaganda and the Role of the State*, 11–13.

the physical deterioration, is by so much the more dangerous'.[19]
Many people shared this concern, including Arthur Ponsonsby,
whose study of propaganda appeared in 1928:

> In calm retrospect we can appreciate better the disastrous effects of the
> poison of falsehood, whether officially, semi-officially, or privately
> manufactured. It has rightly been said that the injection of the poison
> of hatred into men's minds by means of falsehood is a greater evil in
> war-time than the actual loss of life.[20]

For Ponsonby, 'The deception of whole peoples is not a matter
which can be lightly regarded', and his book focuses on a particular
kind of lying: the false information which circulated in newspaper
articles, pamphlets, verbal rumours, official reports. An enormous
amount of inaccurate information appeared during the war; Ponsonby examines just a few of the most famous and sensational examples. Every country used propaganda 'to deceive its own people, to
attract neutrals, and to mislead the enemy'.[21] It was also used to
delay or prevent peace settlements, as Buitenhuis has recently
argued:

> In the latter part of 1916 and throughout 1917, there were several
> calls for peace by negotiation among the Allies. These attempts all
> failed, largely because of three factors: the alleged military victories
> manufactured by the generals and propagandists, the lack of informa-
> tion about the real conditions on the Western Front, and the climate
> created by the hate and atrocity propaganda against Germany.[22]

The precise effects of propaganda are impossible to measure, but,
whatever it achieved during the war, anxiety about propaganda had

---

19 Cooper Willis, preface (1927), *England's Holy War*, xix–xx. The book examines responses (including propaganda) to the war in the Liberal press and com-
prises material first published in pamphlet form, 1919–21.

20 Arthur Ponsonby, *Falsehood in War-Time*, 13, 18. According to Raymond
Jones, the book was a best-seller and went into eight editions by 1940. Jones,
*Arthur Ponsonby: The Politics of Life* (London, Christopher Helm, 1989),
168–9.

21 Ponsonby, *Falsehood in War-Time*, 13. This argument is developed in Read,
*Atrocity Propaganda*. Ponsonby's own work has been appropriated by a more
recent form of propaganda. In the early 1980s, *Falsehood in War-Time* was
republished by the 'Institute for Historical Review', with an anonymous preface denying the truth of the Nazi holocaust.

22 Buitenhuis, *The Great War of Words*, 141.

become a serious matter by 1928, when universal franchise was established in Britain for the first time.[23] A basic premise of democracy – that people make rational choices based on reliable information – was thrown into question. And, as Grant points out, there was concern that the new electors were easily swayed by propaganda, so that – paradoxically – the extended franchise came to seem a threat to democracy.[24]

Propaganda can seem like an act of betrayal when the state deliberately misleads its subjects, the newspaper its readers. As Freud remarked in 1915, citizens of the supposedly civilised European states were expected to live by high moral standards; above all, people were 'forbidden to make use of the immense advantages to be gained by the practice of lying and deception'. Clearly, citizens assumed that the state would obey its own rules. People become disillusioned, says Freud, when they realise that 'the state has forbidden to the individual the practice of wrong-doing [in this case, lying], not because it desires to abolish it, but because it desires to monopolize it, like salt and tobacco'. Freud's turn to an economic metaphor is particularly striking. Lies, rumours, and propaganda become commodities – valuable assets taken under state control – while citizens become passive consumers, treated 'like children by an excess of secrecy and a censorship upon news and expressions of opinion'.[25] This leaves them extremely vulnerable to propaganda and rumour – almost the only information in circulation in a society at war.

In some ways the manufacture of propaganda – especially atrocity stories – was simply an extension of the sensational journalism of the nineteenth century.[26] Some stories were deemed too obscene to publish and were circulated as rumour or folk myth. Trevor Wilson points out that many of these stories involved 'sexual-sadistic fan-

23 The Representation of the People Acts of 1918 and 1928 extended the vote to all women and men over twenty-one.

24 This led to debates about education. Education was seen as necessary to arm people against propaganda, yet 'the growth of literacy had made it much easier to spread misinformation'. Grant, *Propaganda and the Role of the State*, 12, 15.

25 Sigmund Freud, 'Thoughts for the Time on War and Death' (1915), Pelican Freud Library 12, *Civilization, Society and Religion* (Harmondsworth, Penguin, 1985), 62, 66.

26 Cooper Willis, *England's Holy War*, xvi.

tasies' which entered public discourse, especially among middle-class people, 'under the guise of patriotic warnings'. Wilson speculates that this kind of rumour provided a strong *frisson* of enjoyment as well as horror or disgust.[27] Harold Lasswell's influential study, *Propaganda Technique in the World War* (1927), makes the point more strongly:

> Stress can always be laid [in propaganda] upon the wounding of women, children, old people, priests and nuns, and upon sexual enormities [...]. These stories yield a crop of indignation against the fiendish perpetrators of these dark deeds, and satisfy certain powerful, hidden impulses. A young woman, ravished by the enemy, yields secret satisfaction to a host of vicarious ravishers on the other side of the border. Hence, perhaps, the popularity and ubiquity of such stories. (82)

Lasswell's characterisation of entire nations as would-be rapists is both startling and facile, and owes something to popular misunderstandings of psychoanalysis. Yet it identifies, however clumsily, the element of sexual fantasy at work in much atrocity propaganda – what H. D. Chalmers described in 1914 as 'sensational outrages which please the public'.[28]

After the war, many writers were concerned that citizens had been treated like children by the state, the newspapers, and other institutions. As people struggled to recover from the mental and physical suffering of the war, this realisation produced a good deal of bitterness. There were serious political reasons for objecting to institutional lying, and writers such as Ponsonby, Lasswell, and Cooper Willis made their cases very strongly. But the language of outrage and indignation which appears in a number of studies of propaganda suggests that something else is at stake in these writings. Terms such as *defilement, degradation, contamination, desecrated, polluted, germs of hate, poison, evil*, and *hysteria* appear in many of the analyses of propaganda after the war, uncannily repeating some of the outraged language of the propaganda itself, drawing on metaphors of disease, dirt, and sexual depravity. Sometimes they imitate the methods of propagation, too, repeating hearsay,

---

27  Wilson, *Myriad Faces of War*, 739–40, 185–90.
28  Chalmers, letter to Lord Bryce, December 1914, quoted in Wilson, *Myriad Faces*, 185. Chalmers was a barrister who worked with the Bryce Committee.

retelling unverified rumours, citing incomplete sources – and, in some cases, exhibiting a kind of relish in the horrible material.

In *The Propaganda Menace* (1933), for example, Frederick Lumley quotes material drawn third-hand from other sources about a French firm which supposedly manufactured atrocity photographs.

> Its principal work consisted in making photographs and cuts of wooden figures with cut-off hands, torn-out tongues, gouged-out eyes, crushed skulls and brains laid bare. The pictures thus made were sent as unassailable evidence of German atrocities to all parts of the globe, where they did not fail to produce the desired effect. In the same rooms fictitious photographs were made of bombarded French and Belgian churches, violated graves and momuments and scenes of ruins and desolation. The staging and painting of those scenes were done by the best scene-painters of the Paris Grand Opera.[29]

It seems remarkable that anyone should need to forge such scenes of devastation, but propaganda frequently preferred fakes. Real mutilated bodies were not hard to come by, either, though these were often unsuitable for propaganda. Lumley does not comment on this incongruity, nor on the astonishing name of the institution involved: the House of Propaganda and Prostitution. He is as unsuspicious of the story and its sources as earlier readers had been of the propaganda itself. James Morgan Read later argued that the original anonymous source, *Behind the Scenes of French Journalism*, was unconfirmed by any other evidence.[30] And even a study as careful as Ponsonby's, according to Read, contains errors of fact; inaccurate stories continued to circulate long after the war had ended.[31]

## Rumour in *Parade's End*

What has *Parade's End* to say about these concerns? It is a highly unsettling novel, teetering, as Max Saunders argues, on the brink between tragedy and absurdity.[32] It also locates itself on another brink – between anxiety and pleasure – an ambivalent position

---

29  Lumley, *Propaganda Menace*, 230; Lumley's notes refer to *Behind the Scenes of French Journalism*, quoted in *The Progressive*, 1 January 1926.
30  Read, *Atrocity Propaganda*, 24.
31  Read, *Atrocity Propaganda*, 24–5. Read misnames Ponsonby's book here.
32  Saunders, *Ford*, vol. 2, 219.

which gives the work much of of its power, and which is highly resonant when read against the debates around propaganda after the war. One source of its ambivalence, perhaps, is Ford's unease about his own propaganda work in the early stages of the war. He contributed a series of articles to *Outlook* in 1914–15, and was commissioned by Masterman to write two propaganda books: *When Blood is Their Argument* (1915) and *Between St. Dennis and St. George* (1915). Many respected writers produced serious books which argued, directly or indirectly, in support of the war, often on secret commission from government propaganda committees: Wells, Bennett, Galsworthy, Kipling, Mrs Humphry Ward, Conan Doyle, and many others.[33] This was quite a different kind of writing from the atrocity stories discussed earlier, but it was an important element in the great propaganda machine, and its disguised origins were another kind of lie. In *Between St. Dennis and St. George*, Ford pillories some leading pacifists, accusing H. N. Brailsford of lies and 'forgery' and Shaw of repeating unfounded gossip; this surely raised some ethical questions when Ford began to recognise the consequences of the war.[34] Perhaps the pacifists deserved support rather than ridicule and attack. Peter Buitenhuis argues that Ford, like Wells, Kipling, and Bennett, looked back on the war and felt 'some dismay at [his] own complicity'.[35] Ford's own propaganda work was very slight, but it raised questions about collusion and official lies which are addressed, often in a highly displaced form, in *Parade's End*.

'You can't get ahead of rumour', says Christopher Tietjens, the central character of *Parade's End*, and the novel's four volumes are filled with gossip about his sexual life, his politics, his marriage, his money. Most of the stories are untrue – 'foul and baseless rumours', as his estranged wife Sylvia puts it, but they have a material effect on the course of Tietjens' life.[36] Gossip drives the various plots and organises the relationships among the central characters. Rumours about Tietjens diminish his reputation, isolate him from his social

33 For a detailed discussion of writers' propaganda activities, see Buitenhuis, *The Great War of Words*, ch. 4; Samuel Hynes, *A War Imagined: The First World War and English Culture* (London, The Bodley Head, 1990), ch. 2.
34 *Between St. Dennis and St. George: A Sketch of Three Civilisations* (London, Hodder and Stoughton, 1915), 227, 282.
35 Buitenhuis, *The Great War of Words*, 151.
36 Ford, *Parade's End* (1924–8; Harmondsworth, Penguin, 1982), 196, 166.

class, damage his finances. Yet, at the same time, the gossip enlarges him, placing him at the centre of the stories his society tells itself. Gossip is fundamental to social organisation; it is an important source of pleasure as well as a mechanism for policing people. Throughout the novel, Tietjens' friends and family tell lies about him, then behave as if the stories were true. The processes of gossip are like 'the smooth working of a mechanical model' (202).

Generically, *Parade's End* moves between soldier's memoir and modernist fiction. Published as four separate novels – *Some Do Not* (1924), *No More Parades* (1925), *A Man Could Stand Up* (1926), and *The Last Post* (1928) – it did not appear as a single volume until 1950. Although much of its war material is based on Ford's own experiences at the front, its central character is only partly autobiographical, and it is quite unlike the other famous soldiers' narratives of the Great War. Even in the sections set in battle in *No More Parades* and *A Man Could Stand Up*, in method *Parade's End* more closely resembles Dorothy Richardson's *Pilgrimage* (1915–38) – a book Ford admired – than Remarque's *All Quiet on the Western Front* (1929), Barbusse's *Under Fire* (1916), Blunden's *Undertones of War* (1928), or Graves' *Goodbye to All That* (1929). (These works are discussed in Chapter 3.)

Ford enlisted in the army in July 1915 and was sent to the war in July 1916. He was in his forties – a generation older than most men who enlisted – and he had joined the army, according to Buitenhuis, partly to escape from 'the financial and patriotic necessity to write propaganda for C. F. G. Masterman's office'.[37] Being a soldier was Ford's first real job. Like many soldiers in the trenches, Ford did not actually fight in the sense of using weapons against enemy soldiers. He worked with battalion transport, just behind the front lines – a position which was subject to frequent attack. Not long after he arrived, it seems he was blown into the air by a shell, sustaining minor injuries and a concussion which was to affect his memory for many years afterwards.[38] He was also to suffer from war neuroses until 1923.[39] Yet the experience was also oddly healing, as Saunders notes. After several periods of mental suffering before the

37 Buitenhuis, *The Great War of Words*, 119.
38 Saunders, *Ford*, vol. 2, 1–2.
39 Judd, *Ford*, 280–1; Saunders, *Ford*, vol. 2, 216. Saunders also notes that when he was dying Ford imagined himself back in the war. *Ford*, vol. 2, 228–9.

war, Ford had 'no more mental breakdowns after the war; and from the mid-1920s onwards he was much less prone to depression'.[40]

When *Parade's End* begins the young Tietjens is working in the Civil Service in a job which requires him to fake statistics (47, 57, 60), and is married to Sylvia, who has run off with another man. As a husband Tietjens considers it ungentlemanly to divorce his wife, and insists on protecting her reputation. The novel repeatedly draws attention to Tietjens' adherence to an anachronistic moral code. Although he is one of the few members of his circle who is monogamous, he develops a reputation for indiscreet affairs. People want to drop him from their visiting lists – not for the fictional affairs so much as for being the subject of malicious gossip. This pattern is repeated throughout the novel, and accords with Tietjens' own statement at the beginning that society distrusts the 'cuckold' and blames him for his own misfortunes (10, 11). As a wealthy member of the ruling class who refuses to defend himself against libel, Tietjens is an unusual victim. His unyielding belief in the correct codes of behaviour often makes him unsympathetic. He defends his wife's honour as a point of principle, for example, but fails to do the same for Valentine, the woman he loves; nor will she defend him (258).

Much of the gossip in the novel focuses on illicit sexual practices. Tietjens is said to be 'a bloody pimp living on women' (217); to have taken Mrs Duchemin (later Mrs Macmaster) as his mistress (161, 207, 209, 215, 220, 270, 271) and to have made her pregnant before her marriage to Macmaster (222, 261). Many people think that Valentine has had a war baby to Tietjens (158, 209–10, 212). 'Seven people in the last five weeks have told me you have had a child by that brute beast', says Mrs Duchemin to Valentine, calling her a 'shameless thing' and a harlot (260–1); Valentine in turn considers Mrs Duchemin a 'foul whore' (265). Before he has even met Valentine, Tietjens is alleged to be her lover (107, 117): 'He was said to have ruined himself, broken up his home and spent his wife's money on her' (87). 'Those were lies', reflects Tietjens, patiently. 'On the other hand they were not inherent impossibilities' (87). To some extent, it is the gossip – 'the pressure of suggestion' – which

40  Saunders, *Ford*, vol. 2, 258.

makes the affair between Tietjens and Valentine possible (88). 'The whole world conspired to force them together!' (214). Later, in the war, Tietjens is sent up the line, despite being medically unfit, because the scandals attached to his private life are thought to be demoralising the army (476–8). One of the Welsh soldiers, O Nine Morgan, discovers that his wife has taken up with a prize fighter. He applies for leave, but Tietjens refuses, on the grounds that 'the prize-fighter would have smashed him to bits' (310). O Nine Morgan is killed shortly afterwards, his face smashed by a shell (308). Tietjens will be haunted by this death, caused, indirectly, by the workings of gossip.

The worst rumours have a physical effect on Teitjens' family: his brother Mark feels 'sickish' when he thinks of Tietjens and the stories which surround him (738), and the gossip is said to have killed their father (178, 490, 739). Even in the war, Tietjens himself suffers less from the violence of battle than from malicious stories, most of which originate from his wife. Sylvia's attacks on Tietjens are key elements in the movement of the plot, yet their causes remain enigmatic. Her main purpose in life is to torment him for reasons which change in the course of the novel: because he bores her; because she hates him; because she loves him; because he is the only real man she knows; because she wants him to notice her; because she enjoys the spectacle of suffering. Most of the characters in *Parade's End* attempt to injure Tietjens in some way; their motives, too, are often obscure. Early in *Some Do Not*, General Campion questions Tietjens about his alleged affair with Valentine. Tietjens has been seen 'lolloping' in central London with an unknown woman; is this the same one? The woman is actually one of Macmaster's unsuitable mistresses, and Tietjens tries to protect his friend without lying to the General: '"I was trying to get that young woman … I was taking her out to lunch from her office at the bottom of the Haymarket … To get her off a friend's back. That is, of course, between ourselves"' (72). The General is astonished by such an implausible excuse:

> 'Upon my soul,' he said, 'what do you take me for?' He repeated the words as if he were amazed. 'If,' he said, ' my G.S.O.II – who's the stupidest ass I know – told me such a damn-fool lie as that I'd have him broke tomorrow. […] Damn it all, it's the first duty of a soldier

– it's the first duty of all Englishmen – to be able to tell a good lie in answer to a charge. But a lie like that […] Hang it all, I told that lie to my grandmother and my grandfather told it to *his* grandfather.' (72)

But of course the story is true. One reason Tietjens is persecuted is because he refuses to tell the right sort of lies. Such scruples are beyond the General, who says 'I only want a plausible story to tell Claudine. Or not even plausible. An obvious lie as long as it shows you're not flying in the face of society' (74).

Sylvia's lies about Tietjens are designed to discredit him. Early in the novel, they leave him literally so, and his bank refuses to honour his cheques (161, 182–3, 194, 202). Much is made of the relationship between credit and discredit. Without social and financial credit, the individual cannot function within society. Society itself is being transformed through the processes of lying; members of the old ruling class (land-owners such as Tietjens) are being displaced by lower-middle-class people such as Macmaster who gain power by fraud. Macmaster, for example, is awarded a knighthood for his war work: a set of bogus statistics designed to prove that the French have barely suffered during the war. He has not even faked the figures himself, but has stolen the calculations from Tietjens (256).

Tietjens formulates the statistics as an intellectual exercise, but they will have a profound effect on many people's lives. The aim of the statistics is to prevent reinforcements being sent, and to delay the introduction of a single command. Tietjens explains the reasoning to Valentine, the woman everyone (at this stage, wrongly) believes to be his mistress:

> They had wanted to rub into our allies that their losses by devastation had been nothing to write home about […] Well, if you took just the bricks and mortar of the devastated districts, you could prove that the loss in bricks, tiles, woodwork and the rest didn't – and the figures with a little manipulation would prove it! – amount to more than a normal year's dilapidations spread over the whole country in peace time … House repairs in a normal year had cost several million sterling. The enemy had only destroyed just about so many million sterling in bricks and mortar. And what was a mere year's dilapidations in house property! You just neglected to do them and did them next year.
>
> So, if you ignored the lost harvests of three years, the lost industrial output of the richest industrial region of the country, the smashed

machinery [etc. ...] – and the loss of life! – we could go to our allies and say:

'All your yappings about losses are the merest bulls. You can perfectly well afford to reinforce the weak places of your own lines. We intend to send our new troops to the Near East, where lies our true interest!' And though they might sooner or later point out the fallacy, you would by so much have put off the abhorrent expedient of a single command. (253)

When Valentine wonders if it isn't dangerous to tell Macmaster these ideas, Tietjens emphatically defends his friend: 'Oh, no, no. No! You don't know what a good soul little Vinnie is. [...] He'd as soon think of picking my pocket as of picking my brains. The soul of honour!' (253). As it turns out, Macmaster picks his pocket as well as his brains, and is rewarded for his corruption while Tietjens is further discredited. Yet Tietjens is not simply a helpless victim; here, as elsewhere, the distinction between innocence and guilt, honour and dishonour becomes blurred. After all, it was Tietjens who calculated the bogus statistics; does he bear no responsibility for their consequences? The novel is aware of precisely this question, and deliberately makes it impossible to untangle the lines of responsibility; at the same time, it demonstrates repeatedly that the texts and stories people produce – rumours, lies, statistics – are integral to the war, and can affect the lives and deaths of large numbers of people.

*Parade's End* appeared in a period in which several key propaganda stories were exposed as inventions, and it expresses some of the anxieties they aroused. What does 'democracy' mean if you do not have reliable information upon which to base your judgements, if the state in which you are now a democratic citizen has been systematically telling you lies? Ford wrote in his preface to *A Man Could Stand Up* that he hoped that war could be prevented in the future; but how can this be achieved if propaganda and censorship make one's knowledge of the war so imperfect? The novel suggests that even the most privileged of individuals can be seriously damaged by lies and rumours. And yet, as I have suggested, Tietjens is an unusual victim who is oddly liberated when he is mistreated by his society; he derives some pleasure from relinquishing responsibility, being told what to do, and subjecting himself to the large, impersonal, and violent structures of the war.

When Tietjens returns from the war his affair with Valentine can begin, but their first opportunity to sleep together is thwarted by Sylvia, who turns up to announce she is to have an operation for cancer. Sylvia is 'a *maîtresse femme*' who knows how to choose a 'good lie' – like a successful propagandist (776). But lying can harm the liar, too, and towards the end of *The Last Post* Mark Tietjens reflects that inventing 'that sort of sex-cruelty stuff' leaves your mind 'a little affected'. People 'who invent gossip frequently' end up going 'dotty'. Christopher is a saint, thinks Mark, and providence 'invents retributions of an ingenious kind against those who libel saints' (727–8). Elsewhere he is likened to Christ (379) – an image which was particularly freighted as a result of the circulation (and later exposure) of stories about crucified soldiers. Tietjens is often compared to a saint or a martyr, much to Sylvia's irritation. He is even likened to the most famous military martyr of the previous generation, as General Campion remarks:

'A regular … what's 'is name? A regular Dreyfus!'
'Did you think Dreyfus was guilty?', Tietjens asked.
'Hang it,' the General said, 'he was worse than guilty – the sort of fellow you couldn't believe in and yet couldn't prove anything against. The curse of the world [...] fellows like that *unsettle* society. You don't know where you are. You can't judge. They make you uncomfortable'. (75)

Later he says to Sylvia, 'You're too young to have heard of Dreyfus … But I always say that Christopher is a regular Dreyfus … I shouldn't be astonished if he didn't end by being drummed out of the army' (409). Here, as elsewhere, the General is satirised for his ignorant prejudice. Yet Dreyfus really was a martyr – an innocent man vilified and imprisoned for five years on Devil's Island for crimes he never committed. The Dreyfus case, it is often argued, created profound divisions in French society and created a new wave of anti-Semitism in the late nineteenth century.[41] *Parade's End* takes up this cultural memory and shifts the idea of the victim away from the figure of the persecuted Jew towards an English Tory gen-

---

41 Eric Cahm, *The Dreyfus Affair in French Society and Politics* (1994; London, Longman, 1996); Guy Chapman, *The Dreyfus Trials* (London, Batsford, 1972). Saunders argues that Ford often returned to the Dreyfus affair 'as a touchstone of true conspiracy and persecution.' *Ford*, vol. 2, 237, but its use in *Parade's End* seems to me to be rather more ambiguous than Saunders suggests.

tleman struggling for Anglican sainthood (187, 483). Here, too, the novel is hard to pin down. Tietjens has a number of relationships with Jewish men; like Scots, the Jews are cast as duplicitous aliens within English society – social inferiors who will use an honourable Englishman to help them rise, only to betray and discredit their patron. These 'inferior' men (Macmaster, Ruggles, Levin, Schatzweiler) are frequently represented as feminised, hysterical, and deceitful. On the one hand the book claims the moral ground occupied by the traduced Jew Dreyfus; on the other it casts the Jew – like the femme fatale – as a source of damage and betrayal.[42]

*Parade's End* is often read as a nostalgic study of the disappearance of the old, prewar England Tietjens supposedly represents. But it might be more useful to think about this as a cultural fantasy, and to ask how the book takes up other anxieties of the 1920s, including the re-emergence of anti-Semitism. Its relationship to anti-Semitism is, characteristically, highly ambivalent, both mobilising and mocking its ideas, and perhaps alludes to Ford's own experience as the (non-Jewish) butt of some bizarre anti-Semitic attacks. In 1916, for example, *The New Witness* published a hostile review of *Zeppelin Nights*, a book co-written by Ford and Violet Hunt. 'It is generally supposed that Mr. Hueffer [Ford] is not exactly of pure European extraction', wrote the reviewer, 'and this book tends to confirm such impression.' She went on to accuse Ford of 'abjection', referring enigmatically to 'the foreign quarters of Whitechapel – and by "foreign" I mean those parts which are inhabited by non-Europeans'. This set off an anti-Semitic debate in the letters page, starting with J. M. Barrie's claim that, while *Zeppelin Nights* was a bad book, 'That is no reason why you should go out of your way to insult Mr. Hueffer by calling him a Jew and a coward'.[43] Later, in

42  On representations of Jews in this period, see Bryan Cheyette, *Constructions of 'the Jew' in English Literature and Society: Racial Representations, 1875–1945* (Cambridge University Press, 1993); Linda Nochlin and Tamar Garb, eds, *The Jew in the Text: Modernity and the Construction of Identity* (London, Thames and Hudson, 1995).

43  'J. K. Prothero' [Ada Elizabeth Jones], 'Mr. Hueffer and his Cellar *Garnis'*, *New Witness*, 6 January 1916, 293; 'J. M.' [J. M. Barrie], letter, *The New Witness*, 13 January 1916, 321; both rpt in F. MacShane, ed., *Ford Madox Ford: The Critical Heritage* (London, Routledge and Kegan Paul, 1972), 122–5. The original reviewer never mentioned Jews, but her response to Barrie confirms that this is indeed what she meant. 'J. K. Prothero', letter, *The New Witness*, 20 January 1916, 352.

1926, a review of *No More Parades* called it 'not a thoroughly English book', likening it to the work of 'one of those aliens in the British Empire, Celt or Semite, who in their souls resents what England stands for'.[44] The attacks are absurd, hysterical, weirdly entertaining as well as potentially harmful; all these possibilities are present in *Parade's End*, too. It is not Tietjens, however, but the 'womanish' men (the Scots and Jews) and Sylvia, the gossiping woman, who are finally removed from the world of the text. Perhaps that is why some readers consider the fourth novel unsatisfying: the rumours, lies, and sexual cruelty have disappeared.[45]

Towards the end of *Some Do Not*, Valentine's mother, Mrs Wannop, is approached by 'one of the more excitable Sunday papers to write a series of articles on extravagant matters connected with the hostilities' (269) – in other words, to write propaganda. It is easy work, and well paid. The subjects proposed are 'war babies' and 'the fact that the Germans were reduced to eating their own corpses'. Valentine Wannop is a pacifist, yet oddly seems to have no ethical objection to her mother writing propaganda. The morality of the issue is raised by Tietjens, for whom the topics are 'below the treatment of any decent pen'. Furthermore, the stories are not true: 'The illegitimacy rate, he had said, had shown very little increase; the French-derived German word "*cadaver*" meant bodies of horses or cattle; *leichnam* being the German for the word "corpse". He had practically refused to have anything to do with the affair' (269).

His objection to the 'war babies' story seems clear enough – they don't exist, therefore it would be dishonest to write about them. The second matter is less straightforward. The question of the German word for 'corpse' had been a matter of debate in 1917, when it was falsely reported in the newspapers (and later presented in a government pamphlet) that the Germans were converting battlefield corpses into oil, fertiliser, and animal food (the use varied from one report to the next). Ponsonby called this 'one of the most revolting lies invented during the war' (102), and it generated intense interest. There were several reports and letters about the 'corpse factory' in *The Times* during April 1917; the matter was also

---

44 Mary Colum, 'New Worlds and Old', *Saturday Review of Literature*, 30 January 1926, 523; rpt in MacShane, ed., *Ford: The Critical Heritage*, 94.
45 Whether *The Last Post* belongs in the novel has been a matter of some debate; see Saunders, *Ford*, vol. 2, 249, 252–4.

raised in Parliament, and an article was published in *The Lancet* as to the technical aspects of utilising human corpses.[46] Much of the debate focused on whether the word *Kadaver* referred to human or animal bodies.[47] In *Disenchantment* (1922), C. E. Montague cites the story as evidence that you 'can't believe a word you read' in the newspapers.[48] It was not until 1925 (the year after *Some Do Not* was published) that the story was officially exposed as a lie; even then, a number of different stories circulated about the exact nature of the fraud.[49] In *Some Do Not*, the 'excitable paper' attempts to exaggerate the story even further, into cannibalism. (A variation on this story appears in Remarque's *All Quiet on the Western Front* in which the German soldiers are accused of eating Belgian babies. The narrator calls the authors of such propaganda 'the real culprits' of the war (136).)

In the event, Mrs Wannop can drop the atrocity story when she is asked to write propaganda for a respectable journal instead (269). The ethics of writing propaganda are not confronted here, nor anywhere else in the novel. Even its most moral figures (Valentine, Mrs Wannop) find themselves contributing to the propaganda machine without, it seems, compromising their integrity. Yet, structurally, *Parade's End* is troubled by precisely this issue. It worries at the idea that stories – both true and false – can have a material effect in the world, and can cause serious damage. On the other hand, lies can be comforting. In the final paragraphs of the novel, Tietjens' brother Mark breaks his long silence to speak kindly to Valentine as he dies. Valentine tells the doctor Mark has spoken, but asks him not to tell Mark's wife, Marie-Léonie. 'She would have liked to have his last words', says Valentine, 'But she did not need them as much as I' (836).

46  *The Lancet*, 21 April 1917, 635. Ponsonby, *Falsehood in War-Time*, 103–13; see also *The Times*, 4 November 1925, 16; 'Kadaver', *The Nation*, 38 (1925), 171–2; Read, *Atrocity Propaganda*, 38–41; Marwick, *The Deluge: British Society and the First World War*, 2nd edn (Basingstoke, Macmillan, 1991), 252–3.
47  'The "Kadaver" Controversy', *The Nation*, 19 May 1917, 168; 'Kadaver', *The Nation*, 26 May 1917, 198.
48  C. E. Montague, *Disenchantment* (London, Chatto and Windus, 1922), 94.
49  This story, too, had long-term consequences; British newspapers would not print early reports of Nazi gas chambers because they believed them to be another version of the 'corpse-conversion factory'. Arthur Marwick, *The Deluge*, 253.

*Parade's End*'s concern with propaganda is not simply a citique of its practices. Ford goes beyond Ponsonby or Cooper Willis in being more conscious of the pleasures involved in the circulation of outrageous stories. Both the atrocity propaganda and its critiques are, as I have argued, ambivalent, unsettling, and sometimes duplicitous forms of writing. But how might this help us to understand the ambivalences of *Parade's End*? An incident from the life of another young man who went to the Great War is useful here. In 1907, Ernst Lanzer, the Rat Man, went into analysis with Freud. Shortly before this, he had been on military manoeuvres, where he heard a terrible story. A captain who was fond of cruelty said that 'he had read of a specially horrible punishment used in the East'. The Rat Man finds it very difficult to retell the story to Freud. After many hesitations, he manages to indicate that ''a criminal was tied up [...] a pot was turned upside down on his buttocks ... some *rats* were put into it ... and they [...] *bored their way in* ...'. As he speaks, the Rat Man shows 'every sign of horror and resistance', says Freud; at the most important moments of his story, his face 'took on a very strange, composite expression. I could only interpret it as one of *horror at pleasure of his own of which he himself was unaware*'.[50] The rat story is a characteristic piece of atrocity propaganda. Its source is vague and it is located somewhere loosely designated 'the East' at an unspecified time. Like the Rat Man's story, as analysed by Freud, both the propaganda of the Great War and some of the criticism which followed seem to articulate a *horror at pleasure of its own* of which the writing itself is unaware. This may be a further reason why atrocity stories were so fascinating, and so disturbing, and why they received so much attention.

The debates around propaganda are particularly troubled after the war. Democracy is supposed to be organised around rational choices based on accurate information; just as democracy is fully established, the sources of supposedly reliable information are found to be shameless liars. Moreover, the bogus atrocity stories displace the suffering of millions of real bodies. Even more troubling, however, is the realisation that to criticise propaganda requires the repudiation of a fantasmatic pleasure which dare not speak its name (fantasies about mutilation, sexual sadism, and so

---

50 Freud, 'Notes Upon a Case of Obsessional Neurosis' (1909), Penguin Freud Library 9, *Case Histories II* (London, Penguin, 1991), 47–8.

forth). Criticism of the war reveals some of the obscene pleasures which drive the war's psychic economy. But it also mobilises them in its own writings. *Parade's End* enacts this contradiction, not only by exposing the damage done by rumours, lies, and sensational stories, but also because it is covertly interested the pleasures they generate. It both enjoys and repudiates the idea of pleasurable representations of war – what Gringoire in *No Enemy* calls 'the most horrible of crimes' and Sylvia likens to pornography, repeated 'with the lust of men telling dirty stories in smoking-rooms' (439). Often praised as one of the great critiques of the war, *Parade's End* is not simply or self-evidently an anti-war novel. It is powerful for the same reason that it is disturbing, expressing anxiety at a pleasure of its own of which it is only partially aware.

# II

# Corporeal fantasies

# 3

# Vile bodies

N THE DECADE that has passed since the Peace Treaty was signed', wrote John Brophy in 1929, 'the three chief belligerent countries have yielded a rich harvest of narratives and philosophic examinations. The "war book" has become as well recognised a category as the disparaging biography, the "thriller" or the fantasy.' For Brophy, the war book might be seen as a slightly disreputable literary form – like the thriller or fantasy – but it has an important political function, providing evidence in the debates around 'the prime ethical and international problem of the age – whether war is to cease or not'.[1] But what kind of evidence does this new category of literature offer to its readers? What is it that the writings think they have seen?

Two sights are figured repeatedly in the soldiers' narratives of the Great War: corpses and bodies in pieces. For Frederic Manning, the most troubling sight of the war is the spectacle of men dying. It is not the mere fact of death, but the manner in which it occurs. 'Whether a man be killed by a rifle-bullet through the brain, or blown to fragments by a high-explosive shell, may seem a matter of indifference to the conscientious objector, or to any other equally well-placed observer' – that is, to those who do not actually *see*

---

1 John Brophy, introduction to *The Soldier's War: A Prose Anthology* (London, Dent, 1929), viii, vii. Brophy's comment was made at the height of what Samuel Hynes calls 'the great period of English prose-writing about the war', 1926 to 1933. Hynes, *A War Imagined: The First World War and English Culture* (London, The Bodley Head, 1990), 424. Works published during this period include Edmund Blunden, *Undertones of War* (1928); the four books of Ford Madox Ford's *Parade's End* (1924–8); Robert Graves, *Goodbye to All That* (1929); Ernest Hemingway, *A Farewell to Arms* (1929); Mary Borden, *The Forbidden Zone* (1929); Richard Aldington, *Death of a Hero* (1929); Frederic Manning, *The Middle Parts of Fortune* (1930); Helen Zenna Smith, *Not So Quiet* (1930); Vera Brittain, *Testament of Youth* (1933).

what happens – but it matters to the soldier. This might be an illusion, for 'a man is dead or not dead, and a man is just as dead by one means as by another', but for the witness, 'it is infinitely more horrible and revolting to see a man shattered and eviscerated, than to see him shot'. Manning's novel, like the other narratives discussed in this chapter, is obsessed with the sight of the human body at war: 'one sees such things; and one suffers vicariously', even as one refuses to confront what has been seen:

> The mind is averted as well as the eyes. It reassures itself after that first despairing cry: 'It is I!'
> 'No, it is not I. I shall not be like that.'
> And one moves on, leaving the mauled and bloody thing behind.[2]

And yet, paradoxically, for some writers, it is sights such as these which attract men to war in the first place, as Ernst Jünger suggests in *Storm of Steel* (1920):

> The horrible was undoubtedly a part of that irresistible attraction that drew us into the war. A long period of law and order, such as our generation had behind it, produces a real craving for the abnormal, a craving that literature stimulates. Among other questions that occupied us was this: what does it look like when there are dead lying about? (22–3)

This question animates many of the war narratives in one way or another: what does it look like when there are dead lying about? Or, worse, what does it look like when the dead are *not* lying about, but destroyed, atomised, reduced to fragments by the weapons of modern warfare? This chapter examines some of the best-known 'war books' published during and after the war, from Barbusse's *Under Fire* (1916) to Blunden's *Undertones of War* (1928) and Manning's *The Middle Parts of Fortune* (1930). The discussion which follows analyses the representations of this distressing material and asks: what does it mean, conceptually, historically, and within the context of particular narratives?

Of the nine million people who died in the Great War, many disappeared completely, leaving no identifiable body behind. This happened to approximately half of the British dead, for example,

---

2  Manning, *The Middle Parts of Fortune* (1930; London, Penguin, 1990), 10–11.

including Kipling's son John. The absence of a body to bury and to mourn was a source of profound trauma, both for soldiers and civilians. The bodies which did remain were also troublesome, for conditions of trench warfare sometimes made burial impossible and bodies would lie around, decomposing, for weeks or even months.[3] At times the living were surrounded by corpses throughout the trenches and adjacent areas. The dead were underfoot; they were used to reinforce the parapets of the trenches; they were stored in trenches awaiting burial. Some turned up in bizarre places, such as in the latrine, holding up a fragile doorway, or up a tree. All such events appear in the soldiers' writings. Corpses are trodden underfoot in *Undertones of War* and *Under Fire*; bodies support the parapet in *Goodbye to All That* (1929); Blunden refers to a corpse propping up a doorway in *Undertones of War*, and dead men are found in a tree in *All Quiet on the Western Front* (1929). Barbusse frequently depicts the living as completely surrounded by the dead, and Jünger's *Storm of Steel* (1920) is interested in the sight of soldiers' corpses which lie around, visibly, for months.[4]

Remarque's *All Quiet on the Western Front* is a novel set 'on the borders of death' (178). Near the beginning of the novel, the narrator, Paul, witnesses the pitiful death of his close friend, Kemmerich. Paul is suddenly strongly aware of being alive; he enters into a kind of ecstasy:

3 Paul Fussell, *The Great War and Modern Memory* (Oxford University Press, 1975), 47; J. M. Winter, *The Great War and the British People* (Basingstoke, Macmillan, 1986), 298; Winter, *The Experience of World War I* (Oxford, Equinox, 1988), 146. One function of memorials erected after the war was the symbolic reunification of absent and lost corpses of British soldiers. Catherine Moriarty, 'Christian Iconography and First World War Memorials', *Imperial War Museum Review*, 6, n.d. [*c.* 1991], 63–75. See also Hynes, *A War Imagined*, 281; Winter, *Sites of Memory, Sites of Mourning: The Great War in European Cultural History* (Cambridge University Press, 1995); Joanna Bourke, *Dismembering the Male: Men's Bodies, Britain and the Great War* (London, Reaktion, 1996); Adrian Gregory, *The Silence of Memory: Armistice Day 1914–1946* (Oxford, Berg, 1994).

4 Henri Barbusse, *Under Fire*, trans. W. Fitzwater Wray (1916; London, Dent, 1988), 224–8, 253; Blunden, *Undertones of War* (1928; Harmondsworth, Penguin, 1982), 125, 130–1; Graves, *Goodbye to All That* (1929; rev. edn 1957; Harmondsworth, Penguin, 1988), 96; Remarque, *All Quiet on the Western Front*, trans. A. W. Wheen (1929; London, Picador, [1990]), 137; Ernst Jünger, *Storm of Steel*, trans. Basil Creighton (1920; London, Chatto and Windus, 1929), 22.

Outside the door I am aware of the darkness and the wind as a deliverance [*Erlösung*]. I breathe as deep as I can, and feel the breeze in my face, warm and soft as never before. Thoughts of girls, of flowery meadows, of white clouds suddenly come into my head. My feet begin to move forward in my boots, I go quicker, I run. Soldiers pass by me, I hear their voices without understanding. The earth is streaming with forces which pour into me through the soles of my feet. The night crackles electrically, the front thunders like a concert of drums. My limbs move supplely [*sic*], I feel my joints strong, I breathe the air deeply. The night lives; I live. I feel a hunger, greater than comes from the belly alone. (27)

The use of *Erlösung* – relief or deliverance – is striking. It is a term with religious connotations: redemption, blessed relief, relief from suffering (*der Erlöser* means 'saviour'). And it is curious to find that it is Paul – who is alive and not physically suffering – who feels relief or redemption in response to the death of his friend. He simultaneously identifies with and rejects the condition of being dead, and asserts himself and the world around him as aggressively alive. Indeed, the sight of death leads, perversely, to romantic visions of girls and flowery meadows, just as Bourne in *The Middle Parts of Fortune* finds himself dreaming of 'womanly softness' in response to a disgusting memory of unburied bodies (11). In Barbusse's *Under Fire*, men celebrate 'the Feast of the Survivors. The boundless glory in which they rejoice is this – they still stand straight' (50). Some survivors of a battle 'seem to be dancing as they brandish their knives'; they are 'elated, immensely confident, ferocious', when they have just been trampling over the bodies of the dead (253). For Jünger, battle is followed by a period of quiet pleasure:

These drink-offerings on the morrow of well-fought fights count among an old soldier's happiest memories. And though ten out of twelve had fallen, still the last two, as sure as death, were to be found on the first evening of rest over the bottle, drinking a silent health to their dead companions, talking and laughing over all they had been through. For dangers past – an old soldier's laugh. For those to come – a full glass, though death and the devil grin there, as long as the wine was good. Such has ever been the custom of war. (140–1)

In *The Middle Parts of Fortune*, Manning describes a loss of appetite amongst survivors of a battle, followed by a rush to eat stale food 'ravenously'. 'Gradually their apathy cleared and lifted, as first their bodily functions, and then their habits of life asserted themselves. One after another they started shaving' (13). (And it is notable that their 'habit of life' here – shaving – is also a mark of adult manhood, distinguishing the men from women and boys.) In these examples we find the living defining themselves in relation to the dead, and celebrating their difference. Yet at the same time, the soldier's sense of his bodily identity is threatened by the mere presence of a corpse, as Julia Kristeva has recently suggested in *Powers of Horror*.

Kristeva describes the corpse, 'the most sickening of wastes', as a border, but 'a border that has encroached upon everything'.[5] It is the most powerfully affecting example of the *abject*. The abject is that which is excluded in the processes of constituting the subject, but which none the less lingers 'at the borders of our existence',[6] at once guaranteeing our subjectivity (for 'How can I *be* without border?'[7]) and threatening it with dissolution. This metaphor also functions at the level of an entire culture, which marks its boundaries by casting as abject – and rejecting – certain people or things which then hang around at the edges, marking the margins of society *as* margins by their very presence. Being rejected as a form of rubbish is precisely how soldiers see themselves at certain moments in the war narratives, especially in Barbusse's novel; it is particularly disturbing to find the living being cast as abjected, like the dead.

For the physical body, the abject (bodily fluids, waste, sweat, tears, etc.) simultaneously marks its boundaries and threatens to dissolve them. The abject is that which must be fully rejected; yet complete rejection is, paradoxically, always impossible. The living body 'extricates itself' from the 'theater' of waste and corpses – from the border between life and death. And yet some aspects of the abject (bodily fluids, waste) are also signs of being alive: 'Such wastes drop', writes Kristeva, 'so that I might live, until, from loss to loss, nothing remains in me and my entire body falls beyond the limit – *cadere*, cadaver.'[8] Producing and rejecting waste keeps one physically alive until the time one is 'waste'; similarly, one psychically

5  Julia Kristeva, *Powers of Horror: An Essay on Abjection*, trans. Leon S. Roudiez (1980; New York, Columbia University Press, 1982), 3.
6  Elizabeth Grosz, *Sexual Subversions: Three French Feminists* (Sydney, Allen and Unwin, 1989), 71.
7  Kristeva, *Powers of Horror*, 4.
8  Kristeva, *Powers of Horror*, 4, 3.

rejects the corpse (and the idea of the corpse) until one's own death. In *Goodbye to All That*, Graves supervises the collection of corpses for burial. As an officer, he does not have to handle them, but the sight and smell of the bodies make him vomit – a physical and psychic rejection of the abject (137). A similar scene occurs in A. P. Herbert's *The Secret Battle* (1919).[9]

Yet the corpse is, paradoxically, 'something rejected from which one does not part, from which one does not protect oneself as from an object. Imaginary uncanniness and real threat, it beckons to us and ends up engulfing us.'[10] On the one hand, the corpse as abject marks the threshold between subject and object and threatens to contaminate or dissolve the subject. It breaks down the distinction between being and non-being: the corpse exists, but in what sense can it be said to 'be'? The corpse is like an object, says Kristeva, in only one sense: it is 'opposed to I'.[11] But, on the other hand, the corpse marks the border which confirms the living person as alive, and can thus be a source of strength and affirmation to the subject. Survivors often felt guilty at being alive when their comrades were dead, as J. M. Winter points out,[12] but that guilt is sometimes figured in highly ambivalent terms. Survivors in the war writings are faced with trauma, guilt, and sorrow, but they also find some strange forms of pleasure. More than this: the war writings describe the fantasy relationship between the living and the dead, understood through the troubling figure of the corpse – inert matter which looks uncannily like a person.

## Body politics: Barbusse, *Under Fire*

*Under Fire* was one of the most influential novels of the Great War and appeared more than a decade earlier than most of the well-known English narratives of the war. Barbusse joined the French army at the age of forty-one, despite being exempted on the grounds of ill health, and worked as a stretcher-bearer in the front lines. He was awarded the Croix de Guerre for bravery in 1915 and

9   A. P. Herbert, *The Secret Battle* (1919; London, Chatto and Windus, 1970), 105.
10  Kristeva, *Powers of Horror*, 4.
11  Kristeva, *Powers of Horror*, 1.
12  Winter, *The Great War and the British People*, 300–2.

was invalided out of the war in 1917. From October 1915 he kept a diary of observations and conversations in the trenches. This formed the basis of his most famous novel, *Le Feu* (1916) which won the Prix Goncourt in 1917; the English translation, *Under Fire*, appeared in July of that year.[13]

Early admirers of the novel included Lenin, Sassoon, Owen, and Wyndham Lewis. By the end of the war it had sold nearly 250,000 copies.[14] It made a powerful impression on reviewers in Britain. For Muriel Ciolkowska in *The Egoist*, *Le Feu* made other war books seem like 'impertinencies'; similarly, Gerald Gould in the *New Statesman* felt that 'to "review" such a book in the ordinary sense of the term would be an impertinence'. Gould concluded that 'Everybody should read this book; but, most of all, politicians and journalists who advocate at their ease the compulsion of other people into unimaginable suffering'.[15] Even the conservative *Bookman*, which usually preferred middle-brow, patriotic works, declared it 'a great book; the most intensely and wonderfully realised revelation of the war', as well as an insight into 'the soul of the common French soldier' – the last comment effacing the internationalist politics so central to the argument of the book.[16] The *Times Literary Supplement* was struck by Barbusse's refusal to hate the enemy, and found it difficult to imagine such a work being written by an English writer or winning a prize in Britain – 'the "tendency" might have told against it'.[17]

*Under Fire* is fascinated by the bodily appearance of the ordinary soldiers, both alive and dead, and it frequently draws on corporeal metaphors to describe the trenches and the environment of war (the dug-out, for example, is like a human mouth, 'foul of

13 *Le Feu: Journal d'une Escouade* was published in parts in the left-wing periodical *L'Oeuvre* from August 1916, then as a book in December 1916. Hynes, *A War Imagined*, 203–6.

14 J. E. Flower, *Literature and the Left in France: Society, Politics and the Novel since the Late Nineteenth Century* (London, Methuen, 1983), 32; Frank Field, *Three French Writers and the Great War: Barbusse, Drieu La Rochelle, Bernanos: Studies in the Rise of Communism and Fascism* (Cambridge University Press, 1975), 38–9.

15 Muriel Ciolkowska, 'Le Feu', *The Egoist*, 4, 4 (May 1917), 55.

16 'Under Fire', *Bookman*, October 1917, 40.

17 'If an Englishman hated war as M. Barbusse hates it, he would not only not write about it, he would almost certainly not take part in it.' 'Le Feu', *Times Literary Supplement*, 5 April 1917, 164.

breath' (5)). It is through the spectacle of the human body – suffering, taking pleasure, and shaped by the experience of war – that Barbusse mobilises his political arguments for peace. When the soldiers first appear, the narrator describes them as 'shadows', 'huge and misshapen lumps, bear-like, that flounder and growl. They are "us". We are muffled like Eskimos. Fleeces and blankets and sacking wrap us up, weigh us down, magnify us strangely' (5–6). The soldiers are changing from their original human, French shapes: they are 'misshapen'; they are like bears, like Eskimos; their clothes distort them, make them seem larger. The layers they wear over their clothes 'mask and magnify the men, and wipe out their uniforms almost as effectively as their skins' (11), transforming their shape both as men and as soldiers. And they are not simply different from their former selves: *Under Fire* also emphasises their difference from one another:

> 'I say,' [says Barque,] 'we don't resemble each other much.'
> 'Why should we?' says Lamuse. 'It would be a miracle if we did.'
> (14)

And yet:

> Yes, we are truly and deeply different from each other. But we are alike all the same. In spite of this diversity of age, of country [i.e. region], of education, of position, of everything possible, in spite of the former gulfs that kept us apart, we are in the main alike. Under the same uncouth outlines we conceal and reveal the same ways and habits, the same simple nature of men who have reverted to the state primeval. (17)

The book frequently draws attention to the paradox of sameness and difference. In *The Secret Battle*, too, A. P. Herbert's narrator emphasises this paradox, but concludes that difference, especially class difference, is ultimately more important. Soldiers need as companions 'men who make the same kind of jokes' (25, 152). In *Under Fire*, the men begin to lose the alienating trappings of modern life which kept them apart (seen as a good change), but they are also reverting to a lower point on the evolutionary scale – becoming 'primeval'. This change is not seen as altogether bad, for to be 'more wild, more primitive' is to be 'more human' (40). The 'terrible narrowness of the common life' in war 'binds us close, adapts us, merges us one in the other', yet: 'It is a sort of fatal contagion' (17).[18] Barbusse keeps returning to the idea of equality – understood partly as *sameness*, whereby foreign men, including the present enemy, are recognised as the same as 'us' (335).

The first description of a corpse appears near the beginning of the novel when one man explains how he acquired a pair of boots from a dead German:

> Old man, he was there, his arse in a hole, doubled up, gaping at the sky with his legs in the air, and his pumps offered themselves to me with an air that meant they were worth my while. 'A tight fit,' says I. But you talk about a job to bring those beetle-crushers of his away! I worked on top of him, tugging, twisting and shaking, for half an hour and no lie about it. With his feet gone quite stiff, the patient didn't help me a bit. Then at last the legs of it – they'd been pulled about so – came unstuck at the knees, and his breeks tore away, and all the lot came, flop! There was me, all of a sudden, with a full boot in each fist. The legs and feet had to be emptied out. [...] We shoved our arms inside the boots and pulled out of 'em some bones and bits of sock and bits of feet. (13)

Here, the body and its parts are represented as grotesque, comical, but inoffensive. The scene teeters on the edge of disgust yet the body of the dead German ('the patient') is described with affection rather than revulsion. The second reference to a death is also comical and turns up during a discussion of cooks and their unfortunate tendency to be the dirtiest men in the army. Someone asks after a particular cook. 'He's dead,' is the reply. 'A bomb fell on his stove. *He* didn't get it, but he's dead all the same – died of shock when he saw his macaroni with its legs in the air. Heart seizure, so the doc' said' (30). This scene lacks the grotesque element of the boots scene, partly because the cook's body is not described. But there are echoes of the previous scene through the image of the legs in the air, rendered even more absurd and untroubling by being used to describe the macaroni.

It is not until nearly half-way through the book that the disturbing material for which Barbusse is famous begins to appear. This happens when the narrator and his friend unexpectedly come across 'rows of dead' waiting to be taken for burial.

18  See Geoffrey Gilbert, *A Career in Modernism: Wyndham Lewis 1909–1931* (Ph.D. dissertation, Cambridge, 1995), ch. 4.

They are close against each other, and each one indicates with arms or legs some different posture of stiffened agony. There are some with half-mouldy faces, the skin rusted, or yellow with dark spots. Of several the faces are black as tar, the lips hugely distended – the heads of negroes blown out in goldbeaters' skin. Between two bodies, protruding uncertainly from one or the other, is a severed wrist, ending with a cluster of strings. (146–7)

Death creates new kinds of difference amongst the soldiers, figured in terms of a fictional 'race' or colour which Barbusse reports without comment. In Herbert's *The Secret Battle*, by contrast, the English officers are revolted at the sight of dead white bodies at Gallipoli turning black in the heat. This spectacle kills the 'Romance of War' for the central character, turning war into a 'necessary but disgusting business, to be endured, like a dung-hill' (70–1). Yet the bodies in *Under Fire* are simultaneously undifferentiated: it is impossible to see which corpse is attached to the severed wrist. A more extreme account of the loss of human shape follows:

Others are shapeless larvae of pollution, with dubious items of equipment pricking up, or bits of bone. Farther on, a corpse has been brought in in such a state that they have been obliged – so as not to lose it on the way – to pile it on a lattice of wire which was then fastened to the two ends of a stake. Thus was it carried in the hollow of its metal hammock, and laid there. You cannot make out either end of the body; alone in the heap that it makes, one recognises the gape of a trouser-pocket. An insect goes in and out of it. (147)

The individual body is figured in terms of an absence. Although material enough to be collected as a single entity – and those collecting it treat it as one object, which they are trying not to lose – it has no recognisable shape or coherence. The only familiar part is itself an absence, a space – 'the gape of a trouser pocket'. The comical 'legs in the air' of the earlier chapters is now represented seriously as a 'posture of stiffened agony', the moment of death frozen in the body's posture.

Most important for Barbusse is the effect of this sight on those who survive. Towards the end of the scene just quoted, the corpse marks the boundaries of the bodies of the living. Two stretcher-bearers appear out of the fog, 'joined together by something they are carrying' (147–8). It is a 'new' corpse.

73

LIVERPOOL JOHN MOORES UNIVERSITY
LEARNING SERVICES

They put down the body, which is dressed in new clothes.

'It's not long since, now, that he was standing', says one of the bearers. 'It's two hours since he got his bullet in the head for going to look for a Boche rifle in the plain. He was going on leave on Wednesday and wanted to take a rifle home with him.' (148)

The bearer removes a covering from the dead face: 'It is quite young and seems to sleep' – a scene from a pastoral poem, 'except that an eyeball has gone, the cheek looks waxen, and a rosy liquid has run over the nostrils, mouth and eyes'. Of all the terrible sights, this corpse alone affects the viewers: 'The body strikes a note of cleanliness in the charnel-house, this still pliant body that lolls its head aside when it is moved as if to lie better; it gives a childish illusion of being less dead than the others' (148). Marking the threshold, this corpse blurs the boundaries between life and death. It seems 'nearer to one, more intimate, as we look'. The men look at it with pity, but do not speak: 'And had we said anything in the presence of all that heap of beings destroyed, it would have been "Poor boy!"' (148). Yet the act of looking is an attempt to turn the abject into an object; to reassert the boundaries of the living body. Elsewhere, this is taken further, when the dead become the enemies of the living, threatening the living both psychically and physically. This relationship is complicated, however, when the corpses are the bodies of the characters' beloved comrades. When four of the central characters in *Under Fire* are killed, their bodies are kept in the trench with their living friends. And though the bodies are not really the 'selves' of the dead – 'they are too far disfigured,' says the narrator, 'for us to say truly "It is *they*"' (228) – they are none the less described as 'definitely distinct'. Each corpse has its own look and behaviour; the narrator reads its posture and appearance as a kind of characterisation (227–8). Lamuse, in particular, with his arm protruding from the 'heap of dead', touches people in the face as they walk by (228). But it is not really 'Lamuse', nor any of the narrator's friends. The corpses are 'motionless monsters'. The living must 'turn away' from the corpse in order to accept the death of their friends and 'feel the void they have left among us'. The corpse *represents* the dead man; its presence signifies his absence.

Shortly after this, the dead threaten the living directly: 'Like posts and heaps of rubbish, corpses are piled anyhow on the wounded, and press them down, suffocate them, strangle them' (253). Yet this is not the only cause of the inert killing. On top of the dead are the narrator and his 'living ragged band' of comrades, trampling 'soft bodies underfoot, some of which are moving and slowly altering their position; rivulets and cries come from them' (252–3). And, as in Remarque's text, the survivors assert themselves aggressively as not-dead: 'There is some change working in them. A frenzied excitement is driving them all out of themselves. [...] They shake themselves like banners. They carry the luck of their survival as [if] it were glory; they are implacable, uncontrolled, intoxicated with themselves' (252–3).

Finally, it is in the presence of yet another corpse that the men resolve to build a new world on the ruins of the war, recognising the common interest amongst the men who have been sent to fight – and die – in a war that seems to serve none of their interests. 'It is we who are the material of war', argues the narrator. 'War is made up of the flesh and the souls of common soldiers only. It is we who make the plains of dead and the rivers of blood, all of us, and each of us is invisible and silent because of the immensity of our numbers. [...] Yes, war is all of us and all of us together' (334). 'The people – they're nothing, though they ought to be everything', says another, struggling to come to a political understanding of the physical suffering of the war (335). As this discussion takes place, the men are joined by the silent presence of a corpse, exhumed by a landslide in a pile of mud. The body is broken and sits in their midst 'folded the wrong way' (333). They are momentarily disturbed by the corpse's face – until they realise it is the back of its head – but continue their discussion, which has been 'revived by this fearful sleeper'. They speak as though 'the corpse were listening' (333). Rather than turning away from the corpse, they incorporate it into their analysis of the war and the need for a new order. A version of this idea is common in a lot of writing about the war – the dead are better than the living; they must not have died in vain, etc. – but *Under Fire* is one of the few works to confront the material body rather than an abstract idea of the 'glorious dead'.

## Repression and fascination: Blunden, *Undertones of War*

Blunden's *Undertones of War* is one of the least explicitly violent of the famous soldiers' narratives. It was written in Tokyo in 1924 and published in 1928 in London, where it sold out in one day.[19] *Undertones of War* is a curious book, well respected by critics even as it generates a distinct sense of unease.[20] Blunden rarely describes the violence of the war directly, and often resorts to euphemism or studied nonchalance: 'a man had gone west' (75); 'Outside, men were killed from time to time' (172). The remains of a mangled body are described thus: 'the skeleton seemed less coherent than most' (27). British weapons 'do mischief' or are 'conjuring-tricks'; bombardments are 'disturbances' (68) or 'ungentle interludes' (107). The trauma of warfare is made bearable through the use of a knowing, upper-middle-class understatement, working against the fantasy of the combatant as 'a harmless young shepherd in soldier's coat' (242).

Most of the details of the war's violence are suppressed. Even the disgusting memory which haunts Blunden is described in relatively mild terms. Characteristically understated as 'my own unwelcome but persistent retrospect', Blunden's recurring vision is the sight of two 'flattened' German corpses lying in a shell-hole which the British use as a latrine. These corpses are remembered as 'tallow-faced and dirty-stubbled, one spectacled, with fingers hooking the handle of a bomb' (128). The actual sight of the bodies is mentioned four pages earlier, but there no detail is given, and the 'sprawling corpses' are said to be overlooking the latrine hole, rather than lying in it, as they are in memory. Blunden does not comment upon this discrepancy, and it is quite striking to find the bodies shifted into an even more abjected state – lying in the British men's excrement – in his memory of the scene.

Blunden's memoir is partly an attempt to repress the horrible sights of war and to contain them within the reassuring conventions of pastoral narrative. Yet the book is also fascinated by the vision of horror. This emerges in chapter 5, when Blunden's battalion is based near the 'tattered' village of Richebourg St Vaaste: 'The large church, and the almost rococo churchyard, astonished everybody: they had been

---

19 Preface, *Undertones of War*, 8; Fussell, *The Great War and Modern Memory*, 256.

20 Hynes, for example, calls it 'one of the best' of the English autobiographies of the war (*A War Imagined*, 426), and Fussell argues that it is widely agreed to be 'one of the permanent works engendered by memories of the war' (*The Great War and Modern Memory*, 255). The unease is noted by Tylee, *The Great War and Women's Consciousness* (Basingstoke, Macmillan, 1990), 227.

bombarded into that state of demi-ruin which discovers the *strongest fascination* (56; emphasis added). The description continues:

> At the foot of the monolith-like steeple stood a fine and great bell, and against that, a rusty shell of almost the same size; the body and blood of Christ, in effigy of ochred wood, remained on the wall of the church. Men went to contemplate that group, but more to stare into the very popular tombs all round, whose vaults gaped unroofed, nor could protect their charges any longer from the eye of life. Greenish water stood in some of these pits; bones and skulls and decayed cerements there attracted frequent soldiers past the 'No Loitering' notice board. Why should these mortalities lure those who ought to be trying to forget mortality, ever threatening them? Nearly corpses ourselves, by the mere fact of standing near Richebourg Church, how should we find the strange and the remote in these corpses? I remember these remarks: 'How long till dinner, Alf?' 'Half an hour, chum.' 'Well, I'll go and 'ave a squint at the churchyard.' (56)

The wreckage and bodies in this scene 'lure' the soldiers there; like the bombed building at the beginning of the passage, they are irresistible, fascinating. This idea appears in a good many war narratives. In Barbusse's *Under Fire*, one character is 'attracted towards the dead by a strange curiosity' (266); A. P. Herbert in *The Secret Battle* notes the 'hideous fascination' of dead bodies (105); tank driver Arthur Jenkin is 'curious' to see the dead in a civilian cemetery. Charles Carrington describes how one man gloats at the sight of dead bodies; 'There's some good ones over there', he says, 'enjoying himself'. Of his own experience of seeing dead bodies for the first time, Carrington comments: 'I felt neither afraid nor unhappy, but fascinated. These things were less like men than the friendly earth to which they were returning. They were unclean. I returned satisfied; I had seen a corpse.'[21] Corpses are a spectacle, uncanny and fascinating, that the men keep returning to see. In other writings, this vision has precisely the opposite effect; Herbert Read, for example, writes of a soldier rendered 'impotent' by the sight of a body which is accidently dug up.[22]

---

21  Jenkin, *A Tank Driver's Experiences: Or Incidents in a Soldier's Life* (London, Elliot Stock, 1922), 165; Charles Edmonds [pseud. of Charles Carrington], *A Subaltern's War* (London, Peter Davies, 1929), 55.

22  Read, 'Kneeshaw Goes to War', *Naked Warriors* (1919), rpt in *Collected Poems* (1966; London, Sinclair-Stevenson, n.d.), 32.

## Bodies in pieces

Every war is historically specific. The technology and ideology of warfare change over time, as do cultural ideas about warfare, the individual subject, and social organisation. Perhaps the most enduring image of the Great War is of the male body in fragments – an image in which war technology and notions of the human body intersect in horrible new ways. Developments in weapons technology made it possible for unprecedented numbers of men to be blown apart in battle; many more were witness to such sight. 'I saw 'im, sir', says a character in Manning's *The Middle Parts of Fortune* (1930), "'e were just blown to buggery. [...] 'e were a chum o' mine, sir, an' I seen 'im blown into fuckin' bits' (21). Some bodies were atomised completely and disappeared out of sight. Sometimes just one part of the body (often the feet) remained behind while the rest vanished,[23] or the entire body might be dismembered and scattered around (or upon) the men nearby – this is one reason that so many of the dead were never found for burial. These were new experiences of war, and the combatants' narratives worry at what this means for those who survived and were witness to such sights.

Blunden's *Undertones of War* is less overtly violent than the other war narratives, but its tone of poetic melancholy is occasionally disrupted by scenes of extreme and unexpected violence. An example of this occurs quite early in the novel, in chapter 6:

> Not far away [...] a young and cheerful lance-corporal of ours was making some tea as I passed one warm afternoon. Wishing him a good tea, I went along three firebays; one shell dropped without warning behind me; I saw its smoke faint out, and I thought all was as lucky as it should be. Soon a cry from that place recalled me; the shell had burst all wrong. Its butting impression was black and stinking in the parados where three minutes ago the lance-corporal's mess-tin was bubbling over a little flame. For him, how could the gobbets of blackening flesh, the earth-wall sotted with blood, with flesh, the eye under the duck-board, be the only answer? At this moment, while we looked with dreadful fixity at so isolated a horror, the lance-corporal's brother came around the traverse. (67)

23 Percy Smith's etching *Death Awed* (1918) represents the figure of Death arrested in his tracks by the sight of a pair of boots with splinters of leg sticking out and no sign of the rest of the body anywhere in the empty landscape.

The horror of the man being blown to pieces is turned into a kind of grim comedy when the brother turns up at precisely the wrong moment. And the focus is shifted to Blunden feeling caught out, like a guilty schoolboy, looking at something intimate or forbidden. The scene is extremely controlled and makes its devices quite obvious, setting up the lance-corporal (young and cheerful), the afternoon (warm) and Blunden (kindly wishing the lance-corporal a 'good tea') as almost excessive in their pleasantness. Even the shell seems benign at first: its smoke seems simply to 'faint out' and enhance Blunden's sense of everything being 'lucky'. This pleasant world is suddenly blown apart; the shell, though doing precisely what it is designed to do, is seen as having 'burst all wrong'.

The setting of such a benign scene increases the horror of the event but also renders it curiously aesthetic. The language, too, is rather poetic: 'bubbling', 'gobbets', 'sotted'. Aesthetic pleasure and disgust are here merged, as they are in the passage depicting the men's fascination with civilian corpses, discussed above. The scene continues:

> He [the brother] was sent to company headquarters in a kind of catalepsy. The bay had to be put right, and red-faced Sergeant Simmons, having helped himself and me to a share of rum, biting hard on his pipe, shovelled into the sandbag I held, not without self-protecting profanity, and an air of 'it's a lie; we're a lie'. (67)

What are they putting into the sandbag? We know from the beginning of the scene that it is the fragments of a dead man, but there is a conscious refusal to name it here, even though the grammar of the sentence seems to demand an object for the verb 'shovelled'. This in fact intensifies the horror of the event by partially veiling it; the act of suppression draws the reader's attention to that which has been suppressed. A similar veiling occurs near the beginning of the war section in *Goodbye to All That*, when Graves first arrives in the trenches. As he is being guided into the front line, an injured man is carried past on a stretcher. 'Who's the poor bastard, Dai?' the guide asks one of the stretcher-bearers.

> 'Sergeant Gallagher', Dai answered. 'He thought he saw a Fritz in No Man's Land near our wire, so the silly booger takes one of them new issue percussion bombs and shots it at 'im. Silly booger aims too low, it hits the top of the parapet and bursts back. Deoul! man, it breaks his

silly f—ing jaw and blows a great lump from his silly f—ing face, whatever. Poor silly booger! Not worth sweating to get him back! He's put paid to, whatever.' (84)

'The wounded man had a sandbag over his face', says Graves. 'He died before they got him to the dressing-station' (84). The man's mutilated face is not described; the reader is given merely a tantalising allusion to a disgusting sight. Later, however, the veil will be lifted and such sights will be described in abundance. Graves is at once disgusted by the violence of the war and compelled to describe it. His novel is deeply interested in the horrible sights and uncomfortably aware of the pleasure which lies on the other side of disgust.[24] *Goodbye to All That* provides descriptions of destroyed and decomposing bodies which fascinate and sicken simultaneously; part of the text's power comes from its consciousness of the relationship between these two sensations.

Dismembered bodies and body parts are described in many of the war narratives. Sometimes they are grotesquely comical – two rats tussling over a severed hand in *Goodbye to All That*, for example; the legs in the air in *Under Fire* discussed above – but more often they are used to signify the terror and sorrow of the frail human body facing the machinery of war. In Remarque's *All Quiet*, for example, Paul watches a French soldier falling into the barbed wire. 'His body collapses, his hands remain suspended as though he were praying. Then his body drops clean away and only his hands with the stumps of his arms, shot off, now hang in the wire' (77). Parts of the body which might be grotesquely funny in isolation elicit horror and pity when they are seen to be lost from a dying person. This is reinforced by Paul's reading of the dead man's final gesture as the supplication or piety of prayer. Elsewhere in *All Quiet*, bodies are reduced almost to nothing; here the horror teeters on the edge of hysterical laughter when two men are 'smashed so' that one

---

24 Ned Lukacher, 'The Epistemology of Disgust', foreword to Monique David-Ménard, *Hysteria from Freud to Lacan: Body and Language in Psychoanalysis*, trans. Catherine Porter (1983; Ithaca NY, Cornell University Press, 1989), viii. Lukacher notes that the link between pleasure and disgust was made by Freud in the late 1890s, leading him 'to the very threshold of the pleasure principle'. See also Ernest Jones, 'War and Individual Psychology', *Sociological Review*, 8 (1915), discussed in Daniel Pick, *War Machine: The Rationalisation of Slaughter in the Modern Age* (New Haven, Yale University Press, 1993), 256.

character remarks 'you could scrape them off the wall of the trench with a spoon and bury them in a mess tin' (87).

## These men were men

Frederic Manning's *The Middle Parts of Fortune* and Richard Aldington's *Death of a Hero* are both fascinated by the spectacle of men at war. Aldington is concerned about how this might be interpreted, however, and near the beginning of the novel the narrator warns against certain kinds of reading.

> Let me at once disabuse the eager-eyed Sodomites among my readers by stating emphatically once and for all that there was nothing sodomitical in these friendships [between soldiers]. I have lived and slept for months, indeed years, with 'the troops', and had several such companionships. But no vaguest proposal was ever made to me; I never saw any signs of sodomy, and never heard anything to make me suppose it existed.[25]

That homosexual desire and practice should be completely invisible or even non-existent is historically questionable, to say the least. Homosexuality and homoeroticism were present among soldiers in the Great War, just as among any other section of society. Indeed, the war provided opportunities for erotic relationships among men which were not necessarily available in peacetime. But the implausibility of the narrator's denial is precisely what makes it so arresting. The idea of homosexuality is resisted by Winterbourne, the central character, too. When his wife Elizabeth wants to start a 'crusade' against the persecution of homosexual men, Winterbourne refuses to support her, arguing that 'ordinary' relations need to be put 'on a decent basis first' (197). Moreover, he says he is afraid that to support the rights of homosexual men would make him 'suspect'. 'It's a damned dangerous thing to do in England; in most cases the suspicion is far too likely to be true!' (198). Winterbourne is prepared to tolerate homosexual men only if they 'keep jolly quiet about it, and [do] not try to make themselves martyrs, and flaunt

25  Richard Aldington, *Death of a Hero* (1929; London, Hogarth, 1984), 30–1. On Aldington's war experiences, see Hugh Cecil, *The Flower of Battle: British Fiction Writers of the First World War* (London, Secker and Warburg, 1995), ch. 2; Charles Doyle, *Richard Aldington: A Biography* (Basingstoke, Macmillan, 1989), ch. 5.

themselves publicly'. 'I respect their freedom, of course, but I don't like them. As a matter of fact, I don't know any, at least so far as I am aware. No doubt some of our friends are homosexual; but as I'm not personally interested in it, I never notice it' (198). The contradictions here are interesting. Winterbourne claims to respect the 'freedom' of gay men, as long as they keep their desires secret and don't demand the same freedoms as heterosexuals. He says he does not know any homosexual men, yet he is certain he does not like them. His inability to 'notice' homosexuality among his friends seems peculiarly unobservant. The shaky logic in these passages suggests that homosexuality might be something of a problem for this text. It certainly worried Aldington. In a letter to his ex-wife, HD, written in the same year as *Death of a Hero*, he argues:

> Derek [Patmore] is a homosexual, and knows quantities of effeminate pederasts, the kind of men who simply make me sick. It's so absolutely different in women, something quite normal and natural. But these little vindictive half-men are intolerable, especially to me, since I have lived and suffered with real men, and know how magnificent they are. Out of loyalty to Derek, Brigit [Derek's mother] accepts and is influenced by these miserable little scented worms, and that makes a rather difficult situation. I WON'T accept them. Out of loyalty to the dead I won't accept them.[26]

The hysterical repudiation of homosexuals as 'half-men' and 'scented worms' reappears in *Death of a Hero* and is particularly striking when set against Aldington's celebration of the bodies of 'real' men. When Winterbourne, the central character, first sees soldiers returning from the Front, he is 'charmed' by the sight of them:

> These men were men. There was something intensely masculine about them, something very pure and immensely friendly and stimulating. They had been where no woman and no half-man had ever been, could endure to be. There was something timeless and remote about them, as if [...] they had been Roman legionaries or the men of Austerlitz or even the invaders of the Empire. They looked barbaric, but not brutal; determined, but not cruel. Under their grotesque wrappings, their bodies looked lean and hard and tireless. They were Men. (253)

26  Richard Aldington, letter to HD, 20 May 1929, *Richard Aldington and HD: The Later Years in Letters*, ed. Caroline Zilboorg (Manchester University Press, 1995), 40.

Beside such Men, writes Aldington, the 'fresh faces of the new drafts seemed babyish – rounded and rather feminine'. Soldiers become objects of erotic interest for the man watching, even as Aldington anxiously repudiates the very idea of homosexuality; masculinity takes many forms in the novel, even as Aldington tries to formulate a single model of real manhood.

Quite a different vision of returned soldiers can be found in Herbert's *The Secret Battle*, where the narrator observes 'some of them with slight bodily wounds, but all of them with grievous injury staring out of their eyes' (3). Like Aldington, Herbert is concerned by the injustice of the war; unlike Aldington, he locates the effect of suffering in the damaged gaze of returned soldiers. Mary Borden's memoir of nursing, *The Forbidden Zone*, published in the same year as *Death of a Hero*, is similarly interested in the eyes and bodies of groups of soldiers. But where Aldington celebrates a breed of virile Men, Borden sees 'a column of hunchbacks, a herd of deformed creatures'.[27]

> They did not look quite like men. One could not be certain what kind of men they were. [...] They had not quite the colour nor the shape of men. [...] And they were all deformed, and certainly their deformity was the deformity of war. They were not misshapen in different ways. They were all misshapen in the same way. Each one was deformed like the next one. Each one had been twisted and bent in the same way. [...] The same machine had twisted and bent them all. They did not look quite like men, and yet they were men. (24–5)

> I saw in their eyes that they were men. [...] And in their deep fixed eyes [...] there was a strange expression, the expression of profound knowledge. (26)

For Borden, the soldiers' eyes express a trauma and a masculinity which is somehow separate from the suffering body. Their 'stupified, patient, hopeless eyes' also signify 'how boring it is to be a hero' (2). Later, she describes how civilian men and women in a hospital near the Front care for the soldiers with an extraordinary blend of gentleness and cruelty. 'This is the place they are mended', she writes, likening the wounded men to clothes which are sent to

---

27  Borden, *The Forbidden Zone* (London, William Heinemann, 1929), 23. For a discussion of Borden, see Tylee, *The Great War and Women's Consciousness*, 98–101.

the laundry (117). The medical staff take complete control of the soldiers' bodies:

> We lift him on to a table. We peel off his clothes, his coat and his shirt and his trousers and his boots. We handle his clothes that are stiff with blood. We cut off his shirt with large scissors. We stare at the obscene sight of his innocent wounds. He allows us to do this. He is helpless to stop us. (119)

The staff work with tenderness, fascination, and an eroticised horror on this body which is in their power:

> We experiment with his bones, his muscles, his sinews, his blood. We dig into the yawning mouths of his wounds. Helpless openings, they let us into the secret places of his body. We plunge deep in his body. We make discoveries within his body. (119–20)

Enid Bagnold's nursing memoir, *Diary Without Dates* (1918), comments on the significance of the sight of the wounded men, the hidden knowledge 'beneath the dressings'.[28] Bagnold criticises a pacifist friend for thinking that 'his and his "movement's" are the only eyes to see the vision of horror. Why, these others [the patients] *are* the vision!' (104); for Bagnold, a Voluntary Aid Detachment nurse in England, the sight of injured male bodies *is* the war. Even some of the wounded men in this book come to regard their injuries as spectacle: ''Tisn' no more me arm', comments one soldier of his 'unrecognizable' limb; ''Tisn' me arm, it's me wound' (115).

The soldiers' and nurses' narratives display a similar kind of interest in damaged soldiers, and they all pay homage to representations of suffering in the poetry of Sassoon, Owen, Gurney, and Rosenberg. The difference between viewer and spectacle – or between subject and damaged object – is frequently more important than the difference between women and men. The war alters bodies in disturbing new ways; the difference between someone who is wounded and someone who is not is far more profound and psychically disturbing than the distinctions of sexual difference. This in turn raises questions about how we might understand the theorising of sexual difference during this period – by Freud, for example – and I will return to this in the following chapter.

The war narratives I have discussed all focus on the sight of the

---

28  Enid Bagnold, *Diary Without Dates* (1918; London, Virago, 1979), 90.

male body, suffering, in pieces, as a corpse. There are obvious historical reasons for this, since the vast majority of combatants were men, yet the Great War also killed women who worked in munitions factories or volunteered as nurses, workers, and ambulance drivers at the Front. Women civilians were injured and killed in the war zones, in aerial attacks on civilian areas, and at sea. Dead women are rarely represented in the narratives discussed here, but when they do appear they help us to see how the bodily difference of death or injury often outweighs the notion of sexual difference.

## Dead women

In Helen Zenna Smith's *Not So Quiet* (1930), the narrator imagines her generation as 'a race of men bodily maimed and of women mentally maimed', a distinction which has become a commonplace about the First World War. Yet when the women workers at the Front in *Not So Quiet* are caught in an air raid, they suffer exactly the same kinds of injuries as the men.[29] Sexual difference disappears in the face of modern weaponry; all human bodies become mangled flesh and blood. Smith's women are volunteers in the war zones – VADs, ambulance drivers, Women's Army Auxiliary Corps – like soldiers, they are vulnerable to physical and mental trauma.[30]

Barbusse's *Under Fire* is one of the few well-known war narratives to represent a civilian woman in the trenches. She first appears in chapter 4. After the matter-of-fact tone used to describe the men, the prose suddenly becomes mock-lyrical: 'She was slender, her head all afire with fair hair, and in her pale face we could see the

29  Smith, *Not So Quiet* (1930; London, Virago, 1988), 167, 159, 237–8.
30  For discussions of writings by and about women in the war zones, see Tylee, *The Great War and Women's Consciousness*; Sharon Oudit, *Fighting Forces, Writing Women: Identity and Ideology in the First World War* (London, Routledge, 1994); Margaret Randolph Higonnet *et al.*, eds, *Behind the Lines: Gender and the Two World Wars* (New Haven, Yale University Press, 1987); Helen M. Cooper *et al.*, eds, *Arms and the Woman* (Chapel Hill, University of North Carolina Press, 1989); Dorothy Goldman, ed., *Women and World War I: The Written Response* (Basingstoke, Macmillan, 1993); Jane Potter, 'A Great Purifier: The Great War in Women's Romances and Memoirs', Helen Small, 'Mrs Humphry Ward and the First Casualty of War', Suzanne Raitt, '"Contagious Ecstasy": May Sinclair's War Journals', and Con Coroneos, 'Flies and Violets in Katherine Mansfield', all in Raitt and Tate, eds, *Women's Fiction and the Great War*.

night-dark caverns of great eyes. The resplendent being gazed fixedly upon us, trembling, then plunged abruptly into the undergrowth and disappeared like a torch' (56). Her name is Eudoxie; Lamuse is attracted to her and thinks she is interested in him even though she runs away whenever she sees him. The narrator sees her following another of their comrades, Farfadet, and believes she is attracted to him (58). We never learn what she actually wants, however. When Lamuse eventually declares his interest in Eudoxie, she seems revolted:

> 'Leave me alone – you disgust me!'
> [...] He draws her to him. His head bends towards her, and his lips are ready. His desire – the wish of all his strength and all his life – is to caress her. He would die that he might touch her with his lips. But she struggles, and utters a choking cry. She is trembling, and her beautiful face is disfigured with abhorrence. (79–80)

Her face is 'disfigured', in uncanny anticipation of her own death. Much later in the novel, the narrator comes across Lamuse in a state of distress. He wants to speak to the narrator privately: 'When I am by him he whispers to me, very low, and as if in church, "I have seen Eudoxie again." He gasps for breath, his chest wheezes, and with his eyeballs fast fixed upon a nightmare, he says, "She was putrid."' (196). Lamuse has found her body as he cleared out the debris from a caved-in trench. Something 'like a big sandbag', a 'queer sack' falls on him: it is Eudoxie's corpse, moulding, dead 'for a month perhaps' (197). Her body seems to *want* to fall on him:

> 'Old man, she wanted to kiss me, and I didn't want – it was terrible. She seemed to be saying to me, "You wanted to kiss me, well then, come, come *now*!" She had on her – she had *there*, fastened on, the remains of a bunch of flowers, and that was rotten, too, and the posy stank in my nose like the corpse of some little beast.
> 'I had to take her in my arms, in both of them, and turn gently round so that I could put her down on the other side. The place was so narrow and pinched that as we turned, for a moment, I hugged her to my breast and couldn't help it, with all my strength, old chap, as I should have hugged her once on [*sic*] a time if she'd have let me.
> 'I've been half an hour cleaning myself from the touch of her and the smell that she breathed on me in spite of me and in spite of herself. [...]'
> He turns over on his belly, clenches his fists, and slumbers, with his

face buried in the ground and his dubious dream of passion and putre-
faction. (197–8)

Like the dead soldiers, the dead civilian woman turns into a piece of
rubbish. But even as a corpse she is still an object of love and some
desire; even without a 'self', the woman is still a woman. Her femininity is located in her body (which is at once inert and involun-
tarily active) and its trappings (the decorative posy, her hair). Yet the
text also mocks this simplistic notion of femininity through the
sheer excess of manner in the passages quoted above.

If the soldier's corpse in Barbusse is an uncanny man – a subject
fallen into abjection, which the viewer tries to recast as an object –
the female corpse crosses the boundaries of subjectivity from the
opposite direction. In death, Eudoxie's body goes through the
motions of a desiring subject – something it is not permitted to do
in life. None the less, they are Lamuse's discarded desires, rather
than her own, that her body enacts. Like the political discussion in
the final chapter which tries to include the male corpse, *Under Fire*
attempts here to use the woman's corpse to rethink the structure of
sexual difference. The scene is shocking and perverse and raises
challenging questions about gender and sexuality in the war, unsettling the distinctions between subject and object; desiring and
desired, active and passive; masculine and feminine. The representation of the corpse disturbs the narrative which seeks to contain it;
at the same time, the narrative itself is an act of ritual, a fantasy
cleansing of abjected matter; these contradictions are never fully
resolved.

## Bodies in the earth

In many scenes in the war novels we find the living and the dead
brought together into uncomfortable proximity, jumbled together
within the earth of the trenches. A strange relationship is established
between the body and the earth. The earth is where the dead are (or
will be) buried, but it is also the place in which the living are located
– literally in and under the ground – in trench warfare.[31] The spatial

---

31 Fussell notes that some soldiers spent most of the war underground; *The Great
War and Modern Memory*, 41, 51; see also Winter, *The Experience of World War
I*, 145.

distinctions between the living body and the corpse are broken down, threatening the boundaries of the 'clean and proper body'.[32] 'The whole zone was a corpse, and the mud itself mortified', writes Blunden of an area near Thiepval (131). Living in the earth is often a claustrophobic experience. In Remarque's *All Quiet*, one of the young recruits goes mad from being enclosed in a dug-out under fire, and tries to escape into the open. 'It is a case of claustrophobia', says the narrator, 'he feels as though he is suffocating here and wants to get out at any price.' His comrades know, however, that he would fail to protect himself outside and soon be killed; they beat him up, 'to bring him to his senses', and make him stay inside (75–6). The other men, too, feel they are sitting in their own graves in the dug-out, 'waiting only to be closed in' (76). (The recruit goes mad again and 'butts his head against the wall like a goat'; the others tie him up for his own safety and theirs.) In 'The Refuge', a chapter in *Under Fire* set in an underground field hospital, the place of refuge is also malign and claustrophobic. The men enter it in an inverted image of being born: 'Once inside you have a first impression of being trapped [...]. As you go on burying yourself in the gulf, the nightmare of suffocation continues [...]. On all sides you bump and scrape yourself, you are clutched by the tightness of the passage, you are wedged and stuck' (277). Yet the earth is often the only place of safety in trench warfare and is figured as a welcoming, encompassing, safe place. The soldier's relationship to the land is ambivalent and oddly eroticised, as Remarque suggests:

> To no man does the earth mean so much as to the soldier. When he presses himself down upon her long and powerfully, when he buries his face and his limbs deep in her from the fear of death by shell-fire, then she is his only friend, his brother, his mother; he stifles his terror and his cries in her silence and her security [*Geborgenheit*]; she shelters him and releases him for ten seconds to live, to run, ten seconds of life; receives him again and often for ever.
>
> Earth! – Earth! – Earth!
>
> Earth with thy folds, and hollows, and holes, into which a man may fling himself and crouch down. In the spasm of terror, under the hailing of annihilation, in the bellowing death of the explosions, O Earth,

---

32 Kristeva, *Powers of Horror*, viii, 72: the 'corps propre'. An injured man in *Under Fire* complains that 'up to last week I was young and I was clean. [...] Now, I've got nothing but a dirty old rotten body to drag along' (281).

thou grantest us the great resisting surge of new-won life. Our being, almost utterly carried away by the fury of the storm, streams back through our hands from thee, and we, thy redeemed ones, bury ourselves in thee, and through the long minutes in a mute agony of hope bite into thee with our lips! (41–2)

The earth protects men from dismemberment and death, yet is here subjected to a biting of the maternal breast as well as to a figurative invasion or rape. It is both mother and (feminine) lover, yet is also brother and masculine friend (*sein einziger Freund*). It gives birth to the men many times over and enfolds them in death. And in return for the earth's ambiguous nurturing the men will attack it with their bombs, guns, fire, etc. in a frenzy of infantile destructiveness.[33] The novel is not simply imagining violence against the maternal body, however; its representations of Paul's mother, for example, are full of gentleness and compassion.

In Manning's *The Middle Parts of Fortune*, the earth is sexualised in different terms:

> Bourne, floundering in the viscous mud, was at once the most abject and the most exalted of God's creatures. The effort and rage in him, the sense that others had left them to it, made him pant and sob, but there was some strange intoxication of joy in it, and again all his mind seemed focused into one hard point of action. The extremities of pain and pleasure had met and coincided too. (215)

Bourne pants and sobs with effort, rage and joy and is transformed into a 'hard point of action'. He is at once humiliated and elevated, masochistically and sadistically excited, abject and exalted; his ecstasy is both religious and sexual. Moments of terror and suffering are remembered (or imagined) as producing oddly eroticised forms of pleasure which complicate the narratives' relationship to the history of the war. In other words, these writings are as much concerned with war as *fantasy* as with war as an historical event.

Sometimes images of mutilation and suffering are displaced

---

33 Klaus Theweleit also quotes this passage, but he interprets it as portraying the earth as 'the giver of life': *Male Fantasies*, vol. 1, trans. Stephen Conway (Cambridge, Polity, 1987), 239n. See also the section of *Male Fantasies* entitled 'Exploding Earth/Lava' (238–44), and his discussion of the men's Oedipal relationship with the land (205).

from the human body on to the landscape.[34] In *Undertones of War*, the land is 'torn and vile'; the trenches are 'stropped, burned, choked' (99); the battlefield is 'distorted' (101); the roadway 'has a distressed look' (105); the sky is 'desolate' and the landscape 'stricken' (205); Passchendaele is described as undergoing a 'slow amputation' which makes some men weep at the thought of returning to it (220). Similarly, in Barbusse's *Under Fire*, a church is described as 'so thoroughly mutilated by a shell that one can no longer look it in the face' (58). John Dos Passos refers to the 'pitted gangrened soil'.[35] Remarque's *All Quiet* refers to the 'convulsed earth' (91) and, inverting the image, says of the men of his generation: 'We only know that in some strange and melancholy way we have become a waste land' (19).[36]

On the one hand, the earth is figured as a maternal body which protects the men but is also subject to attack by them; and, on the other, it stands in for the men's own bodies as targets of extreme violence. This paradox is strikingly similar to some of the ideas explored in the early writings of psychoanalyst Melanie Klein, who started to publish her work just after the war[37] and whose paper, 'Early Stages of the Oedipus Conflict' was written very close to the time that Aldington, Blunden, Graves, Manning and Remarque were writing their war novels. The paper was delivered as a lecture in 1927 and published in *The International Journal of Psycho-analysis* in 1928. Klein's early writing on the violent fantasies of young children provide useful insights into the preoccupations of the war writings of the same period.[38] I do not propose to offer a Kleinian reading of the fiction; rather, I want to read Klein's early work

---

34 Theweleit sees a parallel between 'the earth's interior' and 'the man's own interior' in the writings of *Freikorps* soldiers. *Male Fantasies*, vol. 1, 240.

35 Dos Passos, *One Man's Initiation: 1917* (1920; Lanham MD, University Press of America, 1986), 36.

36 The German reads: 'Was wir wissen, ist vorläufig nur, dass wir auf eine sonderbare und schwermütige Weise verroht sind'. The term 'waste land' seems to have been introduced by the English translator, perhaps in an echo of Eliot's poem (published 1922), which would have been familiar to English readers.

37 Juliet Mitchell, introduction to *The Selected Melanie Klein* (Harmondsworth, Penguin, 1986), 17.

38 For a discussion of Klein's later work and the Second World War, see Jacqueline Rose, *Why War?* (Oxford, Blackwell, 1993). See also Lyndsey Stonebridge, *The Destructive Element: Psychoanalysis & Modernism* (Basingstoke, Macmillan, 1998).

alongside the war narratives, to try and understand how these different kinds of writings address their historical moment.

## The violence of Melanie Klein

Klein was the first analyst to focus upon the imaginary violence underlying the relationship between the infant (particularly the male infant) and its parents (particularly the mother) during the Oedipus conflict. Before turning to Klein's representations of violence, I need to look briefly at her theories of splitting, projection and introjection – mechanisms which protect the ego[39] – for it is through these processes, especially in the Oedipus phase, that violent fantasies become part of the child's (and adult's) psychic reality. In *splitting*, the infant can separate off and disown 'bad' parts of itself, just as it can split off the 'bad' part of an object to prevent contamination of the 'good' part of that object. The infant is initially incapable of accepting the fact that good and bad can coexist, either in itself or in people and things outside itself. The act of *projection* involves attributing a split-off part of the ego to an external object, filling the object with rejected feelings from within the self. 'It is, however, not only the bad parts of the self which are expelled and projected', wrote Klein in 1946:

> The projection of good feelings and good parts of the self into the mother is essential for the infant's ability to develop good object relations and to integrate his ego. However, if this projective process is carried out excessively, good parts of the personality are felt to be lost. [...]
> The processes of splitting off parts of the self and projecting them into objects are thus of vital importance for normal development as well as for abnormal object relations.[40]

In *introjection*, aspects of an external object are taken within the infant's ego. In this process, 'qualities that belong to an external object are absorbed and unconsciously regarded as belonging to the self'.[41] Klein writes: 'The introjection of the good object, first of all the mother's breast, is a precondition for normal development.' The

---

39  Mitchell, introduction to *The Selected Melanie Klein*, 20.
40  'Notes on Some Schizoid Mechanisms' (1946), *The Selected Melanie Klein*, 183–4.
41  Elizabeth Wright, *Psychoanalytic Criticism* (London, Methuen, 1984), 80.

introjected good object 'comes to form a focal point in the ego and makes for cohesiveness of the ego'.[42] The result of these processes is the creation of an 'ideal object' for the infant's self, for it has expelled all the bad impulses in itself and taken in all the good it perceives in the object outside itself.[43]

These processes involve a great deal of imaginary violence, as Klein suggests in 'Early Stages of the Oedipus Conflict' (1927): 'Oedipus tendencies are released in consequence of the frustration which the child experiences at weaning [...]; they receive reinforcement through the anal frustrations undergone during training in cleanliness.'[44] 'The very onset of the Oedipal wishes' (at about the age of one), Klein argues, 'already becomes associated with incipient dread of castration and feelings of guilt' (70) and sets off anxieties which produce some violent fears and fantasies, including 'a dread of being devoured and destroyed', for:

> The child himself desires to destroy the libidinal object by biting, devouring and cutting it, which leads to anxiety, since awakening of the Oedipus tendencies is followed by introjection of the object, which then becomes one from which punishment is to be expected. The child then dreads a punishment corresponding to the offence: the super-ego becomes something which bites, devours and cuts. (71)

At around the same period, the infant perceives the mother's womb as 'the scene of all sexual processes and developments. The child is still dominated by the anal-sadistic libido-position which impels him to wish to *appropriate* the contents of the womb. He thus becomes curious about what it contains, what it is like, etc.' (72). The child's second major trauma (after weaning) – toilet training – 'strengthens his tendency to turn away from the mother'.

> She has frustrated his oral desires, and now she also interferes with his anal pleasures. It seems as though at this point the anal deprivations cause the anal tendencies to amalgamate with the sadistic tendencies. The child desires to get possession of the mother's faeces, by penetrating into her body, cutting it to pieces, devouring it and destroying it. (73)

These violent fantasies towards the mother's body generate anxiety about a similarly violent retribution, for the feelings are projected

42  Klein, 'Notes on Some Schizoid Mechanisms', 184.
43  Wright, *Psychoanalytic Criticism*, 80.
44  *The Selected Melanie Klein*, 70.

out, on to the mother, and are seen as threatening the infant's body from the outside. For Klein, this is particularly striking in the case of boys; masculinity is founded upon violent fears and fantasies which begin at an early stage and are at crucial moments focused upon the mother's body. Klein describes one such moment in the boy's development as the 'femininity phase' (74). Castration is not the only bodily horror feared by the boy (unlike Freud's account of Little Hans (1909)); according to Klein, he imagines his entire body is under threat.

> The boy fears punishment for his destruction of his mother's body, but, besides this, his fear is of a more general nature, and here we have an analogy to the anxiety associated with the castration wishes of the girl. He fears that his body will be mutilated and dismembered, and amongst other things castrated. Here we have a direct contribution to the castration complex. In this early period of development the mother who takes away the child's faeces signifies also a mother who dismembers and castrates him. Not only by means of the anal frustrations which she inflicts does she pave the way for the castration complex: in terms of psychic reality she *is* also already the *castrator*. (74)

At the same time, there is also an intense fear of the father, whose penis is imagined to be within the womb that the infant wishes to destroy. The boy imagines that the father too will castrate him for his violent desires. The result of this dual anxiety about both parents is 'the tyranny of a super-ego which devours, dismembers and castrates and is formed from the image of father and mother alike'.

For Klein, the Oedipus conflict begins in a period 'when sadism predominates'. In an essay from 1930, she argues:

> The child expects to find within the mother (*a*) the father's penis, (*b*) excrement and (*c*) children, and these things it equates with edible substances. According to the child's earliest phantasies (or 'sexual theories') of parental coitus, the father's penis (or his whole body) becomes incorporated in the mother during the act. Thus the child's sadistic attacks have for their object both father and mother, who are in phantasy bitten, torn, cut or stamped to bits. The attacks give rise to anxiety lest the subject should be punished by the united parents [...].[45]

---

45 'The Importance of Symbol Formation in the Development of the Ego' (1930), *The Selected Melanie Klein*, 96.

Klein considers these 'anxiety situations' in the child's early psychic development to be 'the most profound and overwhelming'. Whereas other psychoanalysts tended to focus upon later parts of the Oedipus conflict, Klein saw the early, pre-Oedipal phase as vitally important, and argued that the Oedipus conflict started much earlier than was generally recognised.

The metaphors she uses for this sadistic period are particularly striking in the context of the war narratives with which this essay, too, is almost contemporaneous: 'In phantasy the excreta are transformed into dangerous weapons: wetting is regarded as cutting, stabbing, burning, drowning, while the faecal mass is equated with weapons and missiles' (96). These 'weapons' are aimed at destroying objects outside the self and are simultaneously perceived as being 'levelled [by the object] at his own person also'. Thus: 'The object of the attack becomes a source of danger because the subject fears similar, retaliatory attacks from it' (97). This image of reciprocal threats of violence is peculiarly appropriate to the idea and experience of the Great War. The soldiers' narratives (and poems such as Owen's 'Strange Meeting') generate a strong sense of the enemy as someone very like 'us' who is engaged in the same kinds of violent actions. The enemy is imagined as outside and different to oneself (not unlike Klein's image of the destructive parents), but also as the *same* – linked to the protagonists through a shared experience and fantasy of reciprocal violence and bodily terror, as we see most insistently in Barbusse's *Under Fire*.

Klein's early essays depict bodily anxieties which are uncannily similar to those found in the war narratives, and both kinds of writing imagine adulthood (especially manhood) as a state in which the entire body is under threat of dismemberment, mutilation or death, whether real or imaginary.[46] Klein posits it as a fantasy of the Oedipus phase, while the war writings represent the body under threat as a real possibility and historical fact of the lives of adult men (and, to a lesser extent, women). Furthermore, Klein's image of the father's body caught within the mother's body – both of which the boy imagines he will destroy and which will attack him in turn – is also a vision of the boy's own future as adult man and father. Simi-

---

46 For further discussion of Klein and masculinity, see Peter Middleton, *The Inward Gaze: Masculinity and Subjectivity in Modern Culture* (London, Routledge, 1992).

lar images recur throughout the war narratives: claustrophobia, entrapment within the (maternal) land, destruction of the protecting land, the sight of men's bodies destroyed. Psychoanalysis, like the literary works, is struggling during this period to address a trauma which it can hardly articulate, and which is expressed as a vision of violence against the body, whether real or in fantasy.

Like modernist fiction of the 1920s and 1930s, the war narratives are troubled by the question of how one is placed in relation to the vast, often incomprehensible events of early twentieth-century history. As education, literacy, the popular press, and the franchise begin to reach the entire population, there is much less autonomy than people might have expected – quite the opposite, in fact, when they find themselves powerless in the face of an inexorable 'war machine'. There is also concern in all these writings as to where the war is located. Is it inside or outside; in the world or in your mind; inscribed upon your own body or upon the bodies you have seen? Like HD, Kipling, and Ford, the soldiers' and nurses' narratives worry about how one bears witness to the events of the war, and this anxiety is expressed most powerfully through the sight of the suffering human body, the place in which history and fantasy meet.

# 4

# Visible differences

NOWHERE DO HISTORY and fantasy meet and clash more strongly than around the figure of the soldier returned from the war. This chapter examines representations of soldiers who come home from the Great War with visible injuries to their bodies. How is this form of physical difference understood in the writings? The Great War was not simply a 'crisis' of masculinity; rather, it made visible – and intensified – differences *within* masculinity in this period. These differences were at once bodily, historical, and fantasmatic, and they emerge with particular force in the writing of two men who did not go to the war: D. H. Lawrence and William Faulkner.

The wounded soldier is a visual reminder of the war. His body carries a complex of meanings back into civilian society. Large numbers of men who survived the First World War were injured. Among British soldiers, the rate of injury was more than twice the death toll: perhaps as many as three-quarters of a million died, while more than 1.6 million were wounded.[1] At least 200,000 men were mentally wounded, suffering from war neuroses or shell shock.[2] Some surviving men were injured in horrifying ways, with portions of their faces or bodies missing. Facial injuries, in particular, were highly visible and not easily repaired. The *Lancet* and the *Dental Record* carried photographs and articles about the medical treatment of injured

---

1 Arthur Marwick estimates 745,000 dead; *The Deluge: British Society and the First World War*, 2nd edn (Basingstoke, Macmillan, 1991), 330. Ian Beckett cites the figure of 570,000; 'The British Army, 1914–18: The Illusion of Change', in John Turner, ed., *Britain and the First World War* (London, Unwin Hyman, 1988), 111.

2 This is according to official figures; the real figure seems to have been much higher than this. Martin Stone, 'Shellshock and the Psychologists', in W. F. Bynum, Roy Porter and Michael Shepherd, eds, *The Anatomy of Madness: Essays in the History of Psychiatry*, vol. 2 (London, Tavistock, 1985), 249.

faces and jaws and analysed improvements in plastic surgery. The large number of new kinds of injuries allowed experimental work to be undertaken, and new techniques were developed.[3]

Postwar societies across Europe, the British Empire, and the United States included significant numbers of men who carried permanent traces of the war, visibly, on their bodies. The wounded returned soldier became a spectacle in civilian society – a sight of both fascination and dread. He was a paradox: as a soldier, he represented a powerful social ideal of manhood, yet the act of soldiering had damaged the bodily basis of masculinity, leaving him scarred, mutilated, paralysed, or blinded. But he was not necessarily a 'feminised' figure – often quite the opposite. Subjectivity and its relation to physical difference are much more complex than this, as the war writings repeatedly demonstrate.

I want to approach the fiction through a brief discussion of Freud's writing about the relationship between seeing and sexual difference in the 1920s. Psychoanalysis was an important body of thinking about war, on the one hand, and sexual difference, on the other, during and after the First World War. It has also been very influential for more recent thinking about sexual difference, and it is useful to pause on some of its historical roots.

## Sexual difference: theories of the visible

It is often argued that psychoanalysis regards sexual difference as a fundamental organising category of identity; indeed, it is what makes identity and language possible in the first place. Sexual difference is predicated upon what is seen, or seen to be absent. For Freud, it is a sight – actual or imagined – which reveals woman's 'castration' to a child. Instead of a penis, she appears to have 'nothing'. In 'Some Psychical Consequences of the Anatomical Distinction Between the Sexes' (1925), Freud's account of sexual difference focuses on a moment of seeing. A girl will 'notice the penis of

---

3 For example Percival Cole, 'Plastic Repair in War Injuries to the Jaw and Face', *The Lancet*, 17 March 1917, 415–17; this article is accompanied by a series of photographs of surgical reconstructions of soldiers' injured faces. H. P. Pickerill, 'Methods of Control of Fragments in Gunshot Wounds of the Jaws', *The Lancet*, 7 September 1918, 313–16; 'Plastic Surgery of the Face', *The Lancet*, 17 March 1917, 419–20; see also *The Dental Record* during and after the war.

a brother or playmate, strikingly visible and of large proportions'. As a result: 'She makes her judgement and her decision in a flash. She has seen it and knows that she is without it and wants to have it.'[4] This knowledge will 'wound' her narcissism and she will develop, 'like a scar, a sense of inferiority'. The boy, on the other hand, when he 'first catches sight of a girl's genital region', starts by seeing nothing, or disavowing what he has seen.[5] Only later does he realise that this was the sight of woman's castration; that he really did see 'nothing'. Freud also discusses the acts of looking and being looked at as sources of infantile sexual pleasure. Scopophilia commonly occurs in children, allowing them to cast other people as 'sexual objects'.[6] Laura Mulvey has argued that the act of looking often underpins gender relationships in modern cultures, casting woman as lacking and man as whole; woman as image and man as bearer of the look. Yet, as Elizabeth Grosz points out, looking is not and cannot be an inherently gendered activity; Mulvey's argument has led to some rather muddled thinking in the past two decades.[7]

What interests me here is the historical context for these debates, especially for Freud's own writing. Like modernism, Freud's work is full of references to the First World War which have received surprisingly little attention. In his essay on 'Fetishism' (1927), for example, Freud draws a direct parallel between the illogical behaviour of the fetishist and the 'grown man' who panics 'when the cry goes up that Throne and Altar are in danger' and goes off to war, or at least supports war.[8] Fetishism is a response to bod-

---

4  Freud, 'Some Psychical Consequences of the Anatomical Distinction Between the Sexes' (1925), Pelican Freud Library 7, *On Sexuality* (Harmondsworth, Penguin, 1983), 335, 336.

5  Freud, 'Some Psychical Consequences', 337, 336.

6  Freud, 'Three Essays on the Theory of Sexuality' (1905), Pelican Freud Library 7, *On Sexuality* (Harmondsworth, Penguin, 1983), 109–13. See Mulvey on Freud's ideas about scopophilia in 'Visual Pleasure and Narrative Cinema' (1975), rpt in Mulvey, *Visual and Other Pleasures* (Basingstoke, Macmillan, 1989).

7  Mulvey, 'Visual Pleasure and Narrative Cinema', 19–24; Grosz, 'Voyeurism, Exhibitionism, the Gaze', in Elizabeth Wright, ed., *Feminism and Psychoanalysis: A Critical Dictionary* (Oxford, Blackwell, 1992), 448–9. For Mulvey's further thinking on this issue, see 'Afterthoughts on "Visual Pleasure and Narrative Cinema"' (1981), rpt in *Visual and Other Pleasures*.

8  Freud, 'Fetishism'(1927), Pelican Freud Library 7, *On Sexuality* (Harmondsworth, Penguin, 1983), 352.

ily difference. In Freud's account, the fetishist is a boy who is trau-matised by the discovery that woman does not possess a penis. He repudiates what he has seen – 'No, that could not be true: for if a woman had been castrated, then his own possession of a penis was in danger' (352). The fetishist manages to sustain the fiction that woman has a penis, however, by imagining it in a new form; other objects come to stand in for woman's missing member. 'He has retained that belief, but he has also given it up' (353). Fetishism simultaneously accepts and denies the possibility of different sexual organs in women and men.

Fear of castration is not unique to the fetishist, as Freud notes a little later in the essay: 'Probably no male human being is spared the fright of castration at the sight of a female genital' (354). In this view, masculinity itself is founded on the simultaneous denial and recognition of woman's genital difference.[9] Representations of fem-ininity, therefore, sometimes strive to represent woman's body as perfect, hairless, without orifices, to minimise the trauma of the sight of her 'castration'[10] and its threat to fantasies about masculin-ity (fantasies which are not necessarily specific to men). Yet the very fact of woman's body being different is what makes this particular notion of masculinity possible in the first place, distinguished by its imaginary wholeness.

In short, sexual difference is both tenuous and founded on con-tradictions; as Rose comments, it is a 'hesitant and imperfect con-struction'.[11] The presence of large numbers of physically damaged men exposes the tenuous and contradictory nature of this construc-tion. More than this: everyone who sees a seriously injured man is reminded of the possibility of *real physical damage* – an image which threatens to outweigh the fiction of sexual difference. The presence of the injured soldier raises serious concerns about the social, political, and cultural structures which send men to war. Such a sight is particularly troubling when people begin to question the value and ethics of a particular war, as many did in the 1920s and 1930s. In Dalton Trumbo's *Johnny Got His Gun* (1939), the injured soldier, limbless and defaced by the war, wants to put his body on display as an 'educational exhibit'. 'People wouldn't learn

9  Kaja Silverman, *Male Subjectivity at the Margins* (London, Routledge, 1992), 3.
10  Rose, *Sexuality in the Field of Vision* (London, Verso, 1986), 232.
11  Rose, *Sexuality in the Field of Vision*, 226.

much about anatomy from him but they would learn all there was to know about war' (287). In this context, it is disconcerting to find Freud writing about woman as castrated and scarred in the mid-1920s – a period in which unprecedented numbers of men were literally castrated, mutilated, and scarred, sometimes in ways which everyone could see. Is the very notion of woman as castrated a fetishistic response to the traumatic sight of damaged men – a response which simultaneously acknowledges the fact of war injury and displaces the image on to woman?

Freud's work has an obvious relationship with the Great War and its writings, but I also want to look briefly at Lacan's writing on the gaze, for this has been central to recent thinking about sexual difference. There has been a lot of critical confusion over the idea of the gaze, as Joan Copjec notes, much of it arising from a fundamental misreading of Lacan.[12] The gaze has frequently been read as something masculine, an act which supposedly affirms men's power. Yet the Lacanian gaze is actually deeply paradoxical, for it is primarily to do with being looked at. 'What we have to circumscribe', writes Lacan in his 1964 seminar, 'The Eye and the Gaze', '[...] is the pre-existence of a gaze – I see from only one point, but in my existence I am looked at from all sides.' Seeing is less something that I do than an act 'to which I am subjected'.[13] This runs directly counter to the Freudian idea of scopophilia, which in its active form is primarily an expression of power, casting other people as objects, and in its passive form (exhibitionism) is a source of pleasure. In *Four Fundamental Concepts of Psychoanalysis*, Lacan represents the gaze as a source of anxiety and a sense of powerlessnesss. The subject is not primarily one who looks, but one who is subject to the gaze of others; indeed, being seen by other people is precisely what constitutes a person as a subject, separate from those others. Above all, 'we are beings who are looked at', in the 'spectacle of the world'. And the spectacle of the world 'appears to us as all-seeing'.[14] For, as

12 Copjec, 'Cutting Up', in Teresa Brennan, ed., *Between Feminism and Psychoanalysis* (London, Routledge, 1989), 228–9. See Grosz, 'Voyeurism, Exhibitionism, the Gaze', 448 on the ways in which Lacan's argument about 'the gaze' has been conflated with Freud on scopophilia and Sartre on 'the look'.

13 Lacan, 'The Eye and the Gaze', *Four Fundamental Concepts of Psychoanalysis*, ed. Jacques-Alain Miller, trans. Alan Sheridan (1973; Harmondsworth, Penguin, 1986), 72.

14 Lacan, 'The Eye and the Gaze', 75.

Slavoj Zizek argues, 'the gaze is always on the side of the object. When I look at an object, the object is always already gazing at me, and from a point at which I cannot see it.'[15]

The sense of objects looking at you emerges from many writings of the First World War. In trench warfare, the enemy is often invisible, hidden from sight. Troops could never be sure when they were being looked at, and they were often under attack from artillery and machine guns which were fired whether or not they were actually within view. Ford Madox Ford remembers a moment at the Somme in which he thinks the ground within his view must contain a million men, all of them hidden from sight. He imagines them 'moving one against the other and impelled by an invisible moral force into a Hell of fear that surely cannot have had a parallel in this world'.[16] The force which takes men to war, like the men themselves, cannot be seen – an uncanny idea which reappears in Ford's own war fiction. Conversely, there were moments in which men thought they safely hidden, but found themselves in the sights of a sniper, as Herbert describes in *The Secret Battle* (44). At other times, the British soldiers at Gallipoli had the paranoid sense that the Turkish troops could somehow see through the walls of the trenches, and were constantly looking at them. Furthermore, as Paul Virilio points out, soldiers were subject to the impersonal gaze of observation balloons, aerial cameras, and aeroplanes – technologies which changed the shape of modern warfare and reconfigured the ways in which the modern subject is imagined.[17]

The act of looking, then, produces subjectivity via the discovery of sexual difference, and the realisation that one is a separate being, looking at and being looked at by other people. But looking also casts the subject in an anxious, powerless position, under the gaze of people and objects in the world. These anxieties surface

---

15 Zizek, *Looking Awry: An Introduction to Jacques Lacan through Popular Culture* (Cambridge MA, MIT Press, 1991), 109. In Lacan's story about the sardine can, he points out that he can see it but it cannot see him, yet it always seems as if objects are looking at the subject. 'The Line and Light', *Four Fundamental Concepts*, 95–6.

16 Ford, 'War and the Mind', ed. Sondra J. Stang, *The Yale Review*, 78, 4 (summer 1989), 499.

17 Paul Virilio, *War and Cinema: The Logistics of Perception*, trans. Patrick Camiller (1984; London, Verso, 1989), 2, 14.

with great intensity in the writings of the First World War, especially around representations of the soldier.

## Soldiers in Lawrence

The war enraged Lawrence and filled him with despair. 'The war is just hell for me', he wrote in August 1914. 'I can't get away from it for a minute: I live in a sort of coma, like one of those nightmares when you can't move. I hate it – everything.'[18] 'I hate and detest the war, it is all wrong, all foolish, all a wicked mistake. Why can't it end? We none of us want it, surely.'[19] Though he hated the war, Lawrence was fascinated by soldiers, and they turn up in his writings even before the war.[20] Many more soldiers appear in his fiction written during and shortly after the war, in *Aaron's Rod* (1922), *The Fox* (1923), *Kangaroo* (1923), *The Captain's Doll* (1923), *The Ladybird* (1923), and 'The Border Line' (1924). In *Lady Chatterley's Lover* (1928), Mellors and Clifford Chatterley both serve in the Great War, and the gypsy in *The Virgin and the Gypsy* (1930) has been in the artillery.

Lawrence's war stories, many of which were collected in *England, My England* (1922) include some striking and unusual portraits of soldiers.[21] Where many of his contemporaries (HD, Aldington, Ford, Woolf, Rebecca West) tend to represent soldiers as traumatised or war neurotic, Lawrence's soldiers are often remarkably serene; indeed, many are less disturbed than his civilian characters. In 'Wintry Peacock' (1921), for example, the central woman character prefers a peacock to her strapping soldier-husband (a preference the story finds decidedly neurotic), while he is sturdily untroubled even though he has recently been wounded. Mellors in *Lady Chatterley's Lover*, the young man in the story 'Hadrian'

---

18 Letter to Edward Marsh, 25 August 1914, *The Letters of D. H. Lawrence*, vol. 2, ed. George Zytaruk and James Boulton (Cambridge University Press, 1981), 211.

19 Letter to Arthur McLeod, 5 January 1915, *Letters*, vol. 2, 255.

20 A number of soldiers appear in the prewar stories in *The Prussian Officer* (1914).

21 Many of the stories collected in *England, My England* (1922) are set during or shortly after the Great War: 'England, My England', 'Tickets, Please', 'The Blind Man', 'Monkey Nuts', 'Wintry Peacock', 'Hadrian', 'Samson and Delilah', 'The Thimble'; of these, in all but 'Tickets, Please' the central male characters are soldiers.

(1920), the husband in 'Samson and Delilah' (1917), and the gypsy in *The Virgin and the Gypsy* all seem to suffer no ill effects from their war service. Even Clifford in *Lady Chatterley's Lover*, who is 'shipped over to England' from Flanders 'more or less in bits', makes a remarkable recovery. 'His hold on life was marvellous. He didn't die, and the bits seemed to grow together again. For two years he remained in the doctor's hands. Then he was pronounced a cure, and could return to life again, with the lower half of his body, from the hips down, paralysed for ever' (5). Despite his disability, the novel insists that he should not become an object of pity.

> Having suffered so much, the capacity for suffering had to some extent left him. He remained strange and bright and cheerful, almost, one might say, chirpy, with his ruddy, healthy-looking face, and his pale-blue, challenging bright eyes. His shoulders were broad and strong, his hands were very strong. He was expensively dressed, and wore handsome neckties from Bond Street. (6)

Later, his injured body is seen as a kind of machine, indistinguishable from the motorised wheelchair to which he is confined. The novel refuses to confront the idea of his pain, but wills it away, as if suffering came in finite quantities. Clifford can then function as a symbol (mind without body; reason without passion) without demanding too much sympathy from the reader. Above all, he does not seem to be traumatised by the war or by his injuries. This is quite unusual in writing of the First World War, and is startling to read alongside Trumbo's *Johnny Got His Gun*, in which the reader is never allowed to forget the material effects of damage to a human body.

In 'Monkey Nuts' (1922), the returned soldier Joe is troubled less by his war experiences than by the 'straight, light-blue gaze' of Miss Stokes, a 'masterful' land-girl. When Miss Stokes and her unsettling hard looks disappear at the end of the story, Joe feels 'more relieved even than he had felt when he heard the firing cease, after the news had come that the armistice was signed' (76). A sexually dominant woman who looks too much is here, absurdly, more threatening than the physical violence of war – something which is remembered as a sound, rather than a sight.[22]

---

22  On Lawrence's ambivalence about looking and seeing, see Linda Ruth Williams, *Sex in the Head: Visions of Femininity and Film in D. H. Lawrence* (Hemel Hempstead, Harvester Wheatsheaf, 1993).

## Lawrence, 'The Blind Man'

'The Blind Man' was written at the end of 1918 and published in 1920 in the *English Review*.[23] The story begins when Maurice Pervin, blinded and scarred in the face, has been back from the war for about a year. This has an unexpected effect on his marriage, bringing him closer to his wife, Isabel. The two characters live in an intensely private world, about which we are told, but not shown. 'He was totally blind. Yet they had been very happy. [...] She and he had been almost entirely alone together since he was wounded. They talked and sang and read together in a wonderful and unspeakable intimacy' (46). Maurice is quite self-contained and content in his blindness; his life is 'still very full and strangely serene [...] peaceful with the almost incomprehensible peace of immediate contact in darkness'. Far from suffering from his injury, Maurice does 'not even regret the loss of his sight in these times of dark, palpable joy' (46). Despite this mystical euphoria, the characters are assailed with madness and depression. Isabel wants to 'possess her husband utterly', but she also wants to ignore him and luxuriate in her pregnancy. His dark presence is at once 'a terrible joy to her, and a terrifying burden' (47). The central characters are constructed around a series of contradictions: they are completely happy and self-contained, yet they suffer from depression and madness. Their relationship is a perfect dyad, yet they are already separated by their unborn child. An acute anxiety occurs at the very level of writing in this text. It moves restlessly from one assertion to another, unable to show the unspeakable, incomprehensible, invisible world the characters inhabit.

Into this peculiar scene comes Bertie Reid, Isabel's old friend and distant cousin, a man quite different from Maurice. Bertie is an 'intellectual', 'quick' and 'ironical' Scot, while Maurice is English, 'passionate, sensitive' with a slow mind, 'as if drugged by the strong provincial blood that beat in his veins' (48). The characters are determined by their origins, nation, and blood, not by historical

23  For this and other bibliographical information, I have drawn on Bruce Steele's introduction to *England, My England* (Cambridge University Press, 1990); Warren Roberts, *A Bibliography of D. H. Lawrence*, 2nd edn (Cambridge University Press, 1982); Mark Kinkead-Weekes, *D. H. Lawrence: Triumph to Exile 1912–1922* (Cambridge University Press, 1996), appendix 1. Dates in brackets in text refer to first publication.

contingency, such as war. And unlike Faulkner in *Soldiers' Pay* (discussed below), Lawrence represents his returned soldier as completely untroubled by his injury. Indeed, Maurice's blindness, though at times explicitly represented as a symbol of castration, actually empowers him. It plunges him into a 'dark, palpable joy' in which his wife becomes pregnant and puts him more deeply in touch with his Englishness and the English land that he owns.

On the evening of Bertie's arrival, Isabel sets out to call Maurice in from work on the farm. It is a stormy November day, and she eventually finds him working in the stable, in the dark. Darkness has become Maurice's element, and it makes Isabel irrationally afraid (51). Looking into the stable, she can see nothing but darkness. She can hear the horses, 'terrifyingly near to her, in the invisible' (52). Darkness is here associated with a mysterious, masculine sexuality ('a strange whirl of violent life'), which makes her feel wild, giddy, almost desperate. She is particularly troubled by the fact she cannot see her husband (52). In 'The Thimble' (1917), the soldier's wife is acutely aware of the 'visual image' of her absent husband, but realises that she knows nothing about him. Later, when he returns with his mouth injured and scarred, she is 'obsessed' by the sight of his disfigurement, as if it were 'photographed upon her mind' (196). Many of Lawrence's stories advise women to stop looking, as Linda Williams points out, even as they share a woman's gaze.

'The Blind Man' inverts the familiar scopic basis of sexual difference. Instead of the man looking at the woman, fascinated and afraid of her as a symbol of difference, 'The Blind Man' sets up the man, blinded and a walking symbol of castration, as the object of the woman's gaze. This position ought to make her powerful, but it has quite the opposite effect. Linda Williams argues that her weakness is located precisely in the fact that she can see.[24] Yet the relationship between sex and looking, darkness and power is by no means stable. The story claims to have discovered a form of absolute knowledge in blind, 'blood-consciousness', yet it also shows that such power is neither complete nor unchanging. Like much of Lawrence's writing of this period, 'The Blind Man' issues a number of uncompromising but contradictory statements which cannot be resolved.

---

24  Williams, *Sex in the Head*, 34.

As the characters leave the stable, Isabel 'longed to see him, to look at him'. And although he is invisible, the narrative tells us what he looks like, as they walk through the darkness:

> He walked erect, with face rather lifted, but with a curious tentative movement of his powerful, muscular legs. She could feel [but not see] the clever, careful, strong contact of his feet with the earth, as she balanced against him. For a moment he was a tower of darkness to her, as if he rose out of the earth. (53)

He is part of the land, like a tree; he is also a kind of erect penis – a 'tower of darkness' – a vision imagined, but not seen, by the woman. To discover a phallic symbol in Lawrence might seem rather clichéd, but it is worth asking how this image is working historically. Lawrence's injured soldier is erect, virile, and powerful, and will stand in defiant (even perverse) opposition to representations of war-injured men in the following two decades.

Maurice's blindness intensifies his relationship with nature, and puts him into 'blood-contact' with the entire world, including the objects within the house. He wants 'no intervention of visual consciousness [...]. He did not try to remember, to visualize. He did not want to' (54), for he has found a richer kind of consciousness – what Mark Spilka calls 'the famous "phallic" or bodily form of consciousness'[25] – located somewhere beyond the scopic structure of sexual difference. Perhaps this is what creates the 'unspeakable intimacy' with Isabel: her 'castration' is no longer visible to him; the sight of her body is no longer a threat. Maurice's masculinity has no need to be fetishistic and he turns into a superman, stalking through the landscape like a mobile penis, strikingly visible and of large proportions. Far from making him suffer, his war injury is a source of deep insight, virility, and joy. Yet some problems remain. What does Maurice want? This question occupies the second part of the story, and is explored through the contrasting figures of Maurice and Bertie: soldier and civilian, figures occupying quite different positions within the understanding of masculinity during the First World War.

---

25  Mark Spilka, 'Ritual Form in "The Blind Man"', in Spilka, ed., *D. H. Lawrence: A Collection of Critical Essays* (Englewood Cliffs NJ, Prentice-Hall, 1963), 114.

Towards the end of the story, Maurice and Bertie confront one another, apparently as rivals for Isabel's affection (61). But Isabel is simply a means by which the men can connect across the horrible sight of Maurice's difference, which Maurice himself is unable to visualise:

> 'I say,' he asked, secretly struggling, 'is my face much disfigured? Do you mind telling me?'
> 'There is the scar,' said Bertie, wondering. 'Yes, it is a disfigurement. But more pitiable than shocking.'
> 'A pretty bad scar, though,' said Maurice.
> 'Oh, yes.'
> There was a pause.
> 'Sometimes I feel I am horrible,' said Maurice in a low voice, talking as if to himself. And Bertie actually felt a quiver of horror.
> 'That's nonsense,' he said.

Maurice then shifts the attention from his own body to Bertie's, away from the act of looking. 'I don't really know you, do I?,' he says, in an 'odd tone'.

> 'Probably not,' said Bertie.
> 'Do you mind if I touch you?'
> The lawyer shrank away instinctively. And yet, out of very philanthropy, he said, in a small voice: 'Not at all.'
> But he suffered as the blind man stretched out a strong, naked hand to him. Maurice accidentally knocked off Bertie's hat.
> 'I thought you were taller,' he said, starting. Then he laid his hand on Bertie Reid's head, closing the dome of the skull in a soft, firm grasp, gathering it, as it were; then, shifting his grasp and softly closing again, with a fine, close pressure, till he had covered the skull and the face of the smaller man, tracing the brows, and touching the full, closed eyes, touching the small nose and the nostrils, the rough, short moustache, the mouth, the rather strong chin. The hand of the blind man grasped the shoulder, the arm, the hand of the other man. He seemed to take him, in the soft, travelling grasp.
> 'You seem young,' he said quietly, at last. (61–2)

This is a curiously erotic moment, full of a suppressed, static violence.[26] Maurice's 'naked' hand enfolds Bertie's head, 'gathering' it

---

26 John Bayley describes this scene as 'one of the most erotic passages in Lawrence, much more so than anything in the novels'. *The Short Story: Henry James to Elizabeth Bowen* (Brighton, Harvester, 1988), 126.

as if it were malleable material, or as if he were a baby, his head as yet unformed. Bertie is paralysed by the intimacy of the encounter; he is 'almost annihilated, unable to answer'. But things get worse:

> 'Your head seems tender, as if you were young,' Maurice repeated. 'So do your hands. Touch my eyes, will you? – touch my scar.'
>
> Now Bertie quivered with revulsion. Yet he was under the power of the blind man, as if hypnotised. He lifted his hand, and laid the fingers on the scar, on the scarred eyes. Maurice suddenly covered them with his own hand, pressed the fingers of the other man upon his disfigured eye-sockets, trembling in every fibre, and rocking slightly, slowly, from side to side. He remained thus for a minute or more, whilst Bertie stood as if in a swoon, unconscious, imprisoned.

At this point we realise that Maurice is not simply blind, but has lost his eyes altogether. This revolts Bertie, but also fascinates him. Touching the scarred face, he falls into a 'swoon', like the heroine of a novelette. Lawrence relentlessly shifts the basis of power away from the visual as the blinded soldier asserts his control over the sighted man. This leaves Bertie terrified, 'lest the other man should suddenly destroy him'. The story concludes with Maurice elated and erect, 'like a strange colossus', and Bertie 'haggard, with sunken eyes', his face now faintly resembling Maurice's disfigurement. Bertie is 'like a mollusc whose shell is broken': an image which suggests that he has been crushed – or perhaps seduced and penetrated, or even raped – by the soldier.

The story is powerfully homoerotic, yet at the same time it tries to suppress its own queer interests by leaving Bertie flattened and miserable. Maurice's symbolic violence towards Bertie is a highly pleasurable moment for the text. It expresses a sadistic enjoyment in destroying the kind of man Lawrence despised as intellectual and sexless (such as Bertrand Russell, who might be the model for Bertie).[27] But some of the pleasure comes from the opposite direction, through a masochistic identification with Bertie. Bertie might

---

27 On the relationship between Lawrence and Russell, see Paul Delany, *D. H. Lawrence's Nightmare: The Writer and his Circle in the Years of the Great War* (Hassocks, Harvester, 1979); Ray Monk, 'The Tiger and the Machine: D. H. Lawrence and Bertrand Russell', *Philosophy of the Social Sciences*, 26, 2 (1996), 205–46; see also Monk, *Bertrand Russell: The Spirit of Solitude* (London, Jonathan Cape, 1996). Bayley suggests that the character might be based on J. M. Barrie. *The Short Story*, 126. Kinkead-Weekes argues that in the unpublished version of the story Bertie bears little resemblance to Russell, *D. H. Lawrence*, 479–80.

think he hates the encounter, but the text finds his humiliation intensely erotic. Lawrence uses the idea of war injury to transform the terror of castration, blindness, or any other kind of physical damage into a source of power. This is perhaps what makes his war writing compelling and even oddly comforting, yet also elusive and troubling. The historical experience of the war is simultaneously present and absent in his work, transformed into erotic fantasies which both confront and efface the damaged bodies it produced.

'The Blind Man' also expresses some of the fantasies which animate the relationships between combatant and non-combatant men in Lawrence's writings of the First World War. The story articulates a powerful erotic interest, both sadistic and masochistic, in the body of the soldier. This interest is present in many other writings of the period, but what makes Lawrence unusual, as I have suggested, is the absence of trauma in his war writings. Like a number of other writers, Lawrence finds that the war makes it possible to imagine sexual difference – visible difference – in new ways. The differences within 'masculinity' become more important, more troubling, and in many ways more fascinating than the differences between women and men.

## Faulkner, *Soldiers' Pay*

Faulkner occupies a curious position as a writer of the First World War, having been both a civilian and a member of the armed forces, but not a combatant. In 1918, he joined the RAF, using forged papers and an acquired accent to persuade the authorities he was English, and left Mississippi for Toronto, to train as a pilot.[28] The war ended not long after he started his training, and there is some doubt as to whether he ever flew an aeroplane at all. He wrote to his brothers, however, that he had celebrated the armistice by taking a plane and a crock of bourbon, getting drunk, executing elaborate tricks with the plane, then crashing into a hangar and injuring his leg. He returned home with a limp and 'numerous versions' of the story of his crash.[29] Later, when he was in New Orleans, he again

---

28  Michael Millgate, 'William Faulkner, Cadet', *University of Toronto Quarterly* (January 1966); Joseph Blotner, *Faulkner: A Biography*, 2 vols (London, Chatto and Windus, 1974), vol. 1, 226.

29  Frederick Karl, *William Faulkner, American Writer: A Biography* (New York, Weidenfeld and Nicolson, 1989), 116. Karl also quotes letters to two different brothers, each containing a different version of the story.

affected a limp and also claimed to have a metal plate in his skull. Frederick Karl notes that these phantom injuries 'precisely duplicated [his brother] Jack's real wounds of a knee and skull injury'.[30] The facts about his war service (or lack of it) were not widely known until after his death. Stories circulated until 1945 that he had been injured at the front; even now there is some uncertainty about his activities in the RAF.

*Soldiers' Pay* was written in New Orleans in 1925, when Faulkner's fictional injuries were at their worst. It traces the return of an American serviceman to civilian society and was reviewed as a war novel when it first appeared – in the United States in 1926, and in Britain in 1930, at the height of the war-fiction boom.[31] Arnold Bennett, writing in the *Evening Standard*, commented: '*Soldiers' Pay* is labelled "Not a war-book." I call it a war book. Its chief male characters are returned soldiers, and the whole story hinges on a terribly scarred aviator, who dies of war.'[32] Reviewers often mentioned that Faulkner himself had supposedly been injured in war service.[33]

*Soldiers' Pay* is set in Georgia, far from the war zones, in 1919.[34] The book is organised around the return and death of Donald Mahon, wounded, disfigured, and deeply traumatised by his experiences as a pilot in France. His war neurosis makes him extremely passive, almost to the point of paralysis. 'It's his apathy, his detachment, that's so terrible', comments Margaret Powers. 'He doesn't seem to care where he is nor what he does' (97). The other charac-

30  Faulkner's brother Jack trained to be a marine and was injured in France; Karl, *William Faulkner*, 112, 116.

31  Faulkner's reputation in Britain was originally as a war writer. See the early reviews reprinted in John Bassett, ed., *William Faulkner: The Critical Heritage* (London, Routledge and Kegan Paul, 1973). Prior to the 1930 publication of *Soldiers' Pay*, he was almost unknown in Britain. For a detailed discussion of Faulkner, the First World War, and American modernism, see John Limon, *Writing After War: American War Fiction from Realism to Postmodernism* (New York, Oxford University Press, 1994), ch. 4.

32  Bennett, 'American Authors "Made" in England', *Evening Standard*, 26 June 1930, 7; rpt in John Bassett, ed., *William Faulkner: The Critical Heritage*.

33  V. F. Calverton wrote in 1938 that Faulkner 'emerged [from the First World War] a lieutenant and a hero with wounds resulting from a plane crash'. Calverton, 'Southerner at Large', *Modern Monthly*, March 1938, 11–12; rpt in Bassett, ed., *William Faulkner: The Critical Heritage*.

34  William Faulkner, *Soldiers' Pay* (1926; London, Picador, 1991), 86.

ters speak of him as a child, but they treat him as an inanimate object, over which they struggle for possession. Donald's return is a double shock for his father and friends, for they believe him to be dead. News of his return brings him back to life, but his severe disability renders him dead again; at first in a metaphorical sense, then literally, when he suddenly remembers his accident, and dies sitting in the garden of his father's house (243–5). As he dies, he silently summons his father, who immediately runs to him. For the first time, Donald is dreaming, or remembering, the fire which brought down his plane. The scene uncannily echoes a story discussed by Freud in *The Interpretation of Dreams* (1900), in which a father dreams about his dead son calling: 'Father, can't you see I'm burning?' Faulkner was reading Freud in 1925, when he wrote *Soldiers' Pay*.[35]

Faulkner also tries to place the returned soldier in relation to domestic political struggles, including the growing pressure for black emancipation and the imminent re-emergence of the Klu Klux Klan (233). The war experience of black men is barely mentioned in *Soldiers' Pay*, but in Faulkner's third novel, *Sartoris* (1929) the returned black soldiers find the war inspiring in their struggle for equal rights. Caspey, a returned soldier, explains:

> I don't take nothn' fum no white folks no mo'. War done changed all that. If us cullud folks is good enough ter save France from de Germans, den us is good enough ter have de same rights de Germans is. French folks thinks so, anyhow, and ef America don't, dey's ways of learnin' 'um. Yes, suh, it wuz de cullud soldier saved France and America bofe. [...] War unloosed de black man's mouf. [...] Give him de right to talk. (45–6)

Like Evelyn Waugh's *Decline and Fall* (published two years later), *Soldiers' Pay* worries about the virility of white men after the war and suspects that power is shifting towards (or being claimed by) other groups within society.

Disfigured, blind, and passive, Donald is a blank space at the centre of the narrative on to which the other characters project their fears and desires. This has irritated some critics, who see the passive

---

35  Watson, introduction to *Thinking of Home: William Faulkner's Letters to his Mother and Father, 1918–1925*, ed. James G. Watson (New York, Norton, 1992), 27.

central character as a failure in narrative technique.[36] But the narrative difficulties are precisely what make the book interesting, as they struggle to express cultural anxieties about severely injured soldiers returning from the war. Donald's passivity is particularly striking in a work set in the spring of 1919 – a period in which returned soldiers were rioting and fighting with civilians in New York, Washington, St Louis, and elsewhere in the United States, as well as in Britain.[37] He occupies two contradictory positions in the novel – a spectacle and a blank space – both of which have been associated with 'femininity' in narrative.[38] But the returned serviceman is not simply a feminised man. His function is more complex than this; as wounded combatant, bearing a shocking symbol of castration across his eyes, he represents the central contradictions underlying ideas about masculinity immediately after the war. This is one of the first meanings allocated to him in the book, through the figure of Cadet Lowe, the first character to appear in the novel.

Julian Lowe, a cadet in a flying squadron, is returning home on a train, disappointed that 'they had stopped the war on him' before he had a chance to participate (7). Donald is also on the train, and his injured body becomes a focus for Lowe's anxiety about his status as a non-combatant man. 'Had I been old enough or lucky enough, this might have been me,' he thinks 'jealously' when he first sees Donald's scarred face and flying insignia (22). Sharing a hotel room with Donald that night, Lowe meditates drunkenly on his own body and its functions. 'In the other bed the man slept beneath his terrible face. (I am Julian Lowe, I eat, I digest, evacuate: I have flown. This man ... this man here, sleeping beneath his scar. ... Where do we touch?)' (38). The two men's bodies are differentiated in terms as profound as sexual difference, through the image of

36  Judith Wittenberg, *Faulkner: The Transfiguration of Biography* (Lincoln, University of Nebraska Press, 1979), 43. Max Putzel, who defends the book against its detractors, none the less finds Donald inexplicable except as one half of a *doppelgänger* (Cadet Lowe being the other half) which represents Faulkner himself. Despite its uncanny topic, this reading effaces much of the novel's strangeness. Putzel, *Genius of Place: William Faulkner's Triumphant Beginnings* (Baton Rouge, Louisiana State University Press, 1985), 33–5.

37  Eric Leed, *No Man's Land: Combat and Identity in World War I* (Cambridge University Press, 1979), 202–3; Hynes, *A War Imagined*, 281.

38  Mulvey, *Visual and Other Pleasures*; Rodowick, *The Difficulty of Difference: Psychoanalysis, Sexual Difference, and Film Theory* (London, Routledge, 1991), 4.

Donald's scar, which is here imagined as separate from his body. The scar becomes a shifting signifier, a sign of difference which both is and is not part of his body, and renders him simultaneously more 'masculine' and more 'castrated' than the man who watches him. (Limon calls the book an 'asexual voyeuristic farce' organised around an 'inverse fetishism'.[39])

Donald's wound is never described to the reader, but remains both glaringly obvious and unimaginable, visible and invisible – uncanny. 'Where do we touch?' asks Lowe. How can the difference between the combatant and non-combatant be mediated? It can't, and Cadet Lowe yearns to occupy the other man's body and identity.

> To have been him! he moaned. Just to be him. Let him take this sound body of mine! Let him take it. To have got wings on my breast, to have wings; and to have got his scar, too, I would take death tomorrow. [...] To be him, to have gotten wings, but to have got his scar too! Cadet Lowe turned to the wall with passionate disappointment like a gnawing fox at his vitals. (38)

Like Manning in *The Middle Parts of Fortune*, Faulkner imagines men at war in terms of religious ecstasy and martyrdom. But the language also hints that Lowe wants to be 'taken', sexually, by the injured soldier. Donald is at once the object of Lowe's desire and the means by which Lowe expresses a desire to be an object. Lowe's homoeroticism is both contained and inflamed by the introduction of a heterosexual narrative, with Donald cast as rival for Margaret Powers' sexual interest. '"Margaret,"' says Lowe, '"are you in love with him?" (Knowing that if he were a woman, he would be.)' (43). But as a man, Lowe is far more fascinated by and in love with Donald than any woman in the novel could be.

Back in Georgia, Donald's wounded body is a remnant, a trace, of a distant European war. *Soldiers' Pay* traces the processes whereby the anxieties generated by the presence of the wounded, war-neurotic soldier are brought under control, and his body finally removed from civilian society. Or, as a contemporary British reviewer put it, invoking an anthropological ritual: 'Soldier's pay is injustice; can hardly be anything else, for is not the soldier the scape-goat for our sins, and why should the scape-goat come

---

39 Limon, *Writing After War*, 117–19.

shambling home out of the wilderness whither he was despatched to die?'[40]

Blind and disfigured, Donald becomes a spectacle for his father and friends at home, but they all see something different, according to their interests. His father refuses at first to acknowledge Donald's illness and insists he is getting better (when in fact he is getting worse, 96–7). Later, when he is planning Donald's wedding, he sees his living son as dead. The civilian transition from son to husband, boy to man – already disrupted by Donald's war experiences – displaces the last of the father's optimistic delusions about his son's health, and replaces it with a new misrecognition: '(This was Donald, my son. He is dead.)' (212–13). Donald's prewar fiancée Cecily can see only his scar – a shocking new form of physical difference which she cannot bear to see (unlike Lawrence's women, who stare with great interest at the male characters' injuries).

Cecily's younger brother Robert is deeply fascinated by the sight of Donald's scarred face. He is a young boy, still at school; the soldier's wounded body shapes the meaning of masculinity for his generation. The little boys come to gawk at the dying soldier, while Gilligan, another returned soldier, tries to protect him from their prurient gazes:

> 'Beat it, now,' [Gilligan] repeated to young Robert Saunders, who, with sundry contemporaries to whom he had promised something good in the way of damaged soldiers, had called.
> 'He's going to marry my sister. I'd like to know why I can't see him,' young Robert protested. He was in the uncomfortable position of one who has inveigled his friends into a gold mine and then cannot produce the mine. They jeered at him and he justified his position hotly, appealing to Gilligan. (124)

'Show's over,' Gilligan tells the boys, and complains to Margaret Powers about 'these damn folks in and out of here all day long, staring at him' (124). For the boys, the injured soldier is a sideshow, a fascinating sight of disfigurement and suffering, but also of manhood and their own possible futures. For Robert, he is also a commodity; a 'gold mine'. Shortly before this scene, the same sight inspires Robert's father to express unusual tenderness towards his

---

40 Proteus, 'Current Literature: New Novels', *New Statesman*, 35 (28 June 1930), 369.

son. And Robert (who has been trying to see Donald, at this stage unsuccessfully) recognises precisely where the embrace is coming from:

> 'Did you see his scar, daddy? Did you see his scar?'
> The man stared at this troublesome small miniature of himself, and then he knelt suddenly, taking his son into his arms, holding him close.
> 'You seen his scar,' young Robert Saunders accused, trying to release himself as the rain galloped over them, through the trees. (99)

*Soldiers' Pay* traces the processes whereby the returned soldier's presence is shorn of its destabilising effect on civilian structures of sexual difference, even though these structures are changing anyway. When the characters attend a dance, for example, the soldiers find themselves relegated to the edges of this social ritual. They talk loudly among themselves,

> drowning the intimation of dancers they could not emulate, of girls who once waited upon their favours and who now ignored them – the hang-over of warfare in a society tired of warfare. Puzzled and lost, poor devils. Once Society drank war, brought them into manhood with a cultivated taste for war; but now Society seemed to have found something else for a beverage [...] (165)

Warfare is something which men have to learn: a 'cultivated taste' which is now out of fashion. It defined their manhood two years earlier (in 1917, when the United States entered the war); now, the meaning of masculinity has changed. The spring of 1919 is the 'day of the Boy, of him who had been too young for soldiering'.

> For two years he had had a dry time of it. Of course, girls had used him during the scarcity of men, but always in such a detached impersonal manner. Like committing fornication with a beautiful woman who chews gum all the while. O Uniform, O Vanity. They had used him but when a uniform showed up he got the air. (156)

Now, the returned soldiers cannot dance; some of them cannot even walk. Women have lost interest in them in preference for the 'Boy'. To complicate matters, there are 'Boys of both sexes' (158) in this 'day of the Boy, male and female' (163).[41] Like Lawrence's war sto-

---

41 In *Lady Chatterley's Lover*, Connie is too womanly to conform to the current fashion for boyish women. Both Lawrence and Faulkner seem to disapprove of these androgynous figures.

ries, *Soldiers' Pay* is troubled by these historical shifts in sexual difference and its intersection with other relationships, such as age, race, or class. But where Lawrence tries to turn the trauma of war into an opportunity for denying or transcending the idea of castration, Faulkner's novel is thrown into a state of deep anxiety which cannot be resolved.

With the exception of Margaret Powers, Faulkner's civilian characters refuse to imagine the war. Margaret is a young woman whose husband of a few days was killed in the war, leaving her with war-neurotic dreams and fantasies of his decomposing body, 'seething' with worms, 'like new milk' (37). She imagines him as a skeleton, his mouth 'hard and shaped as bone' – a figure of Death itself, rendered ironic through the reader's knowledge that his head has been blown off (149), a death far messier than Margaret's fantasy. This is set against the image of Margaret's living, red mouth, which is repeatedly seen by the other characters as a scar (27, 34, 35, 167, 232; similarly, in Barbusse's *Under Fire*, a woman's mouth is perceived as a wound). Like Aldington in *Death of a Hero*, Faulkner satirises his women characters as trivial, cruel, sexually exploitative, indifferent to the soldier's suffering while struggling among themselves for possession of his body. When Margaret Powers first meets Cecily:

> There was that subtle effluvia of antagonism found inevitably in a room where two young 'pretty' women are, and they sat examining each other with narrow care. [...] Cecily, never having been engaged in an unselfconscious action of any kind and being among people whom she knew, examined the other closely with that attribute women have for gaining correct instinctive impressions of another's character, clothes, morals, etc. (67)

Sexual rivalry is one of the few relationships posited between women in *Soldiers' Pay*, and is central to the plot. Cecily is engaged to Donald, but does not love him; Margaret is in love with him and will marry him, shortly before he dies. He is the object of their struggle to attain the feminine prize of wifehood; he has no say in the matter as his will and desire have been destroyed by the war.

*Soldiers' Pay* obsessively returns to the sight of the women:

their clothes, their beauty, their ugliness (especially if they are old), their bodies, their clothes. What effect does this have? Woman as unpredictable, vain and duplicitous – traditional satiric themes – provides a reassuring, familiar background to the text's central anxiety: masculinity and war – or rather, civilian masculinity in a post-war society remote from the place and meaning of the war itself. Yet the traditional satiric view is found to be inadequate to the historical moment, and becomes a further symptom of the novel's anxiety about bodily differences produced by the war.

Both 'The Blind Man' and *Soldiers' Pay* are deeply troubled by the war's effect on vulnerable male bodies. With their symbols of castration inscribed on the central characters' faces, these are stories about men's worst nightmares being rendered visible. For the male body is threatened not only by the terrifying fiction of castration, but by the historical reality of war. But the works are not saying the same thing. In 'The Blind Man', the idea of male castration is externalised in order to be denied. The injured soldier is rendered as aggressively whole, and ends the story as a colossus, able to crush the uninjured civilian man. Lawrence's blind man, unable to see the others seeing him, is blithely unaware of their gaze and thereby empowered. Blindness becomes a way of circumventing the fear of bodily damage whilst appearing to confront it. *Soldiers' Pay* does the opposite. Faulkner's blind man is so traumatised by the war that he ceases to be a subject altogether and can do nothing except die. In both cases, the injured man is intensely under the gaze of other characters, but with different consequences: one becomes a super-subject, the other loses subjectivity altogether.

Most striking, however, are the ways in which these writings unsettle the very idea of sexual difference as the source of all human subjectivity.[42] As I argued at the beginning of this chapter, much of the psychoanalytic basis for current theories of sexual difference dates from this period. The distressing presence of war-injured men surely challenges the idea of woman's body as the basis of all significant difference. Contemporary feminist and psychoanalytic theory pays surprisingly little attention to the fictions, fantasies, and his-

42 Maud Ellmann questions whether 'castration' and sexual difference are adequate models to explain language. *The Hunger Artists: Starving, Writing and Imprisonment* (London, Virago, 1993).

torical experiences of war, yet they have had a profound influence upon the ways in which modern societies live, and how we imagine ourselves.[43]

43 But see Jacqueline Rose, *Why War?* (Oxford, Blackwell, 1993); Jacqueline Rose, *States of Fantasy* (Oxford, Clarendon, 1996); Daniel Pick, *War Machine: The Rationalisation of Slaughter in the Modern Age* (New Haven, Yale University Press, 1993); also Klaus Theweleit, *Male Fantasies*, vol. 1, trans. Stephen Conway (Cambridge, Polity, 1987).

# III

# War and politics

# 5

# The tank and the manufacture of consent

N MAY SINCLAIR's *The Tree of Heaven* (1917), a young man named Nicholas has a 'big Idea': a 'Moving Fortress' which will transform the shape of modern warfare. The idea is with him all day at work, 'hovering like a formless spiritual presence [...]. But in the evenings it took shape and sound. It arose and moved, after its fashion, as he had conceived it, beautiful, monstrous, terrible.' Nicholas is trying to invent the tank, a new weapon of war which was developed in Britain and first used in battle in September 1916. The tank was an idea whose time had come, and May Sinclair's character is one of many real and fictional people who believed they had contributed to its invention.[1]

Literary and cultural history of the First World War has traditionally shown little interest in the development of military technology. But culture is made up of objects as well as writings, and military objects sometimes occupied an important place in the social and intellectual context in which writers such as Woolf, Ford, Lawrence, and HD lived and worked. All the writers discussed in this book would have been aware of the tank; indeed, many of them would have seen one first-hand, as I will discuss shortly. The tank was an imaginative as well as a physical presence, and it turns up in fiction, poetry, and newspapers, as well as military histories and propaganda. In military terms, the success of the first tanks was at best doubtful. But their cultural significance was immense, especially among civilians. If the tank won the war, as its champions claimed, it did so through the mobilisation of fantasy rather than on the battlefield. This in turn raised serious questions about agency, citizen-

---

1 Sinclair, *The Tree of Heaven* (London, Cassell, 1917), 140–1. In Ian Hay's *The Willing Horse* (London, Hodder and Stoughton, n.d.), one character in mid-1916 tries to imagine 'Some sort of armour-plated motor 'bus', 147–8.

ship, and democracy during the war and is an important context for reading the literature which followed.

'For some time past', wrote John Gould Fletcher in 1918, 'various people have been clamouring for a new religion, without seeing that a new one was being born under their noses.' The new religion has been created in the newspapers, and its god, says Fletcher, is the tank. The tank 'has seized upon our imaginations': 'Writers continually hymn for us His virtues. Short stories, sonnets are dedicated to Him. His picture appears everywhere in our papers. Artists paint Him as he appears upon the battlefield, and inventive children experiment with model Tanks of wood and cardboard.'[2] The military and technical history of the tank has been well documented; much less is known about its cultural significance, especially among civilians.[3] How did this new weapon alter the ways in which Britain imagined itself, its citizens, and its relationship to the war? The tank was one of the few innovations in which Britain was more successful than Germany; this alone gave it considerable ideological force.[4] But its significance was far greater than its military value. For Fletcher, its 'commanding personality' had 'captivated' the civilian imagination.

The tank was developed to answer a serious military problem: to break the deadlock on the western front. Not long after the war began, the western front had become paralysed. Two powerful armies faced one another in trenches which extended from the Bel-

---

2  Fletcher, 'The New God', *Egoist*, 5, 3 (March 1918), 45–6.
3  Recent studies include David Fletcher, *Landships: British Tanks in the First World War* (London, HMSO, 1984); David Fletcher, ed., *Tanks and Trenches: First-Hand Accounts of Trench Warfare in the First World War* (Phoenix Mill, Alan Sutton, 1994); George Forty and Anne Forty, *Bovington Tanks* (Wincanton, Dorset, Wincanton Press, 1988); J. P. Harris, *Men, Ideas and Tanks: British Military Thought and Armoured Forces, 1903–1939* (Manchester University Press, 1995); A. J. Smithers, *A New Excalibur: The Development of the Tank 1909–1939* (London, Leo Cooper and Secker and Warburg, 1986); A. J. Smithers, *Cambrai: The First Great Tank Battle 1917* (London, Leo Cooper, 1992); Trevor Wilson, *The Myriad Faces of War* (Cambridge, Polity, 1986). I have drawn my military-historical material from these sources and from F. Mitchell, *Tank Warfare: The Story of the Tanks of the Great War* (1933; Stevenage, Spa Books, 1987) and E. D. Swinton, *Eyewitness* (London, Hodder and Stoughton, 1932).
4  Wilson, *Myriad Faces of War*, 389.

gian coast to the Swiss Alps – a distance of nearly 5 hundred miles. Each side was equipped with machine guns and artillery and was separated from the other by impenetrable barbed wire. Neither side could advance; unprotected troops trying to struggle through the barbed wire were mowed down by machine guns and artillery fire. The war settled into the terrible stalemate of 1915, followed by the failed pushes of 1916. The killing continued, but the war itself was immobilised. To break the deadlock, some kind of armoured vehicle was needed to break through or crush the barbed wire, knock out the enemy's gun emplacements, and allow the infantry to advance – to transform stasis into movement. This need was answered by the tank. Its champions envisaged hundreds of technically efficient tanks launched in a sector of hard ground. The tank was Britain's secret weapon, and would, it was hoped, overwhelm the Germans with surprise and terror as well as technical mastery.

By the late summer of 1916, the high command was desperate for a success at the Somme, following the hundreds of thousands of deaths since July of that year. After intense political struggles within British military circles, tanks were brought into action in September 1916 – about six months before they were ready – at one of the wettest, muddiest sectors of the front.[5] By this date, only sixty machines had been manufactured. Transporting them to the front was a huge undertaking, and many of the crews were physically exhausted before they reached the battle. Several tanks were damaged in transit; others broke down on their way to the starting line. Several more became bogged or broke down, and only eighteen actually took part in the assault.[6] The tank crews were bitterly disappointed; the other troops were sceptical.[7] But hardly anyone actually saw this failure, and it was reported in the newspapers as a remarkable success.

The newspapers were one of the most important sources of propaganda in the Great War, as many historians have docu-

5 Fletcher, *Landships*, 15.
6 Wilson, *Myriad Faces of War*, 344. During and immediately after the First World War, there was considerable debate as to whether the tank could ever be developed into a useful weapon. Smithers, *Cambrai*, 16; see also Swinton, *Eyewitness*; Swinton was an active champion of the tank during and after the war. Later tanks were of course very successful in battle; this has tended to efface the early failures.
7 Mitchell, *Tank Warfare*, 37.

**Plate 1**
An early tank at the front. Reproduced courtesy of the
Trustees of the Imperial War Museum, London. Crown copyright.

mented.[8] It was through the newspapers, too, that civilians' fantas-matic relationship to the war was mobilised – and to some extent *produced*. When the first tanks went into battle, the *Daily Mail* announced a success for 'our glorious infantry, airmen, and gun-ners, and [...] the wonderful new armoured "tanks"', and gave a prominent place to a long report by its correspondent, Beach Thomas:

> The sun rose to-day on a British success and a German defeat. It set on an enhanced victory and a greater rout. [...] We are advancing still, and the enemy still retreating.
>
> [...] Soon after six the spasmodic barking of the cannonade (now normal in spite of its intensity) gave place to a 'kettle-drum bombard-

8 Irene Cooper Willis, *England's Holy War: A Study of English Liberal Idealism during the Great War* (New York, Knopf, 1928); Arthur Ponsonby, *Falsehood in War-Time* (London, George Allen and Unwin, 1928); Philip Taylor, *Munitions of the Mind*, rev. edn (Manchester University Press, 1995); Peter Buitenhuis, *The Great War of Words: Literature as Propaganda 1914–18 and After* (London, Batsford, 1989). See also Chapter 2 above.

ment'. The 'fun' was 'fast and furious', and two minutes after the orchestra opened our men leaped from their trenches. They were not unaccompanied. In spite of the harvest moon we had brought up a certain number of armoured cars which the moonlight transformed into fantastic monsters. 'Autos blindés' is the French term. They looked like blind creatures emerging from the primeval slime. To watch one crawling round a battered wood in the half-light was to think of 'the Jabberwock with eyes of flame' who

> Came whiffling through the tulgey wood
> And burbled as it came.

[... The] enemy ill-distinguished these iron monsters, which in truth amused our men rather than encouraged them. They were a jest, cheering hearts, possibly faithful creatures, but no rival to the bayonet.

[...] With ludicrous serenity they wobbled across the gridiron fields and shook themselves as if the bullets were flies that bit just deep enough to deserve a flick. [...]

Munchausen never approached the stories imagined for them by soldiers. But their pet name is 'tanks', and they were chiefly regarded as a practical joke. Whales, Boojums, Dreadnoughts, slugs, snarks – never were creatures that so tempted the gift of nick-naming. They were said to live in trees and houses and jump like grasshoppers or kangaroos.[9]

The propagandistic quality of the writing seems obvious: the use of 'we' and 'our', the excess of praise ('our glorious infantry', etc.), the duplicitous suggestion that the slow-moving tanks were 'said' (presumably by soldiers) to 'jump like grasshoppers or kangaroos', when they were much more likely to be stuck in the mud. More striking, however, are the metaphors which place the tank simultaneously in a tradition of literary fantasy (Jabberwocky, Munchausen) and somewhere in prehistory. These images appear in a great many newspaper accounts, as well as in tank histories, memoirs, literary works, and even official military communications. *The Times*, for example, describing the same battle, imagines the tanks as 'unearthly monsters, cased in steel, spitting fire'. 'It was as incred-

9 W. Beach Thomas, *Daily Mail*, 18 September 1916, 5. This article is parodied in 'Teech Bomas', 'How the Tanks Went Over', *B.E.F. Times*, 1 December 1916, rpt in *The Wipers Times*, compiled and introd. Patrick Beaver (London: Papermac, 1988), 133. An article in *Punch* also claims that tanks can climb trees: 'The Watch Dogs', *Punch*, 27 September 1916, 214. Mitchell complains about the 'weird and fantastic' press reports which exaggerated the tanks' abilities. *Tank Warfare*, 36, 63. See also W. Beach Thomas, *With the British on the Somme* (London, Methuen, 1917), ch. 13, 'Tanks and Other Engines'.

ible as a nightmare or one of Jules Verne's most fantastic imaginings', it claims, going on to liken the tanks to toad-salamanders, echidna-dragons, mammoths, Leviathan, and various other mythical and ancient beasts.[10] For *Punch*, the tank is a dragon, mounted by St George. Mitchell's tank history remembers the first tanks as 'uncanny brutes emerged from some dim prehistoric age', and Jenkin writes of a tank wallowing 'like some gigantic hippopotamus puffing and bellowing through a reedy swamp'. For Mary Borden, the tanks are 'things of iron' crawling on the earth's naked body; 'obscene crabs, armoured toads, big as houses'. Ford Madox Ford calls them 'ugly, senseless armadillos' which move like 'slow rats [...] snouting crumbs of garbage'.[11]

Almost all the early tank writings compare the machine to some kind of dinosaur emerging out of the primeval mud. As Gertrude Stein remarks, 'war makes things go backward as well as forward';[12] the most advanced weapon of 1916 takes civilisation into a new phase of modern technology at the same time as plunging it back into prehistory – an image both terrifying and pleasurable. It is sometimes argued that the Great War destroyed belief in evolution,[13] but the war's cultural resonances are actually more complex than this. With the tank, especially, evolution begins to run backwards and forwards, simultaneously – a vertiginous notion which informs a number of late modernist writings, from Ford's *Parade's End* (1924–8) to Woolf's *Between the Acts* (1941).

The first tanks also generate a peculiar kind of laughter, as *The Times* correspondent suggests:

> I watched the great things manoeuvre about the field, grotesque and unspeakable; and at each new antic which they performed, each new

10 *The Times*, 16 September 1916, 8; *The Times*, 19 September 1916, 10.
11 'St. George Out-dragons the Dragon', cartoon, *Punch*, 28 November 1917, 367. Mitchell, *Tank Warfare*, 78; Arthur Jenkin, *A Tank Driver's Experiences: Or Incidents in a Soldier's Life* (London, Elliot Stock, 1922), 135; Borden, 'The Hill', in *The Forbidden Zone* (London, WIlliam Heinemann, 1929), 175, 176. See also Swinton, *Eyewitness*, 12; Ford, *Parade's End* (1948; Harmondsworth, Penguin, 1982), 576.
12 Stein, *Wars I Have Seen* (1945; London: Brilliance Books, 1984), 5.
13 Stephen Kern, *The Culture of Time and Space 1880–1918* (Cambridge MA, Harvard University Press, 1983), 291.

capacity which they developed, one could do nothing but sit down and laugh till one's sides ached. Were they only a preposterous joke or were they a serious contribution to modern warfare?[14]

Similarly, the *Southern Daily Echo* reports that 'It makes you roar with laughter to see one of them slide up to a house, go slick-bang through the walls, and come out the other side without a scratch, leaving the house, of course, just a pile of bricks and mortar'.[15] Many of the reports present the tank as comical; a 'preposterous joke', which is said to terrify the Germans and make the British laugh uncontrollably. What is the significance of this laughter? In Bergson's famous definition, laughter is produced by '*Something mechanical encrusted on the living*'.[16] This seems appropriate for the tank, a machine which looks like a 'self-propelling mammoth', 'half battleship, half caterpillar'.[17] But Bergson also points out that laughter is 'above all, a corrective'; it 'intends to humiliate'. Laughter, in other words, has a political function; it helps a society to define itself and its borders, and to regulate behaviour. For Bergson: 'Laughter must answer to certain requirements of life in common. It must have a *social* signification' (8). This was particularly important in the last two years of the war, which produced new demands on the population, and required that they consent, and keep on consenting, to the slaughter.

Very few people saw the tanks in battle, yet almost everyone in Britain knew what they looked like. As Mrs Humphry Ward remarked in 1917, 'London is full of tanks, of course – on the films.'[18] Tank films were extremely popular, reaching an audience of perhaps twenty million people, and tanks made cameo appearances

14  *The Times*, 19 September 1916, 10.
15  *Southern Daily Echo* [Southampton], 4 January 1918, [p. 3]. The *Nation* quotes a newspaper report which praises the tanks for making the British army 'laugh as it fought'. 'The New-Born Tortoise', 23 September 1916, 784–5.
16  Henri Bergson, *Laughter: An Essay on the Meaning of the Comic* (1900; London, Macmillan, 1911), 37. On Bergson's war propaganda, see Geoffrey Gilbert, *A Career in Modernism: Wyndham Lewis 1909–1931* (Ph.D. dissertation, Cambridge, 1995), ch. 4.
17  Jenkin, *A Tank Driver's Experiences*, 14; *Mr Punch's History of the Great War* (London, Cassell, 1919), 110 – an edited version of a piece in *Punch*, 27 September 1916, 214.
18  Mrs Humphry Ward, *Towards the Goal* (London, John Murray, 1917), 31.

in various other war films.[19] An exhibition in London in March 1918 claimed to include the world's largest photograph – 23 foot 6 inches by 17 foot – of tanks on the western front.[20] Many other representations appeared, including an 'exclusive' tank toy for Christmas from Selfridge's.[21] Tanks were used in advertising for headache pills: 'BATTLE HEADACHE. How the TANK Men cure it'.[22] There were tank pleasure rides, tank handbags, tank teapots, tank moneyboxes, paper napkins decorated with pictures of the Royal Family and tanks. Small china models of the tank were produced: these were about six inches long, and often decorated with a small picture – of Peterborough Cathedral, for example.[23] Often witty or parodic, these strange, uncanny objects projected the tank right into the heart of civilian culture.

As well as being surrounded by representations of the tank, a surprising number of civilians saw tanks first hand, at close quarters, in Britain, in one of the more surreal propaganda campaigns of the war. This campaign can be traced through the newspaper reports in the spring of 1918.

## Tank banks

On Friday 1 March 1918, the British newspapers reported a new drive to raise money for the war. The campaign was announced in mock-military terms: 'Business men all over the country are closing their ranks for next week's great offensive to raise One Hundred

---

19  Roger Smither, ed., *The Battles of the Somme and Ancre* (London, Imperial War Museum, 1993), 21, referring to the film *The Battle of the Ancre and the Advance of the Tanks*. Nicholas Reeves notes that 112 London cinemas booked the film. *Official British Film Propaganda during the First World War* (London, Croom Helm and IWM, 1986), 225.

20  'The Prince Sees Himself: War Photographs that Pleased the King', *Daily Express*, 4 March 1918, 3; See also 'The War in Colours', *The Times*, 4 March 1918, 10; 5 March 1918, 9; 6 March 1918, 3; *Daily Telegraph*, 5 March 1918, 5; *Daily Chronicle*, 4 March 1918, 3; *Daily Express*, 4 March 1918, 3. The exhibition was organised by the Ministry of Information.

21  Advertisement in *Daily Express*, 27 November 1916, 2. 'A weird model that goes lumbering fearlessly along' with 'guns which shoot from inside'. The toy tank costs 8s11d.

22  Daisy headache tablets advertisement, *John Bull*, 24 November 1917, 16.

23  These objects (or photographs of them) are on display at the Bovington Tank Museum, Wool, Dorset.

Millions in National War Bonds and War Savings Certificates.'[24] The 'great offensive' was Business Men's Week, which aimed to persuade businesses to invest their entire week's takings in national war bonds.[25] The preliminary responses were promising, as companies jostled to pledge their week's income, and more, to the cause: Selfridge's promised £50,000; Harrod's, £75,000; Ellerman Lines, £1 million.[26] Business Men's Week was the highlight of an intensive campaign to sell war bonds which aimed to raise an average of £25 million per week, every week, for about a year.[27]

Readers were encouraged to buy their war bonds from a tank, parked for the week in Trafalgar Square. *The Times* explained:

> A military pigeon post is being arranged to convey investors' cheques to the Tank in Trafalgar-square. Special baskets of pigeons in charge of soldiers will be on view in the Square. Those who wish to invest amounts over a certain sum can be supplied with a pigeon which will be taken by a soldier to their homes, where the cheque or application for bonds can be inserted in the small metal holder on the leg of the bird, which will then fly with it to the Tank in Trafalgar-square. The pigeons will not accept cheques from outside the Greater London area.

It adds that 'A special telephone exchange is being installed to serve the six Tanks in the London area'. Anyone who was interested simply had to dial 'Tanks, London'.[28]

All over the country, fund-raising targets were set according to the population of each centre. Large cities such as Birmingham and Liverpool promised to raise £2.5 million each, enough to pay for a super-dreadnought, while a tiny Welsh village hoped to raise

---

24 *Daily Mail*, 1 March 1918, 5. 'It is to be the greatest financial push of the war, and everybody, rich and poor, should join in this great offensive', *Weekly Dispatch*, 3 March 1918, 1.
25 See for example *The Times*, 1 March 1918, 3.
26 *The Times*, 1 March 1918, 3; *Daily Mail*, 1 March 1918, 5; 2 March 1918, 6; *Daily Express*, 4 March 1918, 3.
27 *The Times*, 19 January 1918, 10; 21 January 1918, 3.
28 '"Tanks, London": Business Houses' Support', *The Times*, 1 March 1918, 3. Similar reports appear in other papers: 'Flying Cheques: Pigeon Post to Tank', *Daily Mail*, 1 March 1918, 5; '"Chequer" Pigeons: A Novel Way of Investing in War Bonds', *Daily Express*, 1 March 1918, 3; 'Tanks Week: A Fine Start', *Daily Mail*, 2 March 1918, 6. According to one report, only those investing more than £10,000 were entitled to use a pigeon. *Weekly Dispatch*, 3 March 1918, 1.

**Plate 2**
The tank bank in Trafalgar Square, 4–9 March 1918. Miss Marie Lohr buying a
War Bond at the tank bank. Reproduced courtesy of the Trustees of the Imperial
War Museum, London. Crown copyright

enough to buy one aeroplane.[29] The logic of this method of selling
war bonds was explained in an advertisement in the *Daily Express*:

IN THE GOOD OLD DAYS the State *demanded* arms and ships.

TO-DAY, You are only asked to *lend* the money to buy them.
    Until recent times the provision of ships and armour for the defence
of the country was nearly always the duty of the various towns, villages
and individuals.

THE REVIVAL OF ENGLAND'S GLORY.

[...] 'Lend your money' says the State 'and arms and ships will be provided.'[30]

29  *The Times*, 1 March 1918, 3; *Daily Mail*, 1 March 1918, 5.
30  *Daily Express*, 4 March 1918, 2. The advertisement details the pledges received
    for various items of military hardware: 22 cities and towns have promised to
    pay for cruisers at £400,000 each; 32 towns will buy destroyers at £150,000
    each; 67 small towns will buy submarines at £100,000 each; hundreds of little
    towns will buy aeroplanes at £2,500 each. The advertisement appeared in sev-
    eral national newspapers.

Readers were urged to buy as many bonds as possible, to 'help your own city, town or district to carry out the task allotted to it'.[31] The advertisement constructs its readers, somewhat reluctantly, as free citizens rather than feudal subjects, but they were citizens under pressure to renew their consent to the war and to express that support visibly, in public.

The first day of Business Men's Week was very successful; in London alone, £4.5 million was raised.[32] One tank was stationed behind the Royal Exchange, where business men were invited to go 'Over the top of the City Tank' to buy their war bonds.[33] Another tank (called Egbert)[34] remained in Trafalgar Square, while four others roamed the boroughs of London, spending a day in each place, collecting money. Almost all the named tank bank investors in the newspaper reports are large businesses, paying up to £2 million pounds each. But the organisers of Business Men's Week also hoped that working-class people would invest in war bonds, and activities were devised to attract punters from all classes. *The Times* described the 'attractions' provided in Trafalgar Square: a display of model ships, launched by an admiral of the United States navy,[35] and a pigeon race at lunchtime with war bonds as a prize.[36] Another tank was 'in state' at Hackney, where a local shop, 'camouflaged' as a trench, sold 'war trophies'.[37] A few days later, everyone in Fulham who bought war bonds was filmed, and the film screened in a local cinema; the best 'tank smile' won a prize.[38]

On the final days of Business Men's Week, citizens were invited to choose 'British bonds to-day or German bondage to-morrow'. MPs spoke from the top of the tank in Trafalgar Square and the Lord Mayor of London dropped a message from an airship, reminding Londoners of their duty. Altogether, Tank Week raised £135 million, much to the organisers' satisfaction.[39]

31  *Daily Express*, 4 March 1918, 2.
32  *The Times*, 5 March 1918, 7.
33  *The Times*, 5 March 1918, 7.
34  *Daily Mail*, 1 March 1918, 5.
35  *The Times*, 8 March 1918, 7.
36  Other prizes are offered 'with the idea of stimulating buying on the part of the working-classes'. *The Times*, 5 March 1918, 7. The *Daily Express* argues that the public is attracted by the 'sporting chance' of winning certificates or prizes, 6 March 1918, 1.
37  *The Times*, 8 March 1918, 7.
38  'The Best "Tank Smile"', *Daily Express*, 13 March 1918, 3.
39  *The Times*, 9 March 1918, 7.

Not long after they were invented, then, tanks appeared on the streets of all the major British cities. (The first tank banks were introduced the previous autumn, in November 1917, during the battle of Cambrai.[40]) Contemporary reports suggest that civilians rather liked them. Even allowing for newspaper inaccuracies and propaganda, the evidence suggests that large numbers of people visited the tank banks and many bought war bonds.[41] Others were less enthusiastic; Virginia Woolf, for example, acidly described a warm spring day in 1918, in which the sound of 'Richmond worshipping a Tank was like the hum of bees round some first blossom'.[42] John Gould Fletcher complained in the *Egoist* in 1917 that Britain's attempt to destroy the German military machine had led to the invention of other, equally undesirable machines, including the tank and the war loan, 'a machine to empty our pockets'.[43] In his 1918 essay 'The New God', Fletcher likened the tank to a mechanical god, remarking ironically that its ability to collect money was 'miraculous', and that buying war bonds had become a 'religious ceremony'.[44]

In the newspapers, by contrast, tank banks were represented as entertainment for the populace, reported in phrases which weakly parody the language of war: the 'great offensive'; 'go over the top'; and so forth. All over the country, business, the press, and the state worked together to provide official spectacles which aimed to generate laughter and pleasure, and to regenerate support for the war. Tank banks became the centre of a kind of carnival – to which the popular musical *Chu Chin Chow*, for example, sent a camel to buy £10,000 of war bonds.[45] As the *Daily Express* remarked with

40   'Right through the Great Hindenburg Line: Cavalry, Tanks, and Infantry', *Daily Express*, 22 November 1917, 1; 'The Tank-Bank: Attractive Scheme for the Sale of War Bonds', *Daily Express*, 22 November 1917, 3; *Illustrated London News*, 1 December 1917, 661. On Cambrai see Wilson, *Myriad Faces of War*, 491–2; Fletcher, ed., *Tanks and Trenches*, 70; Smithers, *Cambrai*.

41   Enormous sums were collected in all the major cities; the largest amount was collected in Glasgow: £14 million in one week.

42   Woolf, *Diary*, vol. 1, 5 April 1918, 131.

43   John Gould Fletcher, 'The Death of the Machines', *Egoist*, 4, 3 (April 1917), 45.

44   Fletcher, 'The New God', 45–6.

45   'Tank Week Items', *Daily Express*, 8 March 1918, 3. The *Daily Telegraph* reports: 'About two o'clock the animal, with stately step, drew up at the Royal Exchange, where its gorgeously arrayed Eastern attendant handed in a cheque for £10,000 to be invested in National War Bonds, and after a tour of the walks they left by the western steps.' 8 March 1918, 5. The *Daily Chronicle* says that the camel carried £8000 and bore a sign saying 'I am going to the City Tank': 8 March 1918, 3.

LIVERPOOL JOHN MOORES UNIVERSITY
LEARNING SERVICES

approval: 'All that the Tank Fair needs is a coconut shy!'[46] In its editorial – entitled 'Have You Tanked?' – the *Express* argued that people who fail to buy war bonds will 'surely be marked with a blush'; and 'the man without a tank certificate should be as uncomfortable as the man who has not shaved'.[47] People were offered a choice between communal pleasure (however fictitious) and social embarrassment. Consent became a form of personal hygiene, and those who refused should carry a physical mark of shame.

The tank bank campaign was so successful that a similar project was undertaken a few months later. Trevor Wilson describes the 'Feed the Guns' campaign, in which Trafalgar Square was turned into a replica of a bombed French village, with a shell-damaged church tower, wrecked farmhouse, etc. Twenty thousand sandbags were brought in, and visitors were invited to 'feed' the guns on display with bonds and certificates.[48] Here, too, civilians seem to have allowed the state to infantilise them; they enacted a fantasy of the war as circus or fairground, replicated in bizarre simulacra in Trafalgar Square.

Yet tanks were not uncomplicatedly benign or entertaining presences on city streets; the newspapers also admit that they look rather frightening and seem to threaten violence towards the civilian population of their own side.[49] The idea of tanks turning against civilians surfaced just days after the tank first appeared in battle. The *Daily Mail* reported (or perhaps invented) a 'hopeful man who said that after the war is over he will certainly hire one of the "tanks" to clear his wife's relatives out of his house'.[50] Sales

---

46 'All the Fun of the Tank Fair', *Daily Express*, 8 March 1918, 3; see also 'London Sets the Pace', *Daily Express*, 5 March 1918, 3. *Land and Water* noted that some people 'object to what they call "the circus business" in connection with national finance'; implying that the state's money ought to be treated with greater dignity. But, it declared, 'the end has justified the means', and British people are beginning to recognise their 'individual responsibility' to pay for the war. 'The Outlook', *Land and Water*, 14 March 1918, 4. *Land and Water* also published regular propaganda articles by Hilaire Belloc (including attacks on peace proposals) and serialised John Buchan's *Greenmantle*.
47 'Have You Tanked?', editorial, *Daily Express*, 4 March 1918, 2.
48 This campaign raised £29 million in eight days in October 1918. Wilson, *Myriad Faces of War*, 647.
49 This threat was in fact realised shortly after the war, when tanks were used against striking workers in Glasgow early in 1919. Marwick, *The Deluge*, 313.
50 *Daily Mail*, 19 September 1916. John Gould Fletcher suggested sarcastically that when the tank was bored with raising money, it might go 'to the houses of food-hoarders and force them to disgorge for our benefit'. Fletcher, 'The New God', 45.

at the first tank banks were reported in the *Daily Express*, half mockingly, as 'Tank Draws First Blood',[51] and the tank itself described as 'a hungry monster', 'his mouth wide open', like a hippopotamus at the zoo. A frightened child is assured that 'he only bites Germans' and 'purrs' when well fed.[52] Many reports openly acknowledge the fantasy investment in the tank, and one newspaper went so far as to commission cartoonists such as Heath Robinson to imagine the new machine before pictures were made available to the public.[53] In one newspaper advertisement, the tank is represented as a huge, looming presence – disproportionately large in comparison with the human figures around it – shooting money out of its guns.[54] Sassoon's poem 'Blighters' imagines – indeed, hopes for – a tank attack on civilians in a music hall: 'I'd like to see a Tank come down the stalls / Lurching to rag-time tunes, or "Home, Sweet Home"'.[55] This is perhaps the best-known criticism of the use of tanks to trivialise the war, and it locates the blame entirely among civilians – especially women, the 'prancing ranks of harlots' on the stage. Yet the processes which bring comic songs about tanks into popular entertainment are rather more complex than the poem allows.

The winter of 1917–18 was perhaps the most difficult period of the war. With a shortage of food and heating, a very cold winter, and no end to the fighting in sight, there was a real possibility that the war might become unsupportable.[56] The cost was also a problem. How could support for the war be regenerated, especially among civilians, and how was it to be paid for? The early tanks might not have been very successful in battle, but they answered these political problems very nicely and transferred hundreds of millions of pounds out of bank savings and into the war. This had a profound effect on Britain's economy, as John Maynard Keynes later pointed

51 'Tank Draws First Blood', *Daily Express*, 27 November 1917, 3.
52 'Making the Tank Purr', *Daily Express*, 28 November 1917, 3.
53 'My Dream of Tanks', *Weekly Dispatch*, 24 September 1916, 7.
54 Advertisement for Eagle Star and British Dominions Insurance Co., *Daily Express*, 11 March 1918, 1.
55 Sassoon, 'Blighters' (1917).
56 Smithers, *Cambrai*, 5–6. On the shortage of coal and food in 1917 see Wilson, *Myriad Faces*, ch. 46; see Buitenhuis on the importance of propaganda during this period in *The Great War of Words*.

out.[57] Indeed, Britain, like the rest of Europe, ended the war severely in debt; this had serious consequences in the decades which followed.

Overall, between October 1917 and September 1918, war bonds raised £1000 million, an achievement which, as Trevor Wilson argues, caused considerable hardship among poorer people, especially as taxes and postage costs were increased around the same time.[58] This was the tanks' most successful campaign.

## From Little Willie to Mother

Intense secrecy surrounded the development and manufacture of the tank. The name 'tank' was chosen as a disguise, and the early tanks were passed off as water-tanks, supposedly to be exported to Russia in boxes labelled 'With Care to Petrograd'.[59] Strange stories circulated about the origins of the tank; after the war, many different people claimed to have invented it and a Royal Commission was set up to decide on its true parents, and to reward them with large sums of money.[60]

A prototype was tested in the summer of 1915, using the caterpillar track, recently invented for American tractors. As a result of these tests, a track of pressed steel was developed and wrapped around the entire body of the tank, producing the characteristic rhomboid shape. The tracks did not actually move across the ground; rather, a lot of small sprocket wheels drove the body along its own tracks. As Mitchell explains, 'the tank laid its own track, drove along it, then picked it up behind, and passed it over its head before laying it down in front again'.[61] Or as Mary Borden puts it in her tank poem,

---

57  Keynes, *The Economic Consequences of the Peace* (1919; London, Macmillan, 1984), 11–13.
58  The rise in postage was significant because working-class people were writing to relatives at the front, whereas before the war they rarely used the postal service; Wilson, *Myriad Faces of War*, 646.
59  Mitchell, *Tank Warfare*, 12.
60  Many people made claims to have invented the tank, including a medium named Mrs Capron who believed she had invented it while in a trance. A letter about this claim is on display at the Bovington Tank Museum, Dorset.
61  Mitchell, *Tank Warfare*, 18.

They moved slowly along on their stomachs
Dragging themselves forward by their ears.[62]

The tank looks completely self-sufficient; this pleased many early observers. From the outside, the crew is completely hidden; what you see is a machine which appears to drive itself, fire its own guns, and even provide its own road. The tank looked like a completely new kind of mechanical warfare, and it generated intense excitement among journalists and propagandists. It was greeted with less enthusiasm by the army and the war office. Their ambivalence has been dismissed as conservative, narrow-minded, and driven by an excessive love of cavalry;[63] perhaps so, but it is also worth noting that the tank consumed large quantities of money, labour, steel, and so forth at a time of scarcity, and was actually not very good at negotiating a muddy landscape. Even in their most successful battle, at Cambrai in November 1917, the tanks could not hold the ground they had won, and almost all the gains were lost a few days later, with approximately 45,000 casualties on each side.[64] Despite these failures, the tank *appeared* to offer protection to the vulnerable human body. Many writers describe the Great War as a war of machines against men, with the machines always winning. The tank seems, however ineptly, to provide a shield – to protect soldiers from the terrible damage of machine-gun bullets and artillery. In short, the tank promises to reduce the hideous abjection of the war; this alone altered the fantasmatic relationship between the human body and modern warfare, both for soldiers and for civilians.

The Great War is often discussed as if it were a complete break with the past; an abyss which separates the nineteenth century from modernism or modernity.[65] This figure can be traced in a number of writings from the period, but equally we find the war and its objects placed in an almost seamless continuity with the past, especially in military writings. A bizarre range of antecedants was discovered (or

---

62  Borden, 'The Hill', *The Forbidden Zone* (London, William Heinemann, 1929), 176.
63  Smithers, *A New Excalibur*, 6–7.
64  On 20 November 1917 476 tanks were used: 378 for fighting, 98 for supplies, wireless, etc.; 179 were lost that day. Wilson, *Myriad Faces of War*, 485–92.
65  The continuities and discontinuities of the Great War are a matter of contention among historians. For recent discussions see Stephen Constantine *et al.*, eds, *The First World War in British History* (London, Edward Arnold, 1995); Winter, *Sites of Memory, Sites of Mourning*.

invented) for the tank: the Roman testudo, knights in armour, armoured elephants, Leonardo's lost drawings of a horse-drawn tank, Dante's invention of the tank in the *Divine Comedy*, H. G. Wells' land ironclads.[66] Even today, the Bovington Tank Museum locates its objects in antiquity; its exhibition of First World War tanks opens with a quotation from the Bible: 'And the Lord was with Judah: and he drove out the inhabitants of the mountain: but he could not drive out the inhabitants of the valley, because they had chariots of iron.'[67]

The first successful tank was named Little Willie. Little Willie was too short, and was replaced by a larger model: Big Willie.[68] The larger model was the basis of all the early tanks which were used in battle, and was immediately renamed Mother – 'as it was the first of all tanks'.[69] Here the language becomes rather complex, for Mother came in two forms: male and female. (There were also 'hermaphrodite' tanks.) The sex of the tank was determined by relatively minor variations: the male was a little larger and weighed 28 tons; the female weighed 27 tons. The male had two kinds of guns; the female only one (though both carried a total of six guns). Perhaps most significantly from the crew's point of view, in the early models the male had a narrow door in the side, allowing men to escape, with difficulty, if the tank caught fire. The female by contrast had only a small trap door, just two foot high, out of which it was almost impossible to escape.[70] This was soon modified, but in the earliest tanks, being inside a female Mother was one of the men's worst nightmares: it was a place in which they could be trapped and burned alive. Tank driver Jenkin notes that the men 'most favoured' the male Mothers.[71]

66 'Dante the Inventor of Tanks!', *Daily Express*, 30 November 1916, 4; Wells, 'The Land Ironclads' (1903). See Harris, *Men, Ideas and Tanks*, 4–8; Forty, *The Royal Tank Regiment*, 11; Smithers, *A New Excalibur*, 3.
67 Judges I: 19–20; quoted on notice at the entrance of Bovington Tank Museum, Wool, Dorset.
68 Mitchell, *Tank Warfare*, 8. 'Big Willie' and 'Little Willie' were common nicknames for the Kaiser and Crown Prince, but it is also worth noting that 'willie' was documented slang for penis by 1905.
69 Mitchell, *Tank Warfare*, 9. Accounts vary slightly as to the differences between male and female tanks. Jenkin writes that the sex is 'determined by the sponsons and armaments'. *A Tank Driver's Experiences*, 17.
70 Mitchell, *Tank Warfare*, 17, 21.
71 Jenkin, *A Tank Driver's Experiences*, 18.

Drivers took up the terminology, but were inclined to refer to 'my bus' or 'my Willie' rather than 'my Mother'.[72] The language of Willie and Mother, male, female, and hermaphrodite, is scattered throughout the early tank writings with an air of ironic innocence. Mitchell for example writes of the 'adventurous male'; 'determined male'; 'all-conquering female'; 'female man-killers'. 'Would the old "Willie" break down suddenly when in the midst of the enemy?' worries a driver before his first attack. On her first trial, reports Mitchell, Mother 'behaved splendidly'.[73] The *Illustrated London News* presents a picture of a female Mother – '"The Perfect Lady" about to cross a trench'. A book by the engineering firm William Foster and Co. reproduces several photographs of Mother: '"Mother" negotiates her first trench', 'A Supply Tank [...] evolved from "Mother"', and a banner from Foster's factory: 'Welcome to the Birthplace of the Tanks'.[74] Many of the early tank writings employ an excess of metaphors of birth, conception, evolution, and fathering of the tank; the men who will later squabble over the money and glory allocated to the inventor of the tank claim to have given birth – to Mother.[75] Once she is invented, 'Mother' becomes a highly mobile and at times perverse figure – a source of simultaneous pleasure and terror, protection and violence and even a bizarre kind of tenderness. In a piece written long after the war, Henry Williamson tells a tank anecdote from Field-Marshal Hindenburg's autobiography. Hindenburg, says Williamson, recalls the sight, towards the end of the war, of 'a British Tommy sitting wounded by a knocked-out tank, holding the hand of a dying sixteen-year-old German boy, and saying, as the lad cried out *"Mutti – Mutti"*, "It's all right chum, Mother's here with you."'[76]

72  Smithers, *New Excalibur*, 48–50.
73  Mitchell, *Tank Warfare*, 9, 29–31, 33, 39, 107–8. In 1927, the Tank Corps settled on its official marching tune: 'My Boy Willie'. Forty and Forty, *Bovington Tanks*, 46–8.
74  *Illustrated London News*, December 1917; William Foster and Co., *The Tank: Its Birth and Development* (1920; Hinckley, T. E. E. Publishing, 1977), 24, 53, 70.
75  John Gould Fletcher comments that the tank's 'birth was somewhat ridiculous', and that the 'part taken by Winston Churchill therein has never been sufficiently cleared up'. 'The New God', 45.
76  Williamson sees the act as evidence of the 'gentle and kindly [...] attitude towards what was hellish'; a 'virtue' extended even towards the enemy. 'It is a charity which links those who have passed through the estranging remoteness of battle ... men who were not broken, but reborn.' Foreword to facsimile reprint of *The Wipers Times*, x.

## Tank writing

The tank produced new ways of imagining warfare, the human body, and structures of difference. For most British people, both soldiers and civilians, the tank represented an *idea*. Industrial warfare produces new terrors. In theory, at least, you can hide inside a machine known as both Willie and Mother and drive through a dangerous landscape, crushing your enemies in your path. At the same time, you worry that Willie or Mother is threatening to mutilate or destroy you, and possibly take all your money, in uncanny anticipation of the work of Melanie Klein. Such fantasies were available to both women and men *as fantasies*, and are articulated repeatedly in the writings, films, and photographs of the tank. The crucial difference between subjects in an industrial war is located less in sexual difference than in the distinction between combatants and civilians; or, more precisely, between those inside and those outside the sublime object of the tank.

The view from outside could be completely terrifying. Tanks were not easy to manoeuvre and were sometimes obliged to run over wounded soldiers, including men on their own side. For Remarque in *All Quiet on the Western Front*, the tank increases the men's sense of vulnerability in the face of an inexorable machine:

> From a mockery the tanks have become a terrible weapon. Armoured they come rolling on in long lines, more than anything else embody for us the horror of war.
>
> We do not see the guns that bombard us; the attacking lines of the enemy infantry are men like ourselves; but these tanks are machines, their caterpillars run on as endless as the war, they are annihilation, they roll without feeling into the craters, and climb up again without stopping, a fleet of roaring, smoke-belching armour-clads, invulnerable steel beasts squashing the dead and the wounded – we shrivel up in our thin skin before them, against their colossal weight our arms are sticks of straw, and our hand-grenades matches.[77]

Metaphors of the tank turn up in a broad range of writings, from popular fiction such as 'The Pink-Tailed Tank' (1917) and Escott

---

77  Erich Maria Remarque, *All Quiet on the Western Front* (1929; London, Picador, n.d. [1990]), 184. The Germans did not develop their own tanks until 1918. Unlike later German tanks, those of the Great War were not very successful and few were produced.

Lynn's *Tommy of the Tanks* (1919) to Aleister Crowley's *Moonchild* (1929), in which the pedantic Edwin Arthwait adopts the 'literary method' of the tank: 'It was not agile, it was not versatile, it was exposed to artillery attack: but it proceeded.'[78] Virginia Woolf likens pioneering women such as Ethel Smyth to 'the ice breakers, the gun runners, the window smashers' and to the 'armoured tanks, who climbed the rough ground, drew the enemies [*sic*] fire, and left behind her a pathway – not yet a smooth and metalled road – but still a pathway for those who come after her'.[79] Like the tank, Smyth is imagined as anarchic and destructive at the same time as she protects and helps those who follow in her wake.

Those inside the tank often wrote about their experiences. Tank histories and memoirs appeared throughout the 1920s and 1930s and were frequently reviewed alongside other literary and historical works in the *TLS* and elsewhere; here, too, military technology was part of civilian culture.[80] Tank memoirs, especially, offer gripping accounts of how the early tank was imagined long after its technology had been superseded.

All the weapons of the Great War were to some extent spectacles, but none more so than the tank. Unlike machine guns or artillery, the tank actually killed very few people. Its early engagements hinged largely on the question of theatre: how could it best exploit how it looked? The drivers' memoirs are fascinated by the implacable body of the tank and the differences it produces between inside and outside. Both positions are extremely dangerous and each provides a new fantasy relationship between the soldier's body and the sources of danger. Most of the crew are devoted to the machine and determined to make it work; at the same time it inspires a profound terror and rage when it fails to protect them.

78  Crowley, *Moonchild* (1929; London, Sphere, 1972), 151.
79  Woolf, 'Speech Before the London National Society for Women's Service', 21 January 1931, The Pargiters, ed. Mitchell Leaska (London, Hogarth, 1978), xxvii. For a discussion of Woolf and Smyth, see Tracy Hargreaves, 'The Grotesque and the Great War in *To the Lighthouse*', in Raitt and Tate, eds, *Women's Fiction and the Great War*.
80  Early tank histories include D. G. Browne, *The Tank in Action* (1920); J. F. C. Fuller, *Tanks in the Great War, 1914–1918* (1920); John F. Lucy, *There's a Devil in the Drum* (1938); G. Martel, *In the Wake of the Tank* (1931); Murray Sueter, *The Evolution of the Tank* (1937); Albert Stern, *Tanks 1914–1918* (1919); E. D. Swinton, *Eyewitness* (1932). Journals included *Journal of the Royal Artillery*, *Tank Corps Journal* (later *Royal Tank Corps Journal*) and *I Was There!*

Both Jenkin and Mitchell provide detailed descriptions of conditions inside the tank. With the crew crowded around the large engine and heat rising above 100 degrees, the interior of the tank was, as Jenkin remarks, 'a veritable hell' for the men inside:

> machine-gun bullets beat like hail upon the outside, from which hot splinters pricked the gunners' faces, whilst shells could be heard bursting in close proximity. Inside, above the noise of the engine, was heard the sharp cracking of our own machine guns, mingled with the groaning and whining of the gunner who lay stretched along the blood and oil-saturated floor; this, with the vomiting of our second driver, intense heat, exhaust petrol fumes, and nauseous vapour from the guns made an inferno that no outside observer would have thought possible to exist within those steel plates.[81]

The crew are also terrified that the tank will catch fire. Yet the tank is also a place that – in theory, at least – will protect them from danger. Men are placed inside Mother; at the same time they *are* Mother – much is made of the fact that the crew of eight works as a single, disciplined body. All but one of them function as limbs, working the machine and the guns; the eighth is the brains of the outfit and does the navigating. The early tank in action is a completely self-contained unit, cut off from the outside world; a single, complex body within its own carapace.[82]

Sitting inside Mother, the crew could see almost nothing outside. Paul Virilio argues that the technology of cinema began to replace the act of looking in the Great War.[83] In the tank, looking was replaced by aerial photographs, and the commander navigated at one remove. No one inside the tank could actually see where they were going.[84] To protect their faces from sparks and debris, the crew often wore steel or chain-mail masks which reduced visibility even further.[85] Almost blind, navigating with aerial pho-

---

81  Jenkin, *A Tank Driver's Experiences*, 179.
82  Mitchell, *Tank Warfare*, 122.
83  Virilio, *War and Cinema*.
84  Various experiments were tried with slits and loopholes for viewing, but they allowed bullets into the tank under heavy fire, and often had to be blocked off completely.
85  Jenkin describes the 'splinter mask' as 'a steel mask padded in leather, the eyes protected by small flat steel bars one-sixteenth of an inch apart, and a steel chain about six inches by three hangs over the mouth and chin, very similar to the face armour worn by knights in the Middle Ages'. *A Tank Driver's Experiences*, 178.

tographs which could be out of date within hours, the tank crew were, according to Mitchell, 'like an ostrich with its head in the sand' (153) – a position which he says gave them plenty of courage. Yet Mitchell and Jenkin also acknowledge some of the horrible injuries sustained in tank warfare. When Jenkin's tank is hit with a high explosive shell, the steel plate of the tank is severed 'as though it were matchwood' (180). He loses the use of his arm, drags himself out of the tank, and finds himself lying 'exhausted and alone', in terrible pain and suffering from 'the indescribable feelings produced by [engine] fumes upon an empty stomach' (182). Later, in hospital, his arm is amputated without his knowledge (188). Jenkin provides very little description of physical suffering, yet his memoir is disturbing precisely because of its ambivalence. He loves the tank, but it has failed to save him from mutilation.[86]

The tank also produces a new relationship to the notion of work. Tank drivers were required to have a high degree of technical knowledge and training, as Jenkin comments: 'There is scarcely any branch of the Army that demands more brain work from the private than does a complete set of courses in the Tank Corps'. Tank crews learned map-reading, morse code, semaphore and other military skills as well as knowledge about 'how trenches, dug-outs, and machine-gun posts are constructed [... in order] to avoid those parts that would probably get the tank stuck' (48–9, 51). Jenkin and Mitchell each describe the labour involved in driving and maintaining the tank. According to Jenkin, it was the drivers' responsibility at the front to keep the tank in running order at all times, as it had to be ready for use at short notice. This required an enormous amount of continuing repair, even when the tanks were not engaged in battle.[87] Furthermore, it took days of intensive labour transporting the tank from Britain to France, digging it out of ditches, getting it across railway lines, repairing the engine, and so forth. Much of this work was instantly rendered futile when tanks became bogged beyond salvage or wrecked by shell fire. Many tanks never reached a battle, but had to be abandoned; in some areas the landscape was littered with these enormous pieces of

86  Jenkin's modest book irritated the *TLS* reviewer, who called it 'morose' and 'egotistical' and accused Jenkin of 'bitterness': 11 May 1922, 310.
87  Jenkin, *A Tank Driver's Experiences*, 116.

expensive rubbish.[88] After one failed battle, Mitchell recalls the sight of 'eight huge carcasses [...], some battered beyond recognition, others lifting their snouts pathetically beyond the slimy waters'. Derelict tanks blocked the road and had to be blown up – a dangerous undertaking which took about a week.[89] The world's first industrial war generated large-scale industrial waste – a sight which was kept well hidden from the civilians buying their millions of pounds' worth of war bonds at precisely the same time.[90]

The autobiography of the psychoanalyst Wilfred Bion is preoccupied with the strange relationship between inside and outside produced by the tank. Unlike most other tank writers, Bion doesn't like the tank much. He hates being inside 'the cursed thing' – and is frightened of being outside it, as well.[91] (Early tank commanders often walked in front of their tanks into battle; as a new branch of the army, the Tank Corps was trying to establish its reputation for courage and honour, and the crews took considerable risks to achieve this.) When a civilian woman asks what it feels like when his tank runs over people, Bion doesn't know, but he does recall being 'possessed' by the fear that he would fall wounded and be run over by his own tank (130, 266). He also fears, with good reason, that the tanks will get bogged in a swamp 'where the enemy gunners would have them helpless, concentrated like dinosaurs in a prehistoric catastrophe' (240).

Bion represents himself as an incompetent soldier and a hopeless tank commander. All his memories of battle are nightmarish: the men don't know where they are going; the orders don't make sense; men are killed, pointlessly. By the time he comes to his third tank engagement, Bion is simultaneously terrified and cynical about the plans for battle. The crew is exhausted, Bion is confused, the

88  In a letter of 31 August 1917, Ivor Gurney remarks on the 'ruined tanks' in a landscape 'like the last Hell of desolation'. *Collected Letters*, ed. R. K. R. Thornton (Manchester, Carcanet, 1991), 318–19.

89  Mitchell, *Tank Warfare*, 125; Mitchell also details the work involved in salvaging 190 derelict tanks after 3rd Ypres; ch. 10.

90  The problem of waste continued long after the war had ended. Some tanks were turned into war memorials; many others were broken up for scrap metal – a process which was not completed until 1932. Forty and Forty, *Bovington Tanks*, 36.

91  Bion, *The Long Week-End 1897–1919: Part of a Life* (1982; London, Free Association Books, 1986), 245.

**Plate 3**
A Mark IV female tank destroyed by a direct hit before being dealt with by Tank Salvage Company. Reproduced courtesy of the Trustees of the Imperial War Museum, London. Crown copyright.

orders are insane. 'They were not orders', he writes, 'they were sentences of death.' (253) Instead of starting at dawn, the tanks are ordered to attack at 10.30 in the morning. Here Bion provides an unusual description of a tank commander's view from the outside of his tank:

> The tanks were hidden, each under a small clump of trees very conveniently placed, separated by an average interval of fifty yards from each other. At 10.25 they emerged and drove to cross the front line of the division at 10.30. There was no gunfire, no machine-gun fire. As the tanks crossed the line the enemy machine guns opened up. I walked behind Greene's tank hoping, by being as close as possible, to escape the machine-gun fire.
>
> [...] Hauser, who had gone into action sitting on the back of one of the two tanks under his immediate command, had also run back to see what had happened. It was uncanny; nothing had happened – that's what had happened. But he was unmistakably terrified; we both were

– and both perfectly safe in the trench. The troops might have been sleep-walking.

We looked at the tanks; they had nothing wrong with them. They were quietly purring their way forward and were already too far away to catch up with them even if we wanted to do so. As there was no method of communication, wireless or otherwise, we could only stand and watch, the Colonel almost demented, Hauser and I ghost-ridden.

The tanks rolled up a gentle grassy slope. There was a soft muffled explosion. Robertson's tank opened as a flower in a nature film might unfold. Another thud; then two, almost simultaneous, followed. The whole four had flowered. Hard, bright flames, as if cut out of tinfoil, flickered and died, extinguished by the bright sun. One tank, crewless, went on to claw at the back of one in front as if preparatory to love-making; then stopped as if exhausted. (254)

'We stared, fascinated,' says Bion. Later he hears that the Staff have ordered the tanks to carry high explosives, so they can be blown up if they are captured by the Germans, which makes them rather vulnerable if they get hit. The extraordinary vision of the tanks opening 'like blossoms greeting the sun' (257), with his crew inside, disturbs Bion terribly, but it also teaches him something useful. In the next battle, he is inspired to tell the crew to jump out; he will drive the tank alone, steering a zig-zag course. His men leave, then Bion remembers that it takes the entire crew to manoeuvre the tank; all he can do is drive it in a straight line, under the gaze of lots of observation balloons. He opens the throttle, and leaps out. The empty tank races forwards; nothing fires on it; Bion realises he has just made a gift to the enemy of 'a fully equipped tank in complete working order'. He runs after it, presumably in the hope of getting it back again. Then, he says, 'mercifully a shell hit, pierced and burst. The tank stopped, flames spurting everywhere. In a moment it was a total wreck' (262). Bion knows that he (and the crew) should have stayed in the tank, even though they would certainly have been killed. Yet in a way honour is satisfied; the tank went into battle on a useless mission; it was hit, as it must have been. And the crew is alive, rather than pointlessly dead. Here, as elsewhere in this book, tank activity is partly an elaborate masquerade, a simulacrum of warfare, preferably enacted at a safe distance.

One fantasy generated by the tank was that future wars would be fought entirely by machines, who would do the dying for us.

Writing in 1929, John Brophy imagined that 'if another war should be jockeyed or forced upon the world, it will be a scientific, chemical affair; machines will be met by machines, not with the nerves and muscles and wills of mere men'.[92] The tank seems to promise new kinds of agency – enabling the human body to enter zones which were previously impenetrable – at the same time as it negates agency and displaces the human subject from the narratives of war. This human subject, like evolution, is imagined as moving simultaneously forwards into the machine age and backwards into the primeval slime – a movement both frightening and enjoyable. Bion's memoir, written in the 1970s, is written against this fantasy through the knowledge of what war actually did become; he reads the Great War backwards through the human suffering of Vietnam, Korea, the Cold War, Hiroshima, fascism, and other disasters of the twentieth century which emerged from the technical, political, and imaginative developments of 1914–18.

For both soldiers and civilians, contradictory discourses of pleasure, fear, and duty; infantilism, community, and adulthood surrounded the tank. The campaigns around the tank banks, especially, were used to persuade and coerce the British people into renewing their support for the war during its most unpopular period. This in turn raises questions about agency and citizenship during the last few months of the war – a period in which the franchise was extended from eight million to twenty-one million voters.[93] Historians often note that the postwar revolutionary movements were much weaker in Britain than elsewhere in Europe, perhaps because of the extension of the franchise. It is also possible that the particular ways in which civilians were persuaded to consent to the war – including the use of official carnivals around the weapons of war – may have been a factor in postwar politics. Such a claim can only be speculative; we cannot know what would have happened without the propaganda, censorship, tank banks, and so forth. But the success of the pro-war campaigns is highly suggestive; particularly significant is their ability to produce a fantasmatic, infantile, *and pleasurable* relationship

92  Brophy, introduction to *The Soldier's War*, x.
93  Nearly two-thirds of the new voters (8.4 million) were women. Martin Pugh, 'Domestic Politics', in Constantine *et al.*, eds, *The First World War in British History*, 22–3.

to the war and its objects. The tank provided both fictions and fantasies as well as a physical presence and 'commanding personality' around which people gathered, voluntarily, and about which they dreamed.[94] In short, it played a vital role in the manufacture of consent.[95]

94  *Southern Daily Echo*, 31 December 1917, [3].
95  The term comes from Walter Lippmann, *Public Opinion* (New York, Harcourt, Brace and Co., 1922), 248. See also Lippmann, *The Political Scene: An Essay on the Victory of 1918* (London, George Allen and Unwin, 1919).

# 6

# *Mrs Dalloway*
# and the Armenian Question

ON THE DAY of Mrs Dalloway's party, Richard Dalloway MP buys some roses for his wife Clarissa.[1] When he arrives home, he finds Clarissa worrying over whether she should invite a dull cousin to her party. Richard settles her anxieties and puts her down on the sofa, like a child, for an afternoon rest, before returning to his work at the House of Commons. '"Some Committee?" she asked as he opened the door.' '"Armenians", he said; or perhaps it was "Albanians".' What did he say? Clarissa is not sure, but she enjoys looking at the roses.

> And people would say, 'Clarissa Dalloway is spoilt'. She cared much more for her roses than for the Armenians. Hunted out of existence, maimed, frozen, the victims of cruelty and injustice (she had heard Richard say so over and over again) – no, she could feel nothing for the Albanians, or was it the Armenians? but she loved her roses (didn't that help the Armenians?) – the only flowers she could bear to see cut. (157)

This is a startling paragraph to find in a book published in 1925. As I will argue shortly, Clarissa's confusion over Armenia and Albania is an obvious, even heavy-handed, satiric moment in the novel, though the events to which Woolf refers have since become invisible to most British readers. In this chapter, I want to read *Mrs Dalloway*, one of Woolf's most 'aesthetic' novels, as in part a satire on the political climate in Britain shortly after the First World War. But it is satire of a very peculiar kind, and it raises uncomfortable questions about how British civilians were placed in relation to the events of the war and to the settlements which followed.

For many people, the trauma did not end with the war. The peace treaties reshaped the map of Europe, dismantling the Austro-Hungarian and Ottoman empires and creating a number of new

---

1  Virginia Woolf, *Mrs Dalloway* (1925; Oxford University Press, 1992), 150.

nations, including Poland, Hungary, Yugoslavia, Czechoslovakia, Austria.[2] While many people welcomed the independent nation-states, there was also a great deal of dissatisfaction with the new boundaries, drawn up in considerable haste and with much bickering among the victorious nations. Millions of people were displaced or rendered stateless by the treaties; this caused serious hardship and many people were forced to emigrate. To make matters worse, for some months after the armistice of November 1918, Britain helped to maintain a blockade against central Europe, creating poverty and even starvation among civilians.[3] When Harold Nicolson visited Austria in April 1919, he was shocked by what he saw. 'Everyone looks very pinched and yellow: no fats for four years. The other side of the blockade [...] I feel that my plump pink face is an insult to these wretched people.'[4] Even relatively prosperous families such as the Freuds were short of food and warmth after the war; poor people were much worse off.[5]

Nor did the end of the war mean that war had ended. As Nicolson commented, 'The fact is that our Government for electoral reasons allowed the country to imagine that the Armistice meant peace. This it most assuredly was not.'[6] Wars continued after the war, in Poland, Albania, Greece, Turkey, and elsewhere, and the peace settlements raised new sets of problems which contributed to the rise of fascism and another war in 1939. The architects of the peace settlements 'failed in the most spectacular manner'; these effects continue to be felt in central and eastern Europe right up to the present

2 The Treaty of Versailles (June 1919) officially ended the war between Germany and the allies, decided Germany's new borders, and declared Germany responsible for the war. Separate treaties were signed with Austria (September 1919), Bulgaria (November 1919), Hungary (1920), Turkey (1920 and 1923). Andrew Thorpe, *Britain in the Era of Two World Wars* (London, Longman, 1994), 129–32; Eric Hobsbawm, *Age of Extremes* (1994; London, Abacus, 1995), 31–4.

3 Hobsbawm estimates that four to five million people were made refugees between 1914 and 1922. *Age of Extremes*, 51.

4 Harold Nicolson, *Peacemaking 1919* (1933; New York, Universal Library, 1985), 293–4.

5 Peter Gay, *Freud: A Life for Our Time* (1988; London, Papermac, 1989), 379–81.

6 Harold Nicolson, *Peacemaking 1919*, 290. This quotation comes from Nicolson's diary of the Paris peace conference, January to June 1919, published as Book II of the volume.

day.[7] The war had set Europe on the road to ruin, and the Versailles Treaty threatened to complete the process, as John Maynard Keynes warned in *The Economic Consequences of the Peace* (1919). The war had ruined the economies of Europe, leaving countries which had previously been self-sufficient now dependent on the United States for their basic food requirements; the Versailles Treaty made the situation worse.

Keynes had attended the peace negotiations in Paris in the first few months of 1919, and he was concerned that the victorious powers (especially Britain and France) had selfishly pursued their own immediate interests at the expense of the long-term needs of Europe as a whole. The treaty 'must impair yet further, when it might have restored' the 'delicate, complicated organisation' of Europe.[8] The Paris talks were a 'nightmare', writes Keynes, 'and everyone there was morbid' (2). In Britain, however, people seemed oblivious to the dangers posed by the peace settlement; they simply 'received the treaty without reading it' (4). Economically, at least, they appeared strangely untroubled by the experience of the war.

> In England the outward aspect of life does not yet teach us to feel or realise in the least that an age is over. We are busy picking up the threads of our life where we dropped them, with this difference only, that many of us seem a good deal richer than we were before. Where we spent millions before the war, we have now learnt that we can spend hundreds of millions and apparently not suffer for it. Evidently we did not exploit to the utmost the possibilities of our economic life. We look, therefore, not only to a return to the comforts of 1914, but to an immense broadening and intensification of them. All classes alike thus build their plans, the rich to spend more and save less, the poor to spend more and work less. (1–2)

Such an illusion was possible only in Britain and the United States.[9] In the rest of Europe, 'the earth heaves and no one is but aware of the rumblings'. It was a matter of 'life and death, of starvation and existence, and of the fearful convulsions of a dying civilisation' (2).

7  Hobsbawm, *Age of Extremes*, 31–2.
8  Keynes, *The Economic Consequences of the Peace* (1919; London, Macmillan, 1984), 1.
9  Britain's economic complacency was an illusion, of course, as Hobsbawm comments: 'Britain was never the same again after 1918 because the country had ruined its economy by waging a war substantially beyond its resources'. Hobsbawm, *Age of Extremes*, 30.

Britain imagined itself detached from this calamity: 'England still stands outside Europe. Europe's voiceless tremors do not reach her. Europe is apart and England is not of her flesh and body' (2). But this too was an illusion. Britain's future was dependent on the future of Europe (not least because Germany had been one of its major customers). Keynes himself felt he had to shed his 'British preoccupations' and become 'a European in his cares and outlook' (2).

The disillusion of the war is a familiar trope in literary criticism, but the disillusion of the peace should not be underestimated. And the concerns which emerged were international as well as local. For E. H. Carr, the war produced a completely new field of knowledge – the 'science' of international politics. 'The war of 1914–18 made an end of the view that war is a matter which which affects only professional soldiers and, in so doing, dissipated the corresponding impression that international politics could safely be left in the hands of professional diplomats.' International politics became democratised; a topic of popular interest.[10] For Leonard Woolf, writing in 1922, international politics were central to Britain's future prosperity.

> There can be no economic recovery in this country, no beginning to build up an educated and prosperous community, unless there is a complete break with the dangerous and extravagant foreign policy which has been pursued equally by Conservative and Liberal Governments. This country must stand out in Europe and the world as a sincere supporter of a policy of peace and international co-operation. The pivot of its programme must therefore be (1) a real League of Nations, inclusive of all nations, the members of which undertake a definite obligation not to go to war; (2) disarmament, beginning with a drastic limitation of naval and military armaments, coupled with a general guarantee against aggression; (3) an equitable settlement of the reparation problem.[11]

Leonard Woolf believed that political action immediately after the war was even more important than it had been during the conflict,

10  For Carr, anyone who 'reads the political columns of a newspaper or attends a political meeting or discusses politics with his neighbour is to that extent a student of politics'. *The Twenty Years' Crisis 1919–1939* (1939; London, Papermac, 1995), 3–5.
11  Leonard Woolf, election speech given in October 1922, quoted in his autobiography, *Downhill All the Way* (London, Hogarth, 1967), 38.

and he often despaired that the bad decisions which had taken Britain into the war were being made again after it had ended. He saw the 1920s as 'a time of continual crisis';[12] a period also dominated by a particularly unimaginative form of conservatism in parliamentary politics. Trevor Wilson argues that Britain in the 1920s and 1930s was 'massively dominated by the political forces that had come to power during the First World War' – conservatives who were hostile to the liberal tradition which had prevailed before the war.[13] This is the context in which Virginia Woolf wrote *Mrs Dalloway*.[14]

## Postwar satire

*Mrs Dalloway* raises some difficult questions about the ways in which women and men were placed in relation to political power. Who was to blame for the disaster of the war, and who would take responsibility for the peace? Woolf does not simply criticise men and exonerate women, as some critics have suggested;[15] rather, her

---

12  Woolf, *Downhill All the Way*, 40, 94.
13  Trevor Wilson, *The Myriad Faces of War* (Oxford, Plity, 1986), 757–8; Arthur Marwick, *The Deluge: British Society and the First World War*, 2nd edn (Basingstoke, Macmillan, 1991), 350–1.
14  Britain's peculiar relationship with other parts of Europe is registered across a range of writing of the period – in Lawrence's *Women in Love* (1920) and 'The Captain's Doll' (1923), Eliot's *The Waste Land* (1922), Ford's *Parade's End* (1924–8) and *No Enemy* (1929), Wyndham Lewis' *Tarr* (1918; 1928), Jean Rhys' *Good Morning, Midnight* (1939) and Stevie Smith's *Over the Frontier* (1938).
15  For example, Masami Usui argues that 'The bond between Septimus and Clarissa should be understood as a common sense of victimization by the war and by patriarchal values'. 'The Female Victims of the War in *Mrs Dalloway*', in Mark Hussey, ed., *Virginia Woolf and War: Fiction, Reality and Myth* (Syracuse University Press, 1991), 151. It is difficult to make a plausible case for Clarissa as a 'victim' of the war. For Elizabeth Abel, 'Woolf represents the world war as a vast historical counterpart to male intervention in women's lives'. To see the war as simply a metaphor for gender relations in Woolf's work is rather a reductive view of the history she addresses. *Virginia Woolf and Fictions of Psychoanalysis* (University of Chicago Press, 1989), 41. For Toni McNaron, Clarissa's confusion over the Armenians is a symptom of 'her larger fuzziness and disintegration', caused by the loss of her lesbian identity. This argument seems to confuse a number of different issues, and effaces the novel's politics. McNaron, '"The Albanians, or was it the Armenians?": Virginia Woolf's Lesbianism as Gloss on her Modernism', in Vara Neverow-Turk and Mark Hussey, eds, *Virginia Woolf: Themes and Variations* (New York, Pace University Press, 1993), 134–41.

writing directs both satire and sympathy in complex and unexpected ways. Like Ford and HD, Woolf does not formulate a convenient or facile parallel between gender and power when she writes about the complicated experiences of the war, its settlements, and its continuing effects throughout the 1920s.

In the middle of June 1923, Woolf wrote in her diary that she aimed 'to criticise the social system, & show it at work, at its most intense'.[16] *Mrs Dalloway* is set at precisely this period – the middle of June 1923 – a time of profound and troubling change in both domestic and international politics. The novel takes place on a single day, nearly five years after the end of the war.[17] But for many people, the war will never be over.

> For it was the middle of June. The War was over, except for some one like Mrs Foxcroft at the Embassy last night eating her heart out because that nice boy was killed and now the old Manor House must go to a cousin; or Lady Bexborough who opened a bazaar, they said, with the telegram in her hand, John, her favourite, killed. (5)

Women mourn the dead, here represented as young and wealthy – men with titled parents; men who expect to inherit a manor house. The loss is both economic and emotional, with the economic mentioned first.[18] The 'favourite' son being killed is of course a cliché of much war fiction (used in Rosamund Lehmann's *Dusty Answer* (1927), for example), as is the reference to the mother's heroic effort to carry on regardless. However, it is Clarissa who sees Lady Bexborough in these terms, and wants to be like her (12). This is the first of many satiric jabs at her view of the war. Clarissa herself is not in mourning. For her, 'it was over; thank Heaven – over. It was June. The King and Queen were at the Palace' (5). Everything seems to have been returned to its proper place. Mrs Dalloway, married to

16 Woolf, *The Diary of Virginia Woolf*, vol. 2, 1920–1924, ed. Anne Olivier Bell (1978, Harmondsworth, Pengin, 1981), 19 June 1923, 248. This point is explored in Alex Zwerdling's *Virginia Woolf and the Real World* (Berkeley, University of California Press, 1986).

17 Virginia Woolf, *Mrs Dalloway*, 93. On the novel occupying a single day, see Harvena Richter, 'The *Ulysses* Connection: Clarissa Dalloway's Bloomsday', *Studies in the Novel*, 21, 3 (1989).

18 J. M. Winter notes that many wealthy people became poorer in real terms after the war, while the living standards of many working-class people improved. *The Great War and the British People* (Basingstoke, Macmillan, 1986), 281, 279.

a Conservative Member of Parliament, is to give a party that evening for the members and supporters of her class – the politicians, courtiers, professors, Academy artists, physicians, and business people who dominate the political, cultural, and economic life of the nation.

*Mrs Dalloway* takes a hard look at those who managed the social and economic aspects of the war and treated the survivors so badly afterwards.[19] Power might be concentrated in the hands of men such as Richard Dalloway, but it is held in place by women such as Clarissa and Lady Bruton. Without the domestic and social base provided by women, the political system could not function in the same way. The ruling-class women in the novel are profoundly ignorant. Clarissa, with 'the few twigs of knowledge Fräulein Daniels gave them', knows almost nothing outside her own life: 'no language, no history; she scarcely read a book now' (10); 'ask her what the Equator was, and she did not know' (160). She is complacently indifferent to the differences between Armenia, Albania, and Turkey – nations which faced quite distinct sets of problems after the First World War, and which were the subject of a good deal of attention in the British press. Richard Dalloway is sitting on a parliamentary committee on the Armenian Question (156–7).

Clarissa knows nothing about Richard's work on the Armenians, and regards this as a sign of the strength of their marriage; she congratulates herself that she and Richard have kept their identities as separate persons: 'there is a dignity in people; a solitude; even between husband and wife a gulf; and that one must respect, thought Clarissa' (156). But more is at stake here than the status of their marriage. Clarissa has no interest in Armenian suffering as a political or ethical issue in its own right, and the text satirises her mercilessly: 'no, she could feel nothing for the Albanians, or was it the Armenians? but she loved her roses (didn't that help the Armenians?)' (157). In the same passage, she enjoys being infantilised, 'spoilt', settled on the sofa for an afternoon nap. Yet even as she sinks into this childish posture, she reassures herself that the structure of their marriage secures 'one's independence, one's self-

<hr>

19 Alex Zwerdling argues that Woolf represents the governing class as 'engaged in a conspiracy' to deny the effects of the war: 'Woolf gives us a picture of a class impervious to change in a society that desperately needs or demands it'. Zwerdling, *Virginia Woolf and the Real World*, 122, 124.

respect – something, after all, priceless' (156) – because she does not remember the details of Richard's committee work.[20]

The Armenian people were victims of the peace as well as the war. Clarissa's refusal to engage with their suffering is masked by proto-feminist statements about marriage. Two separate arguments are elided. It is one thing to refuse to live vicariously through Richard, and quite another to ignore a political problem simply because he happens to be working on it. Clarissa's comments have proved attractive to some later readers, but we need to be cautious about accepting them at face value, for they are cynically employed as an excuse for refusing adult responsibility. Here Woolf's satire is rather obvious, as Clarissa tries to hide her conservatism and complacency behind a screen of progressive rhetoric.

The idea that Clarissa's love for roses might help the Armenians is so preposterous that it draws attention to itself. People within and across societies are complexly linked, as the novel constantly demonstrates, but one person's good fortune does not necessarily help another. Indeed, in some cases what benefits one may harm others. This is made clear in the novel when characters have conflicting or irreconcilable aims. The struggle between Clarissa and Miss Kilman over Elizabeth's affection, for example, can never be resolved so that both are satisfied or victorious. Towards the end of the novel Clarissa recognises this, and relishes her discovery of the power struggle: 'It was enemies one wanted, not friends' (229).

20 Albania, too, faced serious problems during this period, from the Balkan wars immediately preceding the First World War to struggles over its nationhood and borders during and after the war. Miranda Vickers points out that by 1921 'Albania was devasted and bankrupt, having been continuously at war since 1910'. Britain took a close interest in Albania after oil was found there; according to Vickers, the Anglo-Persian Oil Company provided a large sum of money to support Ahmed Zogu, who became prime minister in 1922, then president of the Albanian republic in 1925. In 1928 Albania turned into a monarchy and Zogu became Zog I, King of the Albanians.

There are many brief references to Albania in the British newspapers in the early 1920s, but there was much less sympathy and interest in the Albanians' claims in the Balkans than for the Armenians' problems in the Transcaucasus. Vickers, *The Albanians: A Modern History* (London, I. B. Tauris, 1995).

Clarissa's confusion over Armenians and Albanians – people who lived in different regions, were caught up in different sets of political questions, and were represented quite differently in the British press – would have been remarkably ignorant for someone in her position in the 1920s.

## The Armenian Question

What was Britain's interest in Armenia in 1923? For many readers, the matter is almost completely forgotten now, but it was important at the time and widely discussed in newspapers and political journals. It raised vital issues about human rights and Britain's quasi-imperial responsibilities, and we need to recall the facts of the case if we are to grasp Woolf's satire. Woolf herself was certainly conscious of the Armenians' situation. Indeed, no one who read the British newspapers could have been unaware of the issue. Apart from dozens of reports in the newspapers between 1915 and 1923, the Armenian Question was a topic of debate in the early 1920s in the *Nation and Athenaeum*, a journal for which Woolf wrote, and for which Leonard Woolf was literary editor from 1923 to 1929.[21] Lyndall Gordon notes that the Armenian massacres, like the Dreyfus affair, were fundamental issues in the shaping of Leonard Woolf's political conscience; this was by no means an uncommon response.[22] The historian Arnold Toynbee was an active supporter of the Armenian cause, and published a number of books and articles on the matter. The Toynbees were friends of the Woolfs, and are mentioned several times in Virginia Woolf's diary in the early 1920s.[23] During the same period, the Woolfs were in contact with an Armenian friend, Ernest Altounyan, for whom they were literary executors.[24]

Armenia is located between the Black Sea and the Caspian Sea, south of the Caucasian mountains, at the 'crossroads' of eastern and western empires.[25] The Armenian people, Christians in a largely

21  Virginia Woolf, *Diary*, vol. 2, 23 March 1923, 240; *Diary*, vol. 3, 24 March 1926, 69 and note 14.
22  Lyndall Gordon, *Virginia Woolf: A Writer's Life* (Oxford University Press, 1984), 139. Leonard Woolf also remembers that a teacher in his early schooling was 'obsessed with the horrors and the barbarism of the Armenian massacres'. Quoted in Virginia Woolf, *Diary*, vol. 3, 274 note 9. Woolf rather trivialises the Armenian issue in her diary entry for 26 December 1929.
23  Toynbee was also a member of the British Armenia Committee, and involved in the Political Intelligence Department of the British Foreign Office. Akaby Nassibian, *Britain and the Armenian Question 1915–1923* (London, Croom Helm, 1984), 48, 49, 111. See also Virginia Woolf, *Diary*, vol. 2, 78, 151, 172; entries for 5 December 1920, 18 December 1921, 24 March 1922.
24  Woolf, *Diary*, vol. 1 (22 May 1919), 276; *Diary*, vol. 2 (3 November 1923), 274.
25  For this section, I have drawn on Nassibian, *Britain and the Armenian Question*.

Muslim area, had been colonised and expelled by various imperial powers since the eleventh century; by 1914, the original area of Armenia lay partly in Russia and partly in Turkey. The events are disputed to this day, but it seems that, during the late nineteenth and early twentieth centuries, the Ottoman authorities made several attempts to clear the area of Armenians, killing and displacing hundreds of thousands of people. In 1878, the Treaty of San Stefano was agreed between Turkey and Russia. Under this treaty, the Armenian lands and population came into the Russian sphere of influence where, historians seem to agree, they would have been safer.

Britain perceived this arrangement as a threat to its interests in the region, and forced a revision of the treaty to keep the Armenian lands within the Ottoman empire. In return, Britain pledged to enforce political reform in Turkey, and to prevent further oppression of minorities. The pledges were not serious, however, and the evidence suggests that the oppression continued and became more intense. In the 1890s large numbers of Armenians were displaced and killed. Worse massacres occurred during the First World War, in 1915. Some historians consider it the twentieth century's first act of genocide, and suggest that it provided a useful model for the Nazis in Germany: proof that an entire civilian population could be killed off without reprisal. Britain was partly responsible for this outcome, as Lloyd George later commented:

> Had it not been for our sinister intervention, the great majority of the Armenians would have been placed, by the Treaty of San Stefano in 1878, under the protection of the Russian flag. [...] The action of the British Government led inevitably to the terrible massacres of 1895–7, 1909 and worst of all to the holocausts of 1915.[26]

Many of those displaced died of hunger and exposure. The massacres during the war were widely reported. On 16 September 1915, *The Times* noted that 'It is believed that it is the official intention that this shall be a campaign of extermination, involving the

---

26 David Lloyd George, *The Truth About the Peace Treaties* (London, Victor Gollancz Ltd, 1938), vol. 2, 1257.

murdering of from 800,000 to 1,000,000 persons'.[27] Often its reports were strongly worded. Historians argue that the massacres were real, but they were also used as propaganda to discredit Turkey – first, during the war, and later during the carve-up of the Ottoman empire. Britain's criticisms of Turkey during this period also need to be read against the long history of the 'Eastern Question' and of European attempts to appropriate portions of the ailing Ottoman empire.

At the end of September 1915, *The Times* described the 'nauseating and appalling character' of atrocities against Armenians. From many Armenian regions came tales of

> men shot down in cold blood, crucified, mutilated, or dragged off for labour battalions, of children carried off and forcibly converted to Islam, of women violated and enslaved in the interior, shot down, or sent off with their children to the desert west of Mosul, where there is neither water nor food [...]. Many of these unfortunates did not reach their destination, because the escort so overdrove their victims that many fell out, and, as flogging and kicking were unavailing, they were left to perish by the roadside, their corpses distinctly defining the route followed. Many were tied back to back in pairs and thrown into rivers alive.[28]

It is difficult to imagine someone in political circles being vague about these matters, especially when they were so widely reported, but the ignorance of ruling-class women is one of Woolf's targets in the novel. Sally Seton, too, 'scarcely ever read the papers' (245).

---

27 'Constantinople in War Time: Conflicting Stories', *The Times*, 16 September 1915, 7, under the subheading 'Exterminating Armenians'. Alan Sharp argues that over a million Armenians were massacred in 1915–16. Evidence of this was used to forge an anti-Turkish consensus in British politics; *The Versailles Settlement* (Basingstoke, Macmillan, 1991), 167. *The Times* was actively engaged in creating public hostility towards the Turks during and after the war, and its reports were not necessarily reliable. Nassibian argues that Britain's publicising of Turkish atrocities was motivated less by concern for human rights than by a desire to discredit its enemies. *Britain and the Armenian Question*, 119. Recent Turkish historians emphasise Britain's use of the Armenian Question for propagandistic purposes. See for example Sinasi Orel and Sureyya Yuca, *The Talat Pasha 'Telegrams'* (Nicosia, K. Rustem and Bro., 1986); Kamuran Gürün, *The Armenian File* (1983; London, Nicosia and Istanbul, K. Ruskin and Bro. and Weidenfeld and Nicolson Ltd, 1985).

28 'Wholesale Murder in Armenia: Exterminating a Race', *The Times*, 30 September 1915, 5. *The Times* claims here that the Turkish leader, Talaat Bey, said of the deportations, 'After this for 50 years there will not be an Armenian question'.

Those who did read the newspapers would have seen a great many references to the Armenian Question during and after the war, especially during 1922 and 1923.

In April 1918, a Transcaucasian Federation was established among the Georgians, Armenians, and Tatars of Azerbaijan; this was dissolved in May 1918 and 'the independent republics of the Caucasus were born', including an independent Armenia.[29] But it was weak and divided, threatened on all sides, and could not survive.[30] After the First World War, Britain and its allies entered into complex negotiations with Turkey over the break-up of the Ottoman Empire, culminating in the London and Lausanne Peace Conferences of 1920 and 1923.[31] One aspect of these negotiations involved protection of minorities in Turkish-controlled areas. A number of Armenian support groups had been established in Britain, arguing for a permanent Armenian national home. The British government and papers such as *The Times* appeared to support this claim, and argued in favour of human rights for oppressed minority groups in the region.[32] The issue was often mentioned in the *Nation and Athenaeum* during the early 1920s, including in a debate on the Greco-Turkish war between Arnold Toynbee and T. P. O'Connor in the letters pages in December 1921 and January 1922.[33] (Albania,

29  Nassibian, *Britain and the Armenian Question*, 104.
30  In December 1922 Armenia became part of the USSR. Michael L. Dockrill and J. Douglas Goold, *Peace Without Promise* (London, Batsford, 1981), 239. By mid-1920, Armenia was internally unstable, 'fatally isolated', and under threat from all sides. Nassibian, *Britain and the Armenian Question*, 207. An independent Armenia was proposed in the Treaty of Sèvres at the 1920 London Peace Conference. Sharp argues that by 1921 this treaty was found to be unworkable. *The Versailles Settlement*, 171–2.
31  Harold Nicolson was involved in the Lausanne negotiations and is another possible source of information for Woolf.
32  The question of an Armenian national home, for example, is mentioned in *The Times* on 13, 14, 15, 16 and 27 December 1922; 8 January and 10 February 1923. See also 'Treatment of Minorities: Turkey and the League', *The Times*, 10 January 1923, 10.
33  See also 'The Liquidation of Mr. Lloyd George', *Nation and Athenaeum*, 23 September 1922, 814–15; 'How Much Longer?', *Nation and Athenaeum*, 7 October 1922, 6–7; 'War on Tap', *Nation and Athenaeum*, 7 October 1922, 7–8; 'Back to '78', *Nation and Athenaeum*, 14 October 1922, 43–4; Wedgwood Benn, 'Mr. Lloyd George's Defence' (letter), *Nation and Athenaeum*, 21 October 1922, 116; 'The Meaning of Lausanne', *Nation and Athenaeum*, 10 February 1923, 710–11. See also 'Events of the Week' during June 1923 for progress reports on the Lausanne Conference.

by contrast, received a much less sympathetic press in Britain during this period.)

The Lausanne Treaty was finally signed on 24 July 1923 – a few weeks after *Mrs Dalloway* is set. By then, Britain had secured its interests in the region – not in Armenia but in the Persian Gulf, partly by creating the new state of Iraq. The Armenians were effectively abandoned by the Lausanne Treaty; those in the Soviet Union were to remain citizens of that state, and the remaining survivors were to stay under the rule of Turkey, under a protectorate agreement. The idea of an Armenian national home in the Anatolia region was simply dropped.[34] For many people, this was a grotesque betrayal of the Armenians, who had suffered so much, and for whom Britain had some responsibility.[35]

In *Mrs Dalloway*, Richard Dalloway MP sits on the committee which is negotiating this final act of betrayal in June 1923. That is where he is going after giving Clarissa the roses.

Clarissa's refusal to think about the Armenian problem is a crucial moment in the novel, and provides us with ways into thinking about the structural relationship between Clarissa and Septimus, the war-neurotic soldier. Who is the victim, who the victimiser; who is responsible for the suffering of others? These questions trouble Woolf's text, just as they do HD's *Bid Me to Live*. But where HD's novel retreats into a private place of writing to contemplate the problem, *Mrs Dalloway* takes it into the heart of the political establishment. Even the Prime Minister is present at the Dalloways' party.

---

34 Sharp, *The Versailles Settlement*, 174. Britain's commitment to an independent Armenia had already begun to disappear, however, in 1920, and it did not provide material support to the fragile republic. Nassibian, *Britain and the Armenian Question*, 210–13. Dockrill and Goold argue that the 1920 Treaty of Sèvres was 'negotiated on the basis of power politics and completely ignored the Allies' professed principle of self-determination. When allied interests were not directly involved, as in the case of Armenia, promises meant nothing, lending weight to charges of Allied hypocrisy'. Dockrill and Goold, *Peace Without Promise*, 213–14.

35 See for example Arnold Toynbee, *Survey of International Affairs 1920–1923* (Oxford University Press, 1925); cited in Nassibian, *Britain and the Armenian Question*, 222. Ernest Hemingway also wrote about the Armenians in 1923. A poem entitled 'They All Made Peace – What is Peace?' begins: 'All of the turks are gentlemen and Ismet Pasha is a / little deaf. But the Armenians. How about the / Armenians? / Well the Armenians'. *Little Review*, 9, 3 (1923), 20

## The Prime Minister

The Prime Minister was originally to have been a central character in the novel.[36] In the final version of *Mrs Dalloway*, he appears only briefly, but he carries a good deal of symbolic weight. Because Woolf dates the novel so precisely, I want to pay attention to its particular historical moment. In the middle of June 1923, Stanley Baldwin had been Prime Minister for about three weeks, having taken over from Bonar Law. Law had retired owing to illness after only six months in office. This was the first non-coalition Conservative government for nearly two decades, and had been elected in November 1922, on a platform radically different from Leonard Woolf's internationalist, pacifist manifesto, quoted above. Indeed, some historians suggest that the Conservatives had policies on nothing at this time apart from tariff reform.[37]

When he became Prime Minister, Baldwin was known mainly for one public act: as Chancellor of the Exchequer under Bonar Law, he had negotiated what many people felt was a disadvantageous agreement in Britain's repayment of war debts to the United States. Some British officials had hoped that all allied war debts to the United States would be cancelled. The US did not agree, and eventually Baldwin agreed to pay £978 million. Other members of the government felt this was a poor deal for Britain. Bonar Law wanted to resign over the matter, and went so far as to write an anonymous letter to *The Times*, attacking the agreement. Baldwin insisted he had secured the best deal possible, but when France and Italy secured better agreements over repayment it looked as if Baldwin had indeed botched the negotiations.[38]

When Baldwin became Prime Minister in May 1923, the *New Statesman* commented:

> Mr. Baldwin is Prime Minister of England. Nothing very much else is known of him. Not half of the electors of Great Britain, we suppose, had ever heard his name until this week. He is said to be an extremely

36 Claire Tomalin, introduction to Oxford University Press edition of *Mrs Dalloway*, xv, xviii. See also Jane Novak, *The Razor Edge of Balance: A Study of Virginia Woolf* (Miami University Press, 1975).

37 T. F. Lindsay and Michael Harrington, *The Conservative Party, 1918–1970* (London, Macmillan, 1974), 53.

38 Lindsay and Harrington, *The Conservative Party*, 48; A. J. P. Taylor, *English History 1914–1945* (Oxford, Clarendon, 1965), 203.

pleasant fellow, and he is an Englishman. He smokes a briar pipe, he is an old Harrovian, and his politics are Conservative.[39]

He is 'an enigma', it says, 'significantly enigmatic'; by the end of that year, the *New Statesman* considered him 'a pygmy' whose administration had achieved 'precisely nothing' – not unlike Bonar Law's rule, which it found to be suffering from 'impotence' and lacking in 'masculine policy'.[40] Baldwin 'presented himself as a simple country gentleman, interested only in pigs'. He read few official documents, and he never read newspapers.[41] His manner was informal for a Conservative prime minister: he was the first to use first names among his colleagues, even if he did not know them well.[42] Trevor Wilson describes him as 'an insular Conservative of no internationalist inclinations'.[43] Later commentators praise aspects of his second and third governments; his first did very little.

Baldwin lost power to Labour in the election of December 1923; his first premiership lasted for about seven months. Perhaps the anonymous grey car which no one can quite identify at the beginning of *Mrs Dalloway* is a wry comment on the greyness and futility of this government during such an important period in world history, a time of intense colonial and anti-colonial struggle in which attempts to construct an effective League of Nations failed, and war debts and reparations crippled several European economies and contributed to the rise of fascism in the following decade. Later commentators suggest that the most significant achievement of the first Baldwin government was the Lausanne Treaty, which restored good relations with Turkey.[44] As I have suggested, however, this treaty was by no means a morally unambiguous act.

---

39  'Mr. Baldwin?', *New Statesman*, 26 May 1923, 188.
40  'Mr. Baldwin?', 188–9; 'Honest Mr. Baldwin', *New Statesman*, 17 November 1923, 168.
41  Taylor, *English History 1914–1945*, 205.
42  Lindsay and Harrington argue that Baldwin tried to make the Conservative party more democratic and less snobbish. *The Conservative Party*, 60. Taylor, *English History*, 173n.
43  Wilson, *Myriad Faces of War*, 757.
44  Lindsay and Harrington, *The Conservative Party*, 47; Taylor, *English History*, 202. Baldwin also provides another link to the Armenian Question for Woolf: his son Oliver was a Lieutenant-Colonel in the Armenian army in late 1920 and early 1921 and published his memoirs, *Six Prisons and Two Revolutions*, in 1924. Nassibian, *Britain and the Armenian Question*, 221.

What is the significance of a Baldwin-figure at the Dalloways' party? He represents the recent restoration to power of a Conservative administration – the Dalloways' set, back in power after sharing it with the Liberals during the war, and now threatened with the rise of Labour. It is also significant that Baldwin was perceived in 1923 to be a nonentity leading a very dull government. Richard Dalloway's inability to get into cabinet, then, would have been a failure of some magnitude.

The Prime Minister's arrival is registered first among the servants.

> The Prime Minister was coming, Agnes said: so she had heard them say in the dining-room, she said, coming in with a tray of glasses. Did it matter, did it matter in the least, one Prime Minister more or less? It made no difference at this hour of the night to Mrs Walker among the plates, saucepans, cullenders, frying-pans, chickens in aspic, ice-cream freezers, pared crusts of bread, lemons, soup tureens, and pudding basins […]. All she felt was, one Prime Minister more or less made not a scrap of difference to Mrs Walker. (216)

For the servants, the Prime Minister is represented as no different from the other guests; he is just another powerful person to whom they are expected to defer, and whom they must feed. Yet there is another narrative at work in this scene. Woolf set the novel during the first Baldwin conservative government, and published it during the second. In between, when most of the writing took place, Britain's first Labour government was in power. It was a minority government, and able to do little;[45] but the very fact that some working-class people had the vote, and were starting to get seats in the cabinet, was a significant political change. The novel suggests that a prime minister more or less might mean a great deal to working women such as Agnes and Mrs Walker in one sense, and very little in another.

Mrs Dalloway's guests take a different view.

> One couldn't laugh at him. He looked so ordinary. You might have stood him behind a counter and bought biscuits – poor chap, all rigged up in gold lace. And to be fair, as he went his rounds, first with Clarissa, then with Richard escorting him, he did it very well. He tried to look somebody. It was amusing to watch. (225)

45 Taylor argues that Labour was 'in office, but not in power'. *English History*, 210.

He is a Conservative, one of them; he represents their current hold on power. Yet he is also slightly ridiculous; he has just come into office, and he doesn't quite look the part – precisely how Baldwin, with his pig-breeding and his briar pipe, was perceived at this time. Where the *New Statesman* sees him as an anthropological misfit (a 'pygmy'), Mrs Dalloway's guests see his inadequacy in class terms: he looks like a shop assistant. As a symbol of real power, however, he makes them feel 'to the marrow of their bones, this majesty passing; this symbol of what they all stood for, English society' (225–6). It is the man, not the gold lace, that the guests find faintly ridiculous. Later, in *Three Guineas* (1938), Woolf attacked the idea of putting on fancy dress in order to govern the country, and she implicitly criticises it here, too. And it is women such as Clarissa Dalloway who play a vital role in keeping this political system in place.

This scene, which I read as satire, reappears a few years later in Evelyn Waugh's *Vile Bodies* (1930). The ruling class gathers at a party: 'a great concourse of pious and honourable people [...] their women-folk well gowned in rich and durable stuffs, their men-folk ablaze with orders; people who had represented their country in foreign places and sent their sons to die for her in battle'; Waugh's characters feel the presence of royalty as 'heavy as thunder in the drawing-room', and wonder stupidly why 'there seem so few young men about' after the war.[46]

Also at Mrs Dalloway's party is Sir William Bradshaw, the doctor who has been treating Septimus Smith's war neurosis. Clarissa consulted him once, we are told, and found him oppressive (240). Her memory of the visit engages our sympathy, but the novel also draws attention to the difference between Clarissa and Septimus. Unlike Septimus, Clarissa's social position allows her to decide for herself whether to obey the doctors, and her spouse has power to protect her. She can reject Bradshaw as her physician, and does so. As a hostess, however, she continues to patronise him and to maintain his position within the social structure. In other words, she is complicit in the processes which legitimate his disciplinary form of med-

---

46 Evelyn Waugh, *Vile Bodies* (1930; London, Penguin, [1991]), 127, 129. Waugh claimed to dislike *Mrs Dalloway*, but there are several echoes of the novel in the party scenes in *Vile Bodies*.

icine – medicine which she knows to be coercive, and which the reader knows has helped to kill Septimus.[47]

Mrs Dalloway's party occurs only hours after Septimus' death. She overhears Sir William Bradshaw talking to Richard Dalloway about a Bill she knows is to be passed through the House of Commons, though she is, characteristically, unclear about the details. 'They were talking about this Bill. Some case Sir William was mentioning, lowering his voice. It had its bearing upon what he was saying about the deferred effects of shell-shock. There must be some provision in the Bill' (240). Mimicking her husband, in a mirror image of the men's conversation, Lady Bradshaw draws Mrs Dalloway 'into the shelter of a common femininity, a common pride in the illustrious qualities of husbands and their sad tendency to overwork'. The disciplinary structures which have killed Septimus simultaneously protect (in class terms) and constrain (in gender terms) women such as these. These structures also pay the bills, and Lady Bradshaw imagines the wall of gold mounting up between her and 'all shifts and anxieties', leaving her comfortably 'wedged on a calm ocean, where only spice winds blow; respected, admired, envied, with scarcely anything left to wish for' (123).

'Sinking her voice', Lady Bradshaw tells Clarissa that 'A young man [...] had killed himself. He had been in the army.' Clarissa's response is enigmatic: 'Oh! thought Clarissa, in the middle of my party, here's death, she thought' (240). What does this mean? The inarticulate 'Oh!' might be interpreted as a schoolgirlish response to an adult tragedy. Like a child, Clarissa thinks about her party first, before confronting the unpleasant news. Her comment is oddly inaccurate: 'in the middle of my party, here's death'. The *idea* of death might have entered her party, but its physical presence remains elsewhere. Septimus' corpse, like those of the other dead millions, is safely out of sight. Most of the people at the party are protected from such spectacles. Even Peter Walsh, witness to the ambulance carrying Septimus' dying body, misunderstands what he has seen:

> One of the triumphs of civilization, Peter Walsh thought. It is one of the triumphs of civilization, as the light high bell of the ambulance sounded. Swiftly, cleanly, the ambulance sped to the hospital, having picked up

---

47  See Sue Thomas, 'Virginia Woolf's Septimus Smith and Contemporary Perceptions of Shell Shock', *English Language Notes*, 25, 2 (1987), 49–57.

instantly, humanely, some poor devil; some one hit on the head, struck down by disease, knocked over perhaps a minute or so ago at one of these crossings, as might happen to oneself. That was civilization. (197)

The satiric force here comes partly from the repetition of the word 'civilization'. Septimus' death is indeed a symptom of the civilisation of the period – not just during the war, but after it, too, well into the 1920s. Like Clarissa, Peter Walsh is preoccupied with his personal affairs and is slow to recognise what is happening to people around him. He enjoys the sight of young men taking a wreath to the tomb of the unknown soldier; boys in uniform, 'carrying guns', marching 'with their eyes ahead of them [...] their arms stiff, and on their faces an expression like the letters of a legend written round the base of a statue praising duty, gratitude, fidelity, love of England'. A 'very fine training', thinks Peter Walsh (65–6). He meditates complacently that the future lies 'in the hands of young men' like he had been, 'thirty years ago; with their love of abstract principles' (65) – young men like Septimus, in fact, who went to the war for an abstract love of Shakespeare. Peter Walsh does not seem to have noticed that many of these young men are now dead or mentally or physically damaged by the war.

When Clarissa hears of Septimus Smith's death, she wanders into another room, looking for Lady Bruton and the Prime Minister. The room is now empty, with no sign but the imprints of the buttocks of greatness. They indicate that Lady Bruton has been sitting 'turned deferentially', while the Prime Minister sat 'four-square, authoritatively' (241). They have been discussing 'India' – a word which carries a complex of imperial values and anxieties in 1923.[48] In

48 People in India were actively campaigning for independence in the early 1920s, and there are many references to the issue in journals such as the *New Statesman* and the *Nation and Athenaeum*. See for example 'The Outlook in India', *New Statesman*, 23 June 1923, 320–1; 'India's Demand', *New Statesman*, 18 August 1923, 539–41; 'The Gathering Crisis in India', *New Statesman*, 22 September 1923, 668–9. In his autobiography, Leonard Woolf comments that independence was granted at least two decades later than it should have been; Britain's refusal to face up to the inevitable led to large numbers of avoidable deaths. In the early 1920s, then, India signifies a place of new political struggles and the decline of empire. See also Zwerdling, *Virginia Woolf and the Real World*, 121; Ruth Henig, 'Foreign Policy' in Constantine *et al.*, eds, *The First World War in British History*, 218–20.

solitude, Clarissa feels a delayed response to the news of the dead soldier. 'There was nobody. The party's splendour fell to the floor, so strange it was to come in alone in her finery' (241). She responds indirectly, through her party. Its splendour falls, like a discarded garment. Away from her party, in an empty room, Clarissa the hostess suddenly ceases to exist. This turns her thoughts back to the news of Septimus' death.

> What business had the Bradshaws to talk of death at her party? A young man had killed himself. And they talked of it at her party – the Bradshaws talked of death. He had killed himself – but how? Always her body went through it, when she was told, first, suddenly of an accident; her dress flamed, her body burnt.

She feels the news, bizarrely, in her clothing, then in her body, then turns to the details of Septimus' death. 'He had thrown himself from a window' she thinks. 'Up had flashed the ground; through him, blundering, bruising, went the rusty spikes. There he lay with a thud, thud, thud in his brain, and then a suffocation of blackness' (241).

Clarissa then begins to mystify death and fantasises that the dead person is better off. 'She had once thrown a shilling into the Serpentine, never anything more. But he had flung it away. [...] They went on living [...]. They would grow old. A thing there was that mattered; a thing, wreathed about with chatter, defaced, obscured in her own life, let drop every day in corruption, lies, chatter. This he had preserved' (241). In living, one becomes corrupted, she thinks. To be dead is to avoid corruption. (The knowledge of what happens to the physical body after death is firmly suppressed.) 'Death was defiance,' thinks Clarissa. 'Death was an attempt to communicate, people feeling the impossibility of reaching the centre which, mystically, evaded them; closeness drew apart; rapture faded; one was alone. There was an embrace in death' (241–2). Two different strands of thought become entwined. Her yearning for her youth at Bourton is elided with thoughts on the death of the unknown young man. Clarissa's romanticisation of death is an attempt to comfort herself for the happiness she feels she has lost. 'There was an embrace in death,' she thinks, yet her own picture of Septimus' death is quite the opposite. His body is pierced, his flesh separated. Far from being embraced, or symbolically reunited with the mother's body (as Makiko Minow-Pinkney suggests), Septimus is completely alone at the moment of death, separated from everyone.

It is worth pausing on Minow-Pinkney's analysis of *Mrs Dalloway* here, for, though it produces a fine Kristevan reading of the text, it does not do justice, in my opinion, to the problem of Septimus Smith. This partly derives from Minow-Pinkney's treatment of Clarissa Dalloway as a predominantly sympathetic figure. As I have argued, the text is also judgemental of her and of her entire class, particularly on the question of the war and its consequences, including distant events, such as the sufferings of the Armenians. We need to recognise that she is a strongly paradoxical figure. The text constructs her quite explicitly as someone with whom we are invited to sympathise *and* whom we are forced to judge. If we fail to address both aspects of her function, then we miss much of the text's political force. More alarmingly, we are in danger of replicating her romanticisation of Septimus' death. This problem surfaces towards the end of Minow-Pinkney's chapter on *Mrs Dalloway*. Citing the scene in which Clarissa thinks of death a 'defiance' and an 'embrace', Minow-Pinkney writes:

> In psychoanalytic terms, the 'embrace' which Septimus aims at in death may be regarded as an embrace with the Mother. [...] What is crucial is not how Clarissa deciphers Septimus' suicide, but *that* she deciphers it, that a relation is established between the two figures. If Septimus does indeed 'embrace' the Mother in death, it is because he now in a sense has a 'mother' who acknowledges him: 'She felt somehow very like him'.[49]

This reading is unduly positive, it seems to me, and makes the soldier's death too easy to bear. It draws too much comfort from the imagined familial structure, allowing Clarissa's self-justification and refusal to confront her own complicity to pass unchallenged. 'The young man had killed himself', thinks Clarissa, 'but she did not pity him. [...] She felt glad that he had done it' (244).

Clarissa passes through a range of emotions and memories as she considers Septimus' death, and comes to a point in which she feels that she, rather than Septimus, is the one experiencing 'disas-

---

49  Minow-Pinkney, *Virginia Woolf and the Problem of the Subject* (Brighton, Harvester, 1987), 79.

ter' and 'disgrace'. 'It was her punishment to see sink and disappear here a man, there a woman, in this profound darkness, and she forced to stand here in her evening dress' (243). The sinking and disappearance of Septimus is of course precisely what she has not seen, though she has pictured it in her imagination. In the midst of her party, from the safety of her wealth and position, she feels as if she is suffering a 'punishment'. Following the representations of Septimus' and Rezia's suffering in the earlier parts of the book, this is surely to be read as satirical. Yet even here the novel is ambiguous. The claim that she is 'forced to stand here in her evening dress' might seem risible. Forced by whom? It is a childish sulk; another example of Clarissa refusing to take responsibility for her own actions. She tries to appropriate Septimus' suffering as her own ('her punishment'). Yet at the same time her denial of responsibility contains some truth. Uneducated, born and married into a particular class, Mrs Dalloway has few options for action. As Rachel Bowlby notes, her daughter will have many more choices in her adult life.[50] Unless Clarissa is willing to sacrifice the comforts and privileges of her class, she is in some sense 'forced' to stand around in an evening dress, feeling foolish.

From imagining herself punished, Clarissa moves into a new phase of emotion, via the memory of Bourton. The next paragraph is full of terms suggesting strength and joy: 'she had never been so happy', 'pleasure', 'triumphs', 'delight' (243). Similarly, when Peter Walsh witnesses Septimus' departure in the ambulance, he thinks: 'Ah, but thinking became morbid, sentimental, directly one began conjuring up doctors, dead bodies; a little glow of *pleasure*, a sort of *lust*, too, over the visual impression warned one not to go on with that sort of thing any more' (my emphasis; 198). The terms linked with death here are very similar to those found in many soldiers' narratives of the war, discussed earlier. Following a battle or a death, the living characters gloat, celebrating the fact they are still alive. This seems to be a necessary process of abjecting the dead; shedding the corpse from the social fabric. In the Dalloways' London in 1923, this is not a difficult task, though the presence of a war corpse is perhaps momentarily more shocking, because more unexpected, than it might have been in the war zone.

---

50  Bowlby, *Virginia Woolf* (Oxford, Blackwell, 1988), ch. 5.

Clarissa's response to Septimus' death needs to be treated with considerable caution. On the one hand she seems to appropriate the experience of his suffering; on the other, the novel keeps pointing towards some kind of parallel between the two characters who never meet. Yet in the end it is the differences, rather than the similarities, which are most important. Most significantly, Clarissa is a survivor (11), while Septimus is a victim; they occupy quite different positions in relation to the war. Clarissa has suffered – though not from the war – and she has also benefited from the 'social system' she actively supports.

I have argued that *Mrs Dalloway* is partly an attack on the Dalloways, their class, and their responsibility for the war. But it is also true that Clarissa Dalloway's character, memories, and experience are treated with considerable sympathy, as other critics have demonstrated. It would be all too easy to construct a purely satiric view of her, a ruling-class woman who lives in Westminster and thinks 'it was very, very dangerous to live even one day' (10); instead, Woolf's representation of Clarissa Dalloway is deeply ambivalent, placing her complexly both on the edges and at the centre of circles of real power.

The satiric element of *Mrs Dalloway* can be traced through Clarissa's attitudes towards political issues of the day: war-neurotic soldiers, the Armenian Question, the new Prime Minister. Yet even if she were keenly interested in these matters, she has very little power to do anything about them. Richard Dalloway, by contrast, is well informed and claims to be deeply concerned about human suffering. He and his government have power to deal with such issues, but choose not to. Is this not where the real responsibility lies? This in turn raises questions about gender and power in the early 1920s, shortly after the vote has been extended to women such as Clarissa Dalloway. Will women's participation in democracy transform politics; or will it transform women? Would readers want women such as Clarissa, who cannot tell the difference between Armenia, Albania, and Turkey, to be making decisions which affect the fate of these nations? Obviously not, yet would their decisions be any worse than those made by the men they support? Would such women be different if they had direct responsibility? Through the figure of Clarissa Dalloway, the novel poses important questions about political power after the war. Taking responsibility, the novel suggests, is extremely difficult, yet needs to be done if Britain is to avoid a repetition of the disastrous decisions which took it into the First World War. By the time the novel was published, it was becoming clear that further disasters – direct consequences of the war and its settlement – were unavoidable. As Hobsbawm comments, the peace settlements were 'doomed from the start, and another war was therefore practically certain' (34).

# BIBLIOGRAPHY

Abel, Elizabeth. 'Narrative Structure(s) and Female Development: The Case of *Mrs. Dalloway*', in Elizabeth Abel *et al.*, eds, *The Voyage In: Fictions of Female Development* (Hanover, University Press of New England, 1983)

Abel, Elizabeth. *Virginia Woolf and the Fictions of Psychoanalysis* (University of Chicago Press, 1989)

'The Air Raid', *The Lancet*, 23 January 1915, 191–2

Aldington, Richard. *Death of a Hero* (1929; London, Hogarth, 1984)

Aldington, Richard. *Roads to Glory* (London, Chatto and Windus, 1930)

Aldington, Richard. *All Men Are Enemies: A Romance* (New York, Doubleday, 1933)

Aldington, Richard. *The Dearest Friend: A Selection of the Letters of Richard Aldington to John Cournos* [1914–18], ed. R. T. Risk (Francestown NH, Typographeum, 1978)

Aldington, Richard. *Richard Aldington and HD: The Early Years in Letters*, ed. Caroline Zilboorg (Bloomington, Indiana University Press, 1992)

Aldington, Richard. *Richard Aldington and HD: The Later Years in Letters*, ed. Caroline Zilboorg (Manchester University Press, 1995)

Alison Phillips, W. 'The Peace Settlements: 1815 and 1919', *Edinburgh Review*, 230 (July 1919), 1–21

'All Quiet on the Western Front', *Times Literary Supplement*, 18 April 1929, 314

Ash, Edwin. *The Problem of Nervous Breakdown* (London, Mills and Boon Ltd, 1919)

'Back to '78', *Nation and Athenaeum*, 14 October 1922, 43–4

Bagnold, Enid. *Diary without Dates* (1918; London, Virago, 1979)

Bailey, Thomas A., and Paul B. Ryan. *The Lusitania Disaster: An Episode in Modern Warfare and Diplomacy* (New York, The Free Press, 1975)

Barbusse, Henri. *Under Fire*, trans. W. Fitzwater Wray (1916; London, Dent, 1988)

Bassett, John. *Faulkner: An Annotated Checklist of Recent Criticism* (Kent, Ohio, Kent State University Press, 1983)

Bassett, John, ed. *William Faulkner: The Critical Heritage* (London, Routledge and Kegan Paul, 1973)

Bate, Jonathan. 'Arcadia and Armageddon: Three English Novelists and the First World War', *Etudes Anglaises*, 39, 2 (1986), 151–62

Bayley, John. *The Short Story: Henry James to Elizabeth Bowen* (Brighton, Harvester, 1988)

Bayliss, Gwyn M. *Bibliographic Guide to the Two World Wars* (London, Bowker, 1977)

Bédier, Joseph. *German Atrocities from German Evidence*, trans. Bernhard Harrison (Paris, Librairie Armand Colin, 1915)

Beer, Gillian. *Arguing with the Past: Essays in Narrative from Woolf to Sidney* (London, Routledge, 1989)

Beer, Gillian. 'The Island and the Aeroplane: The Case of Virginia Woolf', in Homi Bhabha, ed., *Nation and Narration* (London, Routledge, 1990)

Beer, Gillian. 'The Dissidence of Vernon Lee', in Raitt and Tate, eds, *Women's Fiction and the Great War*

Beer, Gillian. *Virginia Woolf: The Common Ground* (Edinburgh University Press, 1997)

Benn, Wedgwood. 'Mr. Lloyd George's Defence' (letter), *Nation and Athenaeum*, 21 October 1922, 116

Bennett, Arnold. 'American Authors "Made" in England', *Evening Standard*, 26 June 1930, 7

Bergonzi, Bernard. *Heroes' Twilight: A Study of the Literature of the Great War* (London, Constable, 1965)

Bergson, Henri. *Laughter: An Essay on the Meaning of the Comic* (1900; London, Macmillan, 1911)

Bernays, Edward. *Propaganda* (New York, Liveright, 1928)

Bersani, Leo. *The Culture of Redemption* (Cambridge MA, Harvard University Press, 1990)

Bevan, Edwyn. 'The Truth about Lies', *The Nineteenth Century*, 80 (September 1916), 612–22

Bion, Wilfred. *The Long Week-End 1897–1919: Part of a Life* (1982; London, Free Association Books, 1986)

Blotner, Joseph. *Faulkner: A Biography*, 2 vols (London, Chatto and Windus, 1974)

Blunden, Edmund. *Undertones of War* (1928; Harmondsworth, Penguin, 1982)

Blunden, Edmund. *Selected Poems*, ed. Robyn Marsack (Manchester, Carcanet, 1982)

Bogacz, Ted. 'War Neurosis and Cultural Change in England, 1914–22: The Work of the War Office Committee of Enquiry into "Shell-Shock"', *Journal of Contemporary History*, 24 (1989), 227–56

Booth, Allyson. *Postcards from the Trenches: Negotiating the Space Between Modernism and the First World War* (New York, Oxford University Press, 1996)

Borden, Mary. *The Forbidden Zone* (London, William Heinemann, 1929)

Bourke, Joanna. *Dismembering the Male: Men's Bodies, Britain and the Great War* (London, Reaktion, 1996)

Bourne, J. M. *Britain and the Great War, 1914–1918* (London, Edward Arnold, 1989)

Bowlby, Rachel. *Virginia Woolf: Feminist Destinations* (Oxford, Blackwell, 1988)

Bradbury, Malcolm. Introduction to *Parade's End* (London, Everyman, 1992)

Breen, Judith. 'D. H. Lawrence, World War I, and the Battle Between the Sexes: A Reading of "The Blind Man" and "Tickets, Please"', *Women's Studies*, 13 (1986), 63–74

Brennan, Teresa, ed., *Between Feminism and Psychoanalysis* (London, Routledge, 1989)

Brittain, Vera. *Testament of Youth: An Autobiographical Study of the Years 1900–1925* (1933; London, Virago, 1978)

Brock, A. J. 'The War Neurasthenic: A Note on Methods of Reintegrating Him with His Environment', *The Lancet*, 23 March 1918, 436

Bronfen, Elisabeth. *Over Her Dead Body: Death, Femininity and the Aesthetic* (Manchester University Press, 1992)

Brophy, John, ed. *The Soldier's War: A Prose Anthology* (London, Dent, 1929)

Brown, William. 'The Treatment of Cases of Shell Shock in an Advanced Neurological Centre', *The Lancet*, 17 August 1918, 197–200

'Brutality of German Warfare', *The Times*, 3 November 1915, 9

Buchan, John. *The Three Hostages* (1924; Harmondsworth, Penguin, 1953)

Buck, Claire. *HD and Freud: Bisexuality and A Feminine Discourse* (Hemel Hempstead, Harvester Wheatsheaf, 1991)

Buitenhuis, Peter. *The Great War of Words: Literature as Propaganda 1914–18 and After* (London, Batsford, 1989)

Burnett, Gary. 'A Poetics out of War: H.D.'s Responses to the First World War', *Agenda*, 25, 3–4 (1988), 54–63

Burnett, Gary. *H.D. Between Image and Epic: The Mysteries of her Poetics* (Ann Arbor, UMI Research Press, 1990)

Burroughs, Megan C. 'Septimus Smith: A Man of Many Words', *University of Windsor Review*, 22, 1 (1989), 70–8

Bury, Judson S. 'Pathology of War Neuroses', *The Lancet*, 27 July 1918, 97–9

Bushaway, Bob. 'Name Upon Name: The Great War and Remembrance', in Roy Porter, ed., *Myths of the English* (Cambridge, Polity, 1992)

Butler, Judith, and Joan W. Scott, eds. *Feminists Theorize the Political* (London, Routledge, 1992)

Butts, Mary. *Speed the Plough and Other Stories* (London, Chapman and Hall, 1923)

Buxton, C. R., and D. F. Buxton. *The World After the War* (London, George Allen and Unwin, 1920)

Buzzard, E. Farquhar. 'Warfare on the Brain', *The Lancet*, 30 December 1916, 1095–9

Cable, Boyd. 'The Pink-Tailed Tank', *Cornhill Magazine*, n.s. 42 (1917), 163–9

Cahm, Eric. *The Dreyfus Affair in French Society and Politics* (1994; London, Longman, 1996)

Cannadine, David. 'War and Death, Grief and Mourning in Modern Britain', in Joachim Whaley, ed., *Mirrors of Mortality: Studies in the Social History of Death* (London, Europa, 1981)

Carr, E. H. *The Twenty Years' Crisis 1919–1939: An Introduction to the Study of International Relations* (1939; London, Papermac, 1995)

Carr, Ian. 'Edmund Blunden and the 1914–18 War', *Stand*, 4, 3 (1960), 48–51

Caruth, Cathy. *Unclaimed Experience: Trauma, Narrative, and History* (Baltimore, Johns Hopkins University Press, 1996)

Caruth, Cathy, ed. *Trauma: Explorations in Memory* (Baltimore, Johns Hopkins University Press, 1995)

Cassell, Richard A., ed. *Ford Madox Ford: Modern Judgements* (London, Macmillan, 1972)

Cather, Willa. *One of Ours* (1922; London, Virago, 1987)

Cecil, Hugh. *The Flower of Battle: British Fiction Writers of the First World War* (London, Secker and Warburg, 1995)

Cesarani, David. 'An Embattled Minority: The Jews in Britain during the First World War', *Immigrants and Minorities*, 8 (March 1989), 61–81

Chapman, Guy. *A Passionate Prodigality* (1933; Southampton, Martins Publishers, 1990)

Chapman, Guy. *The Dreyfus Trials* (London, Batsford, 1972)

Chapman, Guy, ed. *Vain Glory: A Miscellany of the Great War 1914–1918 Written by Those Who Fought in it on Each Side and on All Fronts* (London, Cassell, 1937)

Charteris, John. *At G.H.Q.* (London, Cassell, 1931)

Cheyette, Bryan. *Constructions of 'the Jew' in English Literature and Society: Racial Representations, 1875–1945* (Cambridge University Press, 1993)

Ciolkowska, Muriel. 'Le Feu', *The Egoist*, 4, 4 (May 1917), 55–7

Cole, Percival. 'Plastic Repair in War Injuries to the Jaw and Face', *The Lancet*, 17 March 1917, 415–17

Collie, John. 'The Disabled Soldier', *Edinburgh Review*, 227 (April 1918), 343–58

Collier, Basil. *Arms and the Men: The Arms Trade and Governments* (London, Hamish Hamilton, 1980)

Collier, Peter, and Davies, Judy, eds. *Modernism and the European Unconscious* (Cambridge, Polity, 1990)

Conrad, Joseph. *The Collected Letters of Joseph Conrad, vol. 5, 1912–1916*, ed. Frederick Karl and Laurence Davies (Cambridge University Press, 1996)

Constantine, Stephen, Maurice Kirby, and Mary Rose, eds. *The First World War in British History* (London, Edward Arnold, 1995)

Cooper, Helen M. *et al.*, eds. *Arms and the Woman* (Chapel Hill, University of North Carolina Press, 1989)

Cooper Willis, Irene. *England's Holy War: A Study of English Liberal Idealism During the Great War* (New York, Knopf, 1928)

Cooperman, Stanley. *World War I and the American Novel* (Baltimore, Johns Hopkins University Press, 1970)

Core, Donald. *Functional Nervous Disorders: Their Classification and Treatment* (Bristol, John Wright & Sons Ltd, 1922)

Core, Donald E. 'The "Instinct-Distortion" or "War Neurosis"', *The Lancet*, 10 August 1918, 168–72

Coroneos, Con. 'Flies and Violets in Katherine Mansfield', in Raitt and Tate, eds, *Women's Fiction and the Great War*

Crook, Nora. *Kipling's Myths of Love and Death* (Basingstoke, Macmillan, 1989)

Crowley, Aleister. *Moonchild* (1929; London, Sphere, 1972)

'The Crucifixion of a Canadian: Insensate Act of Hate', *The Times*, 15 May 1915, 7

David-Ménard, Monique. *Hysteria from Freud to Lacan: Body and Language in Psychoanalysis*, trans. Catherine Porter (1983; Ithaca NY, Cornell University Press, 1989)

Dawson, A. J. *Somme Battle Stories* (London, Hodder and Stoughton, 1916)

Dawson, Graeme. *Soldier Heroes: British Adventure, Empire and the Imagining of Masculinities* (London, Routledge, 1994)

Degroot, Gerard. *Blighty: British Society in the Era of the Great War* (Harlow, Longman, 1996)

Dekoven, Marianne. *Rich and Strange: Gender, History, Modernism* (Princeton University Press, 1991)

Delany, Paul. *D. H. Lawrence's Nightmare: The Writer and his Circle in the Years of the Great War* (Hassocks, Harvester, 1979)

Delany, Paul. 'Who Was "The Blind Man"?', *English Studies in Canada*, 9, 1 (1983), 92–9

Demm, Eberhard. 'Propaganda and Caricature in the First World War', *Journal of Contemporary History*, 28 (1993), 163–92

Dockrill, Michael L., and J. Douglas Goold. *Peace without Promise: Britain and the Peace Conferences, 1919–23* (London, Batsford, 1981)

Dos Passos, John. *One Man's Initiation: 1917* (1920; Lanham MD, University Press of America, 1986)

Dos Passos, John. *Three Soldiers* (1921; London, Penguin, 1990)

Dowling, David. *Mrs Dalloway: Mapping Streams of Consciousness* (Boston,

Twayne, 1991)

Doyle, Charles. *Richard Aldington: A Biography* (Basingstoke, Macmillan, 1989)

Doyle, Charles, ed. *Richard Aldington: Reappraisals*, ELS Monograph Series, 49 (Victoria BC, English Literary Studies, 1990)

Droste, C. L. *The Lusitania Case*, ed. W. H. Tantum (1916; London, Patrick Stephens Ltd, 1972)

duPlessis, Rachel Blau. *H.D.: The Career of that Struggle* (Brighton, Harvester, 1986)

Eder, Doris L. 'The Lost Generation Lives Again', *Women's Studies*, 18 (1990), 129–34

Edmonds, Charles (pseud. of Charles Carrington). *A Subaltern's War* (London, Peter Davies, 1929)

Edmunds, Susan. *Out of Line: History, Psychoanalysis, and Montage in H.D.'s Long Poems* (Stanford University Press, 1994)

Eksteins, Modris. *Rites of Spring: The Great War and the Birth of the Modern Age* (London: Bantam Press, 1989)

Ellenberger, Henri. *The Discovery of the Unconscious: The History and Evolution of Dynamic Psychiatry* (1970; London, Fontana, 1994)

Ellmann, Maud. *The Poetics of Impersonality: T. S. Eliot and Ezra Pound* (Brighton, Harvester, 1987)

Ellmann, Maud. *The Hunger Artists: Starving, Writing and Imprisonment* (London, Virago, 1993)

Englander, David. 'Soldiering and Identity: Reflections on the Great War', *War in History*, 1, 3 (1994), 300–18

Enser, A. G. S. *A Subject Bibliography of the First World War*, 2nd edn (Aldershot, Gower, 1990)

'Falsehood in War Time', *Times Literary Supplement*, 14 June 1928, 455

Faulkner, William. *Soldiers' Pay* (1926; London, Picador, 1991)

Faulkner, William. *Sartoris* (1929; London, Chatto and Windus, 1932, 1964)

Faulkner, William. *These Thirteen* (1931; London, Chatto and Windus, 1963)

Faulkner, William. *Thinking of Home: William Faulkner's Letters to his Mother and Father, 1918–1925*, ed. James G. Watson (New York, Norton, 1992)

Felman, Shoshana. 'In an Era of Testimony: Claude Lanzmann's *Shoah*', *Yale French Studies*, 79, *Literature and the Ethical Question* (1991), 39–81.

Felman, Shoshana, and Dori Laub. *Testimony: Crises of Witnessing in Literature, Psychoanalysis, and History* (London, Routledge, 1992)

Fenton, Norman. *Shell Shock and its Aftermath* (London, Henry Kimpton, 1926)

Fergus, David. 'The Zepps are Coming!', *Scots Magazine*, 132 (February 1990), 503–7

Feudtner, Chris. '"Minds the Dead have Ravished": Shell Shock, History, and the Ecology of Disease-Systems', *History of Science*, 31, 4 (1993), 377–420

Field, Frank. *Three French Writers and the Great War: Barbusse, Drieu La Rochelle, Bernanos: Studies in the Rise of Communism and Fascism* (Cambridge University Press, 1975)

Field, Frank. *British and French Writers of the First World War: Comparative Studies in Cultural History* (Cambridge University Press, 1991)

Fieling, Anthony. 'Loss of Personality from "Shell Shock"', *The Lancet*, 10 July 1915), 63–6

Firchow, Peter E. 'Kipling's "Mary Postgate": The Barbarians and the Critics', *Etudes Anglaises*, 29, 1 (1976), 27–39

Firchow, Peter E. 'Rico and Julia: The Hilda Doolittle–D. H. Lawrence Affair Reconsidered', *Journal of Modern Literature*, 8, 1 (1980), 51–76

Fitzgerald, F. Scott. *Tender is the Night* (1934, rev. edn 1951; Harmondsworth, Penguin, 1985)

Fletcher, David. *Landships: British Tanks in the First World War* (London, HMSO, 1984)

Fletcher, David, ed. *Tanks and Trenches: First-Hand Accounts of Trench Warfare in the First World War* (Phoenix Mill, Alan Sutton, 1994)

Fletcher, John, and Andrew Benjamin, eds. *Abjection, Melancholia and Love: The Work of Julia Kristeva* (London, Routledge, 1990)

Fletcher, John Gould. 'The Death of the Machines', *Egoist*, 4, 3 (April 1917), 450

Fletcher, John Gould. 'The New God', *Egoist*, 5, 3 (March 1918), 45–6.

Flower, J. E. *Literature and the Left in France: Society, Politics and the Novel since the Late Nineteenth Century* (London, Methuen, 1983)

[Ford] Hueffer, Ford Madox. 'The Muse of War', *Outlook*, 34 (12 September 1914), 334–5

[Ford] Hueffer, Ford Madox. 'The Scaremonger', *The Bystander*, 25 November 1914, 273–4, 276

[Ford] Hueffer, Ford Madox. 'Enemies', *Outlook*, 35 (16 January 1915), 79–80

[Ford] Hueffer, Ford Madox. *When Blood is their Argument: An Analysis of Prussian Culture* (London, Hodder and Stoughton, 1915)

[Ford] Hueffer, Ford Madox. *Between St. Dennis and St. George: A Sketch of Three Civilisations* (London, Hodder and Stoughton, 1915)

[Ford] Hueffer, Ford Madox. 'Fun! – It's Heaven', *The Bystander*, 24 November 1915, 327–30

Ford, Ford Madox. *Parade's End* (1924–8; Harmondsworth, Penguin, 1982)

Ford, Ford Madox. *No Enemy* (1929; New York, Ecco Press, 1984)

Ford, Ford Madox. *It Was the Nightingale* (1933; New York, Ecco Press, 1984)

Ford, Ford Madox. *The March of Literature* (1938; London, George Allen and Unwin, 1947)

Ford, Ford Madox. *Pound/Ford: The Story of a Literary Friendship*, ed. Brita Lindberg-Seyersted (New York, New Directions, 1982)

Ford, Ford Madox. 'War and the Mind', ed. Sondra J. Stang, *The Yale Review*, 78, 4 (Summer 1989), 497–510

Ford, Ford Madox. *The Correspondence of Ford Madox Ford and Stella Bowen*, ed. Sondra J. Stang and Karen Cochran (Bloomington, Indiana University Press, 1993)

Forty, George. *The Royal Tank Regiment: A Pictorial History 1916–1987* (Tunbridge Wells, Spellmount, 1988)

Forty, George. *The Bovington Tank Collection* (Southampton, Ensign, 1992)

Forty, George, and Anne Forty. *Bovington Tanks* (Wincanton, Dorset, Wincanton Press, 1988)

Freud, 'Three Essays on the Theory of Sexuality' (1905), Pelican Freud Library 7, *On Sexuality* (Harmondsworth, Penguin, 1983)

Freud, Sigmund. 'Notes Upon a Case of Obsessional Neurosis' (1909), Penguin Freud Library 9, *Case Histories II* (London, Penguin, 1991)

Freud, Sigmund. 'Analysis of a Phobia in a Five-year-Old Boy: "Little Hans"' (1909), Penguin Freud Library 8, *Case Histories I* (London, Penguin, 1990)

Freud, Sigmund. 'Thoughts for the Time on War and Death' (1915), Pelican Freud

Library 12, *Civilization, Society and Religion* (Harmondsworth, Penguin, 1985)

Freud, Sigmund. 'Mourning and Melancholia' (1917), Pelican Freud Library 11, *On Metapsychology* (Harmondsworth, Penguin, 1984)

Freud, Sigmund. 'The Uncanny' (1919), Pelican Freud Library 14, *Art and Literature* (Harmondsworth, Penguin, 1988)

Freud, Sigmund. 'Introduction to *Psycho-Analysis and the War Neuroses*', *Standard Edition*, XVII (1917–19), trans. James Strachey (London, Hogarth, 1955), 207–10

Freud, Sigmund. *Beyond the Pleasure Principle* (1920), Pelican Freud Library 11, *On Metapsychology* (Harmondsworth, Penguin, 1984)

Freud, Sigmund. 'Some Psychical Consequences of the Anatomical Distinction Between the Sexes' (1925), Pelican Freud Library 7, *On Sexuality* (Harmondsworth, Penguin, 1983)

Freud, 'Fetishism' (1927), Pelican Freud Library 7, *On Sexuality* (Harmondsworth, Penguin, 1983)

Friedman, Susan Stanford. *Psyche Reborn: The Emergence of H.D.* (1981; Bloomington, Indiana University Press, 1987)

Friedman, Susan Stanford. *Penelope's Web: Gender, Modernity, H.D.'s Fiction* (Cambridge University Press, 1990)

Friedman, Susan Stanford, and Rachel Blau duPlessis, eds. *Signets: Reading H.D.* (Madison, University of Wisconsin Press, 1990)

Friedrich, Ernst. *Krieg dem Kriege* (1924; Frankfurt am Main, Taschenbuch, 1991)

Fuller, J. F. C. *The Conduct of War 1789–1961* (1961; London, Eyre Methuen, 1972)

Fussell, Paul. *The Great War and Modern Memory* (Oxford University Press, 1975)

'The Gathering Crisis in India', *New Statesman*, 22 September 1923, 668–9

Gay, Peter. *Freud: A Life for Our Time* (1988; London, Papermac, 1989)

'Germany's Self-Revelation', review of J. H. Morgan, *German Atrocities*, *Times Literary Supplement*, 30 March 1916, 146

Gibbs, Philip. *Realities of War* (London, Heinemann, 1920)

Gilbert, Geoffrey. *A Career in Modernism: Wyndham Lewis 1909–1931* (Ph.D. dissertation, Cambridge, 1995)

Gilbert, Martin. *The Routledge Atlas of the First World War*, 2nd edn (London, Routledge, 1994)

Gilbert, Sandra, and Gubar, Susan. *No Man's Land*, vol. 2 (New Haven, Yale University Press, 1989)

Gillis, John, ed. *The Militarization of the Western World* (New Brunswick, Rutgers University Press, 1989)

Gliddon, Gerald. *Legacy of the Somme, 1916: The Battle in Fact, Film and Fiction* (Far Thrupp, Sutton, 1996)

Goderez, Bruce I. 'The Survivor Syndrome: Massive Psychic Trauma and Posttraumatic Stress Disorder', *Bulletin of the Menninger Clinic* (Kansas), 51, 1 (1987)

Goldman, Dorothy, ed. *Women and World War I: The Written Response* (Basingstoke, Macmillan, 1993)

Goldstein, Erik. *Winning the Peace: British Diplomatic Strategy, Peace Planning, and the Paris Peace Conference, 1916–1920* (Oxford, Clarendon, 1991)

Goldstein, Laurence. *The Flying Machine and Modern Literature* (Basingstoke, Macmillan, 1986)

Gordon, Lyndall. *Virginia Woolf: A Writer's Life* (Oxford University Press, 1984)

Gosse, Edmund. 'Some Soldier-Poets', *Edinburgh Review*, 226 (October 1917), 296–316

Gould, Gerald. 'Under Fire', *New Statesman*, 8 September 1917, 546–7

Gould, Gerald. 'Fantasy and Effort', *The Observer*, 13 July 1930, 6

Grant, Mariel. *Propaganda and the Role of the State in Inter-War Britain* (Oxford, Clarendon, 1994)

Graves, Robert. *Goodbye to All That* (1929; rev. edn 1957; Harmondsworth, Penguin, 1988)

Gray, Edwyn A. *The Killing Time: The U-Boat War 1914–18* (London, Seeley, Service and Co., 1972)

Gray, Richard. *The Life of William Faulkner* (Oxford, Blackwell, 1994)

Green, Robert. *Ford Madox Ford: Prose and Politics* (Cambridge University Press, 1981)

Green, Roger Lancelyn, ed. *Kipling: The Critical Heritage* (London, Routledge and Kegan Paul, 1971)

Gregory, Adrian. *The Silence of Memory: Armistice Day 1919–1946* (Oxford, Berg, 1994)

Grosskurth, Phyllis. *Melanie Klein: Her World and Her Work* (London, Hodder and Stoughton, 1986)

Grosz, Elizabeth. *Sexual Subversions: Three French Feminists* (Sydney, Allen and Unwin, 1989)

Guest, Barbara. *Herself Defined: The Poet H.D. and her World* (London, Collins, 1985)

Gurney, Ivor. *Collected Letters*, ed. R. K. R. Thornton (Manchester, Carcanet, 1991)

Gürün, Kamuran. *The Armenian File: The Myth of Innocence Exposed* (1983; London, Nicosia and Istanbul, K. Rustem and Bro. and Weidenfeld and Nicolson Ltd, 1985)

Guth, Deborah. '"What a Lark! What a Plunge!": Fiction as Self-Evasion in *Mrs Dalloway*', *Modern Language Review*, 84 (1989), 18–26

Hacobian, A. P. *Armenia and the War: An Armenian's Point of View with an Appeal to Britain and the Coming Peace Conference* (London, Hodder and Stoughton, 1918)

Hall, Radclyffe. *Miss Ogilvy Finds Herself and Other Stories* (London, Macmillan, 1934)

Hamon, Augustin. *Lessons of the World-War*, trans. Bernard Miall (London, T. Fisher Unwin, 1918)

Hanley, Lynne. *Writing War: Fiction, Gender and Memory* (Amherst, University of Massachusetts Press, 1991)

Hanna, Martha. *The Mobilization of the Intellect: French Scholars and Writers During the Great War* (Harvard University Press, 1996)

Hardach, Gerd. *The First World War 1914–1918*, trans. Peter Ross and Betty Ross (1973; Harmondsworth, Penguin, 1987)

Hardwick, Joan. *An Immodest Violet: The Life of Violet Hunt* (London, Andre Deutsch, 1990)

Hardy, G. H. *Bertrand Russell and Trinity: A College Controversy of the Last War* (Cambridge University Press, 1942)

Hargreaves, Tracy. 'The Grotesque and the Great War in *To the Lighthouse*', in Raitt and Tate, eds, *Women's Fiction and the Great War*

Harris, J. P. *Men, Ideas and Tanks: British Military Thought and Armoured Forces,*

*1903–1939* (Manchester University Press, 1995)

Hartcup, Guy. *The War of Invention: Scientific Developments, 1914–18* (London, Brassey's Defence Publishers, 1988)

Hartigan, Richard Shelly. *The Forgotten Victim: A History of the Civilian* (Chicago, Precedent Publishing, 1982)

Haste, C. *Keep the Home Fires Burning: Propaganda in the First World War* (London, Allen Lane, 1977)

Hay, Ian. *The Willing Horse* (London, Hodder and Stoughton, n.d.)

HD. 'Responsibilities' [*c.* 1916], *Agenda*, 25, 3–4 (1987), 51–3

HD. *'Kora and Ka' and 'Mira-Mare'* (Dijon, Darantière, 1934)

HD. 'Kora and Ka' (1934), rpt in Bronte Adams and Trudi Tate, eds, *That Kind of Woman: Stories from the Left Bank and Beyond* (London, Virago, 1991)

HD. 'Two Americans', *The Usual Star* (Dijon, Darantière, 1934)

HD. *Nights* (1935; New York, New Directions, 1986)

HD. *Bid Me to Live* (1960; London, Virago, 1984)

HD. *Palimpsest* (Carbondale, Southern Illinois University Press, 1968)

HD. *Collected Poems 1912–1944*, ed. Louis L. Martz (New York, New Directions, 1983)

HD. *Tribute to Freud*, rev. edn (Manchester, Carcanet, 1985)

HD. 'H.D. by Delia Alton', *The Iowa Review*, HD Centennial Issue, ed. Adalaide Morris, 16, 3 (1986)

HD. Letter to Norman Holmes Pearson, ed. Diana Collecott, *Agenda*, 25, 3–4 (1988), 71

HD. *Paint it Today*, ed. Cassandra Laity (New York University Press, 1992)

HD. *Asphodel*, ed. Robert Spoo (Durham NC, Duke University Press, 1992)

Hemingway, Ernest. *Fiesta* (London, Jonathan Cape, 1927)

Hemingway, Ernest. *Men without Women* (London, Jonathan Cape, 1928)

Hemingway, Ernest. *A Farewell to Arms* (London, Jonathan Cape, 1929)

Henig, Ruth. *Versailles and After, 1919–1933* (London, Methuen, 1984)

Herbert, A. P. *The Secret Battle* (1919; London, Chatto and Windus, 1970)

Herman, Edward, and Noam Chomsky. *Manufacturing Consent: The Political Economy of the Mass Media* (New York, Pantheon Books, 1988)

Hewitt, Andrew. *Political Inversions: Homosexuality, Fascism, and the Modernist Imaginary* (Stanford University Press, 1996)

Hickey, Des, and Gus Smith. *Seven Days to Disaster: The Sinking of the Lusitania* (London, Collins, 1981)

Higonnet, Margaret Randolph *et al.*, eds. *Behind the Lines: Gender and the Two World Wars* (New Haven, Yale University Press, 1987)

Hirschfeld, Magnus, ed. *Sittengeschichte des Weltkriegs*, 2 vols (Leipzig and Vienna, n.d. [1930]), translated as *The Sexual History of the World War* (New York, Cadillac Publishing, 1946)

Hobsbawm, Eric. *Age of Extremes: The Short Twentieth Century, 1914–1991* (1994; London, Abacus, 1995)

Hollenberg, Donna. 'Art and Ardor in World War I: Selected Letters from H.D. to John Cournos', *Iowa Review*, 16, 3 (1986), 126–55

Holton, Robert. *Jarring Witnesses: Modern Fiction and the Representation of History* (New York, Harvester Wheatsheaf, 1994)

'Honest Mr. Baldwin', *New Statesman*, 17 November 1923, 168

'How Much Longer?', *Nation and Athenaeum*, 7 October 1922, 6–7

Hunt, Violet. 'What the Civilian Saw', *Poetry*, 9 (March 1917), 295

Hunt, Violet. 'Love's Last Leave', *More Tales of the Uneasy* (London, Heinemann, 1925)

Hussey, Mark, ed. *Virginia Woolf and War: Fiction, Reality, and Myth* (Syracuse University Press, 1991)

Hynes, Samuel. *A War Imagined: The First World War and English Culture* (London, The Bodley Head, 1990)

'Incidence of Mental Disease Directly Due to War', *The Lancet*, 23 October 1915, 931

'India's Demand', *New Statesman*, 18 August 1923, 539–41

Inge, W. R. 'The Future of the English Race', *Edinburgh Review*, 229 (April 1919), 209–31

'Insanity and the War', *The Lancet*, 4 September 1915, 553

Jameson, Fredric. *The Political Unconscious: Narrative as a Socially Symbolic Act* (London, Methuen, 1981)

Jenkin, Arthur. *A Tank Driver's Experiences: Or Incidents in a Soldier's Life* (London, Elliot Stock, 1922)

Jensen, Emily. 'Clarissa Dalloway's Respectable Suicide', in Jane Marcus, ed., *Virginia Woolf: A Feminist Slant* (Lincoln, University of Nebraska Press, 1983)

Jones, David. *In Parenthesis* (London, Faber and Faber, 1937)

Jones, Ernest. 'War and Individual Psychology', *Sociological Review*, 8 (1915), 167–80

Jones, Ernest. 'War Shock and Freud's Theory of the Neuroses' (1918), *Papers on Psycho-Analysis*, rev. edn (London, Baillière, Tindall and Cox, 1918)

Jones, Raymond. *Arthur Ponsonby: The Politics of Life* (London, Christopher Helm, 1989)

Judd, Alan. *Ford Madox Ford* (1990; London, Flamingo, 1991)

Jünger, Ernst. *Storm of Steel*, trans. Basil Creighton (1920; London, Chatto and Windus, 1929)

'Kadaver', *The Nation*, 26 May 1917, 198

'Kadaver', *The Nation*, 38 (1925), 171–2

'The "Kadaver" Controversy', *The Nation*, 19 May 1917, 168

Karl, Frederick R. *William Faulkner, American Writer: A Biography* (New York, Weidenfeld and Nicolson, 1989)

Keegan, John. *The Face of Battle: A Study of Agincourt, Waterloo and the Somme* (1976; London, Pimlico, 1991)

Kelly, Lionel, ed. *Richard Aldington: Papers from the Reading Symposium* (Department of English, Reading University, 1987)

Kelsey, Nigel. *D. H. Lawrence: Sexual Crisis* (Basingstoke, Macmillan, 1991)

Kemp, Sandra. *Kipling's Hidden Narratives* (Oxford, Blackwell, 1988)

Kent, Bruce. *The Spoils of War: The Politics, Economics, and Diplomacy of Reparations, 1918–1932* (Oxford, Clarendon, 1989)

Kern, Stephen. *The Culture of Time and Space 1880–1918* (Cambridge MA, Harvard University Press, 1983)

Keynes, John Maynard. *The Economic Consequences of the Peace* (1919; London, Macmillan, 1984)

Khan, Nosheen. *Women's Poetry of the First World War* (Hemel Hempstead, Harvester, 1988)

King, Michael, ed. *H.D.: Woman and Poet* (Orono, ME, National Poetry Foundation, 1986)

Kinkead-Weekes, Mark. *D. H. Lawrence: Triumph to Exile 1912–1922* (Cambridge University Press, 1996)

Kipling, Rudyard. *A Diversity of Creatures* (1917; Harmondsworth, Penguin, 1987)

Kipling, Rudyard. *War Stories and Poems*, ed. Andrew Rutherford (Oxford University Press, 1990)

Klein, Holger, ed. *The First World War in Fiction* (1976; rev. edn London, Macmillan, 1978)

Klein, Melanie. *Love, Guilt and Reparation and Other Works 1921–1945* (1975; London, Virago, 1988)

Klein, Melanie. *The Selected Melanie Klein*, ed. Juliet Mitchell (Harmondsworth, Penguin, 1986)

Knapp, Steven. 'Collective Memory and the Actual Past', *Representations*, 26 (spring 1989), 123–49

Knightley, Philip. *The First Casualty: The War Correspondent as Hero, Propagandist, and Myth Maker from the Crimea to Vietnam* (London, Andre Deutsch, 1975)

Kristeva, Julia. *Powers of Horror: An Essay on Abjection*, trans. Leon S. Roudiez (1980; New York, Columbia University Press, 1982)

L., M. A. 'An American Novelist', *Manchester Guardian*, 11 July 1930, 7

'The Laboratory of War-Truth: 1920', *The Nation*, 27 October 1917, 118–19

Lacan, Jacques. *The Four Fundamental Concepts of Psychoanalysis*, ed. Jacques-Alain Miller, trans. Alan Sheridan (1973; Harmondsworth, Penguin, 1986)

Lasswell, Harold D. *Propaganda Technique in the World War* (London, Kegan Paul etc., 1927)

Lasswell, Harold D. *Psychopathology and Politics* (University of Chicago Press, 1930)

Lawrence, D. H. *The Prussian Officer* (1914; Harmondsworth, Penguin, 1981)

Lawrence, D. H. *Aaron's Rod* (1922; Harmondsworth, Penguin, 1960)

Lawrence, D. H. *England, My England and Other Stories*, ed. Bruce Steele (1922; Cambridge University Press, 1990)

Lawrence, D. H. *The Collected Letters of D. H. Lawrence*, vol. 2, 1913–16, ed. George J. Zytaruk and James T. Boulton (Cambridge University Press, 1981)

Lawrence, D. H. *Women in Love*, ed. David Farmer, Lindeth Vasey, and John Worthen (1921; Cambridge University Press, 1987)

'Le Feu', *Times Literary Supplement*, 5 April 1917, 164

Lee, Charles L. *The End of Order: Versailles 1919* (London, Secker and Warburg, 1981)

Lee, Hermione. *Virginia Woolf* (London, Chatto and Windus, 1996)

Leed, Eric. *No Man's Land: Combat and Identity in World War I* (Cambridge University Press, 1979)

Lehmann, Rosamund. *Dusty Answer* (London, Chatto and Windus, 1927)

Levenback, Karen L. 'Clarissa Dalloway, Doris Kilman, and the Great War', *Virginia Woolf Miscellany*, 37 (fall 1991), 3–4

Levenson, Michael. *A Genealogy of Modernism: A Study of English Literary Doctrine 1908–1922* (Cambridge University Press, 1984)

Lewis, Wyndham. 'The French Poodle', *The Egoist*, 1 March 1916

Lewis, Wyndham. 'Cantleman's Spring-Mate', *The Little Review* (October 1917), rpt in *Unlucky for Pringle*, ed. C. J. Fox and Robert T. Chapman (London, Vision Press, 1973)

Lewis, Wyndham. 'William Faulkner, The Moralist with the Corn-Cob', in *Men without Art*, ed. Seamus Cooney (1934; Santa Rosa, Black Sparrow Press, 1987), 37–53

Lewis, Wyndham. *Blasting and Bombadiering: An Autobiography 1914–1926* (1937; rev. edn London, Calder and Boyars, 1967)

Leys, Ruth. 'Traumatic Cures: Shell Shock, Janet, and the Question of Memory', *Critical Inquiry*, 20, 4 (1994), 623–62

Leys, Ruth. 'Death Masks: Kardiner and Ferenczi on Psychic Trauma', *Representations*, 53 (1996), 44–73

'Liberal Idealism', review of Irene Cooper Willis, *England's Holy War*, *Times Literary Supplement*, 20 September 1928, 655

Liddell Hart, B. H. 'The Tale of the Tank', *Nineteenth Century and After*, 112 (1932), 595–607

Limon, John. *Writing After War: American War Fiction from Realism to Postmodernism* (New York, Oxford University Press, 1994)

Lindsay, T. F. and Harrington, Michael. *The Conservative Party, 1918–1970* (London, Macmillan, 1974)

Lippmann, Walter. *The Political Scene: An Essay on the Victory of 1918* (London, George Allen and Unwin, 1919)

Lippmann, Walter. *Public Opinion* (New York, Harcourt, Brace and Co., 1922)

'The Liquidation of Mr. Lloyd George', *Nation and Athenaeum*, 23 September 1922, 814–15

'Literature and the War', *Times Literary Supplement*, 1 June 1916, 253

Littlejohns, Richard. '"Der Krieg hat uns für alles verdorben": The Real Theme of *Im Westen Nichts Neues*', *Modern Languages*, 70, 2 (1989), 89–94

Lloyd George, David. *The Truth about the Peace Treaties*, 2 vols. (London, Victor Gollancz Ltd, 1938)

Longenbach, James. 'Ford Madox Ford: The Novelist as Historian', *Princeton University Library Chronicle*, 45, 2 (1984), 150–66

'Loss of the Lusitania: The Last Scenes', *The Times*, 10 May 1915, 9

'The Lost Cunard Liner', *The Times*, 8 May 1915, 11

Lumley, Frederick E. *The Propaganda Menace* (New York, The Century Co., 1933)

'The Lusitania Victims', *The Times*, 17 May 1915, 5

Lutz, Ralph. 'Studies of World War Propaganda', *Journal of Modern History*, 5 (1933), 496–517

Lynn, Escott. *Tommy of the Tanks* (London, Chambers, 1919)

Macaulay, Rose. *Non-Combatants and Others* (London, Hodder and Stoughton, 1916)

MacCurdy, John. *War Neuroses* (Cambridge University Press, 1918)

MacDonnell, George. *England, Their England* (1933; London, Macmillan, 1946)

McNaron, Toni. '"The Albanians, or was it the Armenians?": Virginia Woolf's Lesbianism as Gloss on her Modernism', in Vara Neverow-Turk and Mark Hussey, eds, *Virginia Woolf: Themes and Variations* (New York, Pace University Press, 1993)

MacShane, F., ed. *Ford Madox Ford: The Critical Heritage* (London, Routledge and Kegan Paul, 1972)

Mallett, Phillip, ed. *Kipling Considered* (Basingstoke, Macmillan, 1989)

Manning, Frederic. *The Middle Parts of Fortune* (1930; London, Penguin, 1990)

Mansfield, Katherine. *The Critical Writings of Katherine Mansfield*, ed. Clare Hanson (Basingstoke, Macmillan 1987)

Manson, Janet. 'Leonard Woolf, the League of Nations Society and the Journal *War and Peace*', in Mark Hussey, ed., *Virginia Woolf Miscellanies* (New York, Pace University Press, 1992)

Marcus, Jane. 'The Asylums of Anteus. Women, War and Madness: Is there a Feminist Fetishism?' in Elizabeth Meese and Alice Parker, eds, *The Difference Within: Feminism and Critical Theory* (Philadelphia, John Benjamins Publishing Co., 1989), 49–83

Marcus, Jane, ed. *Virginia Woolf: A Feminist Slant* (Lincoln, University of Nebraska Press, 1983)

Marwick, Arthur. *The Deluge: British Society and the First World War*, 2nd edn (Basingstoke, Macmillan, 1991)

Masterman, C. F. G. 'The Murder of Armenia', *The Nation*, 20 November 1915, 279–80

'The Meaning of Lausanne', *Nation and Athenaeum*, 10 February 1923, 710–11

'Medical Precautions in Case of Air Raids', *The Lancet*, 9 January 1915, 86

Melson, Robert F. *Revolution and Genocide: On the Origins of the Armenian Genocide and the Holocaust* (Chicago University Press, 1992)

'Men and Soldiers', *The Nation*, 10 March 1917, 759–60

Mensch, Barbara. *D. H. Lawrence and the Authoritarian Personality* (Basingstoke, Macmillan, 1991)

Merskey, Harold. *The Analysis of Hysteria* (London, Baillière Tindall, 1979)

Merskey, Harold. 'Shell Shock', in G. E. Berrios and H. Freeman, eds, *150 Years of British Psychiatry, 1841–1991* (London, Gaskell, 1991), 245–67

Messinger, Gary. *British Propaganda and the State in the First World War* (Manchester University Press, 1992)

Meyer, Eric. 'Ford's War and (Post)Modern Memory: *Parade's End* and National Allegory', *Criticism*, 32, 1 (1990), 81–99

Micale, Mark. *Approaching Hysteria* (Princeton University Press, 1995)

*Microbe-Culture at Bukarest: Discoveries at the German Legation: From the Rumanian Official Documents* (London, Hodder and Stoughton, 1917)

Middleton, Peter. 'The Academic Development of the Waste Land', *Glyph Textual Studies*, 1 (1986), 153–80

Middleton, Peter. *The Inward Gaze: Masculinity and Subjectivity in Modern Culture* (London, Routledge, 1992)

Miller, H. Crichton, ed. *Functional Nerve Disease* (London, Henry Frowde, Hodder and Stoughton, and Oxford University Press, 1920)

Miller, Wayne Charles. *An Armed America: Its Face in Fiction: A History of the American Military Novel* (New York University Press, 1970)

Millgate, Michael. 'William Faulkner, Cadet', *University of Toronto Quarterly* (January 1966)

Minow-Pinkney, Makiko. *Virginia Woolf and the Problem of the Subject* (Brighton, Harvester, 1987)

Minter, David. *William Faulkner: His Life and Work* (Baltimore, Johns Hopkins University Press, 1980)

'Mr. Baldwin?', *New Statesman*, 26 May 1923, 188–9

'Mr. Churchill and the Lusitania', *The Times*, 11 May 1915, 12

*Mr Punch's History of the Great War* (London, Cassell, 1919)

Mitchell, Frank. *Tank Warfare: The Story of the Tanks of the Great War* (1933; Stevenage, Spa Books, 1987)

Mitchell, Juliet. *Psychoanalysis and Feminism* (1974; Harmondsworth, Penguin, 1982)

Mizener, Arthur. *The Saddest Story: A Biography of Ford Madox Ford* (London, The Bodley Head, 1971)

Monk, Ray. *Bertrand Russell: The Spirit of Solitude* (London, Jonathan Cape, 1996)

Monk, Ray. 'The Tiger and the Machine: D. H. Lawrence and Bertrand Russell', *Philosophy of the Social Sciences*, 26, 2 (1996), 205–46

Montague, C. E. *Disenchantment* (London, Chatto and Windus, 1922)

Morel, E. D. *Truth and the War* (London, National Labour Press, 1916)

Morgan, J. H. *German Atrocities: An Official Investigation* (London, T. Fisher Unwin, 1916)

Morgan, Louise. 'Writing a Best-Seller in Seven Weeks', *Everyman*, 4 (1930–1), 101–2

Moriarty, Catherine. 'Christian Iconography and First World War Memorials', *Imperial War Museum Review*, 6, n.d. [*c*. 1991], 63–75

Morrisson, Mark. 'The Myth of the Whole: Ford's *English Review*, the *Mercure de France*, and Early British Modernism', *ELH*, 63, 2 (1996), 513–33

Moser, Thomas. *The Life in the Fiction of Ford Madox Ford* (Princeton University Press, 1980)

Mott, F. W. *War Neuroses and Shell Shock* (London, Hodder and Stoughton, 1919)

Mulvey, Laura. *Visual and Other Pleasures* (Basingstoke, Macmillan, 1989)

Nassibian, Akaby. *Britain and the Armenian Question 1915–1923* (London, Croom Helm, 1984)

'Neurasthenia and Shell Shock' (leader), *The Lancet*, 18 March 1916, 627–8

Nicholls, Peter. *Modernisms: A Literary Guide* (Basingstoke, Macmillan, 1995)

Nicolson, Harold. *Peacemaking 1919* (1933; New York, Universal Library, 1965)

Nicolson, Harold. *Curzon: The Last Phase 1919–1925* (London, Constable, 1934)

Nochlin, Linda, and Tamar Garb, eds, *The Jew in the Text: Modernity and the Construction of Identity* (London, Thames and Hudson, 1995)

'Notes for the Novel-Reader: Fiction of the Month', *Illustrated London News*, 26 July 1930, 175

Novak, Jane. *The Razor Edge of Balance: A Study of Virginia Woolf* (Miami University Press, 1975)

Occleshaw, Michael. *Armour Against Fate: British Military Intelligence in the First World War* (London, Columbus Books, 1989)

Orel, Harold. *A Kipling Chronology* (Basingstoke, Macmillan, 1990)

Orel, Harold. *Popular Fiction in England, 1914–1918* (Hemel Hempstead, Harvester Wheatsheaf, 1992)

Orel, Sinasi, and Sureyya Yuca, *The Talat Pasha 'Telegrams': Historical Fact or Armenian Fiction?* (Nicosia, K. Rustem and Bro., 1986)

Orwell, George. Review of *Death of a Hero*, *New English Weekly*, 20 September 1936; rpt in *Collected Essays, Journals and Letters* (Harmondsworth, Penguin, 1970)

Ouditt, Sharon. *Fighting Forces, Writing Women: Identity and Ideology in the First World War* (London, Routledge, 1994)

'Our "Patriot" Press', *The Nation*, 19 May 1917, 159–60

'The Outlaws of Civilization' (leader), *The Times*, 10 May 1915, 9

'The Outlook in India', *New Statesman*, 23 June 1923, 320–1

Page, Norman. 'What Happens in "Mary Postgate"?', *English Literature in Transition*, 29, 1 (1986), 41–7

Parfitt, George. *Fiction of the First World War: A Study* (London, Faber and Faber, 1988)

Parker, Andrew *et al.*, eds. *Nationalisms and Sexualities* (New York, Routledge, 1992)

Perry, Ralph R. 'The Bonus: A Veteran's Opinion', *Outlook*, 128 (1921), 512–13

Peterson, H. C. *Propaganda for War: The Campaign Against American Neutrality, 1914–1917* (Princeton University Press, 1939)

Phillips, W. Alison. 'The Peace Settlements: 1815 and 1919', *Edinburgh Review*, 230 (July 1919), 1–21

Pick, Daniel. *War Machine: The Rationalisation of Slaughter in the Modern Age* (New Haven, Yale University Press, 1993)

Pickerill, H. P. 'Methods of Control of Fragments in Gunshot Wounds of the Jaws', *The Lancet*, 7 September 1918, 313–16

Pinkney, Tony. *D. H. Lawrence* (Hemel Hempstead, Harvester Wheatsheaf, 1990)

'Plastic Surgery of the Face' (leader), *The Lancet*, 17 March 1917, 419–20

Ponsonby, Arthur. 'Votes for Soldiers', *The Nation*, 15 September 1917, 603–5

Ponsonby, Arthur. *Falsehood in War-Time* (London, George Allen and Unwin, 1928)

Pope, Stephen and Elizabeth-Anne Wheal. *Macmillan Dictionary of the First World War* (Basingstoke, Macmillan, 1995)

Potter, Jane. 'A Great Purifier: The Great War in Women's Romances and Memoirs', in Raitt and Tate, eds, *Women's Fiction and the Great War*

'The Power of the Press' [editorial], *Edinburgh Review*, 227 (April 1918) 383–91

Preston, Peter. *A D. H. Lawrence Chronology* (Basingstoke, Macmillan, 1994)

Price, Alan. *The End of the Age of Innocence: Edith Wharton and the First World War* (London, Hale, 1996)

'Propaganda in the War', review of Harold Lasswell, *Propaganda Technique in the World War*, *Times Literary Supplement*, 12 January 1928, 18

Proteus, 'Current Literature: New Novels', *New Statesman*, 35 (28 June 1930), 369

Putzel, Max. *Genius of Place: William Faulkner's Triumphant Beginnings* (Baton Rouge, Louisiana State University Press, 1985)

Raitt, Suzanne. *Vita and Virginia* (Oxford, Clarendon, 1993)

Raitt, Suzanne. '"Contagious Ecstasy": May Sinclair's War Journals', in Raitt and Tate, eds, *Women's Fiction and the Great War*

Raitt, Suzanne, and Tate, Trudi, eds. *Women's Fiction and the Great War* (Oxford, Clarendon, 1997)

Read, C. Stanford. *Military Psychology in Peace and War* (London, H. K. Lewis, 1920)

Read, Herbert. *In Retreat* (London, Hogarth, 1925)

Read, Herbert. *Collected Poems* (1966; London, Sinclair-Stevenson, n.d.)

Read, James Morgan. *Atrocity Propaganda 1914–1919* (1941; New York, Arno, 1972)

Reeves, Nicholas. *Official British Film Propaganda during the First World War* (London, Croom Helm and IWM, 1986)

Remarque, Erich Maria. *All Quiet on the Western Front*, trans. A. W. Wheen (1929; London, Picador, [1990])

Review of M. D. Eder, *War Shock: The Psychoneuroses in War: Psychology and Treatment* (London, William Heinemann, 1917), *The Lancet*, 1 December 1917, 828

Richter, Donald. *Chemical Soldiers: British Gas Warfare in World War I* (Lawrence, Kansas University Press, 1992)

Richter, Harvena. 'The *Ulysses* Connection: Clarissa Dalloway's Bloomsday', *Studies in the Novel*, 21, 3 (1989)

Rivers, W. H. R. 'The Repression of War Experience', *The Lancet*, 2 February 1918, 173–7

Rivers, W. H. R. *Instinct and the Unconscious*, 2nd edn (Cambridge University Press, 1922)

Roberts, Warren. *A Bibliography of D. H. Lawrence*, 2nd edn (Cambridge University Press, 1982)

Roby, Kinley E. *A Writer at War: Arnold Bennett, 1914–1918* (Baton Rouge, Louisiana State University Press, 1972)

Rodowick, D. N. *The Crisis of Political Modernism* (Urbana, University of Illinois Press, 1988)

Rodowick, D. N. *The Difficulty of Difference: Psychoanalysis, Sexual Difference, and Film Theory* (London, Routledge, 1991)

Roessel, David. '"Mr. Eugenides, the Smyrna Merchant" and Post-War Politics in *The Waste Land*', *Journal of Modern Literature*, 16, 1 (1989), 171–6

Rollyson, Carl E. *Uses of the Past in the Novels of William Faulkner* (Epping, Bowker, 1984)

Rose, Jacqueline. *Sexuality in the Field of Vision* (London, Verso, 1986)

Rose, Jacqueline. *Why War?* (Oxford, Blackwell, 1993)

Rose, Jacqueline. *States of Fantasy* (Oxford, Clarendon, 1996)

Roth, Michael. *Psycho-Analysis as History: Negation and Freedom in Freud* (New York, Columbia University Press, 1987)

Roth, Michael. *The Ironist's Cage: Memory, Trauma and the Construction of History* (New York, Columbia University Press, 1995)

Russell, Bertrand. *The Autobiography of Bertrand Russell*, vol. 2, 1914–44 (London, George Allen and Unwin, 1968)

Rutherford, Andrew. *The Literature of War: Studies in Heroic Virtue* (1978; rev. edn Basingstoke, Macmillan, 1989)

Sagar, Keith, ed. *A D. H. Lawrence Handbook* (Manchester University Press, 1982)

Sanders, Michael L., and Taylor, Philip M. *British Propaganda During the First World War* (Basingstoke, Macmillan, 1982)

'Satisfaction in Germany: Alleged Cargo of Munitions: Victims Themselves to Blame', *The Times*, 10 May 1915, 12

Saunders, Max. *Ford Madox Ford: A Dual Life*, 2 vols (Oxford, Clarendon, 1996)

Sayers, Janet. *Mothering Psychoanalysis* (London, Hamish Hamilton, 1991)

Scarry, Elaine. *The Body in Pain: The Making and Unmaking of the World* (Oxford University Press, 1985)

Schröder, Leena. '*Mrs Dalloway* and the Female Vagrant', *Essays in Criticism*, 45, 4 (1995)

Schwartz, Harvey, ed. *Psychotherapy of the Combat Veteran* (Lancaster, MTP Press Ltd, 1984)

Scott, Joan Wallach. *Gender and the Politics of History* (New York, Columbia University Press, 1988)

Segal, Hanna. *Introduction to the Work of Melanie Klein* (London, Karnac Books, 1988)

Seltzer, Mark. *Bodies and Machines* (London, Routledge, 1992)

Seymour-Smith, Martin. *Robert Graves: His Life and Work* (London, Hutchinson, 1982)

Seymour-Smith, Martin. *Rudyard Kipling* (London, Macdonald, 1989)

Shairp, L. V. 'The Re-Education of Disabled Soldiers', *Edinburgh Review*, 225 (January 1917), 119–38

Sharp, Alan. *The Versailles Settlement: Peacemaking in Paris, 1919* (Basingstoke, Macmillan, 1991)

'Shell Shock in Cows', *The Lancet*, 2 February 1918, 187–8

Showalter, Elaine. *The Female Malady: Women, Madness and English Culture, 1830–1980* (1985; London, Virago, 1987)

Siegel, Carol. *Lawrence Among the Women: Wavering Boundaries in Women's Literary Traditions* (Charlottesville, University of Virginia Press, 1991)

Silverman, Kaja. *Male Subjectivity at the Margins* (London, Routledge, 1992)

Simpson, Colin. *Lusitania* (London, Longman, 1972)

Simpson, Hilary. *D. H. Lawrence and Feminism* (London, Croom Helm, 1982)

Sinclair, May. *The Tree of Heaven* (London, Cassell, 1917)

'The Sinking of the Lusitania: Motive Behind the Crime', *The Times*, 10 May 1915, 5

Skidelsky, Robert. *John Maynard Keynes*, vol. 1, *Hopes Betrayed 1883–1920* (Basingstoke, Macmillan, 1983)

Small, Helen. 'Mrs Humphry Ward and the First Casualty of War', in Raitt and Tate, eds, *Women's Fiction and the Great War*

Smith, Helen Zenna (pseud. of Evadne Price). *Not So Quiet* (1930; London, Virago, 1988)

Smith, Paul. 'HD's Identity', *Women's Studies*, 10 (1984), 321–37

Smith, Stan. *The Origins of Modernism: Eliot, Pound, Yeats and the Rhetorics of Renewal* (Hemel Hempstead, Harvester, 1994)

Smither, Roger, ed., *The Battles of the Somme and Ancre* (London, Imperial War Museum, 1993)

Smithers, A. J. *A New Excalibur: The Development of the Tank 1909–1939* (London, Leo Cooper and Secker and Warburg, 1986)

Smithers, A. J. *Cambrai: The First Great Tank Battle 1917* (London, Leo Cooper, 1992)

Snow, Edward. 'Theorizing the Male Gaze: Some Problems', *Representations*, 25 (winter 1989), 30–41

Sossaman, Stephen, 'Sassoon and Blunden's Annotation of *Goodbye to All That*', *Focus on Robert Graves*, 5 (1976), 87–9

Southgate, Donald, ed. *The Conservative Leadership 1832–1932* (London, Macmillan, 1974)

Spilka, Mark, ed. *D. H. Lawrence: A Collection of Critical Essays* (Englewood Cliffs NJ, Prentice-Hall, 1963)

Spoo, Robert. 'H.D.'s Dating of *Asphodel*: A Reassessment', *H.D. Newsletter*, 4, 2 (winter 1991)

Squires, J. D. *British Propaganda at Home and in the United States* (Cambridge MA, Harvard University Press, 1935)

Stang, Sondra, ed. *The Presence of Ford Madox Ford* (Philadelphia, University of Pennsylvania Press, 1981)

Steele, Bruce. Introduction to D. H. Lawrence, *England, My England* (Cambridge University Press, 1990)

Stein, Gertrude. 'Composition as Explanation' (1926), rpt in *Look At Me Now and Here I Am: Writings and Lectures 1909–45*, ed. Patricia Meyerowitz (Harmondsworth, Penguin, 1984)

Stein, Gertrude. *The Autobiography of Alice B. Toklas* (1933; Harmondsworth, Penguin, 1966)

Stein, Gertrude. *Wars I Have Seen* (1945; London, Brilliance Books, 1984)

Stevenson, David. *The First World War and International Politics* (Oxford University Press, 1988)

Stevenson, Randall. *Modernist Fiction* (Hemel Hempstead, Harvester Wheatsheaf, 1992)

Stone, Martin. 'Shellshock and the Psychologists', in W. F. Bynum, Roy Porter and Michael Shepherd, eds, *The Anatomy of Madness: Essays in the History of Psychiatry*, vol. 2 (London, Tavistock, 1985)

Street, J. C. (Major). 'Propaganda Behind the Lines', *Cornhill Magazine*, n. s. 47 (November 1919), 488–99

Swinton, E. D. *Eyewitness* (London, Hodder and Stoughton, 1932)

Sword, Helen. 'Orpheus and Eurydice in the Twentieth Century: Lawrence, H.D., and the Poetics of the Turn', *Twentieth Century Literature*, 35, 4 (1989), 407–28

Tate, Trudi. '*Mrs Dalloway* and the Armenian Question', *Textual Practice*, 8, 3 (1994)

Tate, Trudi, ed. *Women, Men and the Great War: An Anthology of Stories* (Manchester University Press, 1995)

Tate, Trudi. 'HD's War Neurotics', in Raitt and Tate, eds, *Women's Fiction and the Great War*

Tate, Trudi. 'The Culture of the Tank, 1916–1918', *Modernism/Modernity*, 4, 1 (1997)

Tate, Trudi. 'From Little Willie to Mother', *Women: A Cultural Review*, 8, 1 (1997)

Tate, Trudi. 'Rumour, Propaganda, and *Parade's End*', *Essays in Criticism*, 47, 4 (1997)

Taylor, A. J. P. *English History 1914–1945* (Oxford, Clarendon, 1965)

Taylor, John. *War Photography: Realism in the British Press* (London, Routledge, 1991)

Taylor, Philip. *Munitions of the Mind*, rev. edn (Manchester University Press, 1995)

Taylor, S. J. *The Great Outsiders: Northcliffe, Rothermere and the Daily Mail* (London, Weidenfeld and Nicolson, 1996)

Terraine, John. *White Heat: The New Warfare 1914–1918* (London, Sidgwick and Jackson, 1982)

Theweleit, Klaus. *Male Fantasies*, vol. 1, trans. Stephen Conway (1977; Cambridge, Polity, 1987)

Theweleit, Klaus. *Male Fantasies*, vol. 2, trans. Chris Turner and Erica Carter (1978; Cambridge, Polity, 1989)

Thomas, Sue. 'Virginia Woolf's Septimus Smith and Contemporary Perceptions of Shell Shock', *English Language Notes*, 25, 2 (1987), 49–57

Thomas, W. Beach. *With the British on the Somme* (London, Methuen, 1917)

Thompson, Sylvia. *The Hounds of Spring* (London, William Heinemann, 1926)

Thorpe, Andrew. *The Longman Companion to Britain in the Era of Two World Wars* (London, Longman, 1994)

Tomlinson, Kathleen C. 'New Novels', *Nation and Athenaeum*, 12 July 1930, 477–8

Tomlinson, Nora, and Robert Green, 'Ford's Wartime Journalism', *Agenda*, special issue on Ford (London, Agenda, 1989)

'Torture of a Canadian Officer', *The Times*, 10 May 1915, 7

Toynbee, Arnold. *Nationality and the War* (London, Dent, 1915)

Toynbee, Arnold. *Survey of International Affairs, 1920–1923* (Oxford University Press, 1925)

Toynbee, Arnold. *The Conduct of the British Empire Foreign Relations since the Peace Settlement* (Oxford University Press, 1928)

Tratner, Michael. *Modernism and Mass Politics: Joyce, Woolf, Eliot, Yeats* (Stanford University Press, 1995)

'Treatment of Minorities: Turkey and the League', *The Times*, 10 January 1923, 10

'Treatment of War Psycho-Neuroses', *British Medical Journal*, 7 December 1918, 634

Trotter, David. 'Hueffer's Englishness', *Agenda*, special issue on Ford (London, Agenda, 1989), 148–55

Trotter, David. *The English Novel in History, 1895–1920* (London, Routledge, 1993)

Trumbo, Dalton. *Johnny Got His Gun* (1939; London, Simon and Schuster, 1994)

Turner, John, ed. *Britain and the First World War* (London, Unwin Hyman, 1988)

Tylee, Claire M. '"Maleness Run Riot": The Great War and Women's Resistance to Militarism', *Women's Studies International Forum*, 11, 3 (1988), 199–210

Tylee, Claire M. *The Great War and Women's Consciousness: Images of Militarism and Womanhood in Women's Writings, 1914–64* (Basingstoke, Macmillan, 1990)

'Under Fire', *Bookman*, October 1917, 40.

'Undertones of War', *Times Literary Supplement*, 6 December 1928, 949

Usui, Masami. 'The Female Victims of the War in *Mrs Dalloway*', in Mark Hussey, ed., *Virginia Woolf and War: Fiction, Reality, and Myth* (Syracuse University Press, 1991)

Vickers, Miranda. *The Albanians: A Modern History* (London, I. B. Tauris, 1995)

Viereck, George Sylvester. *Spreading Germs of Hate* (London, Duckworth, 1931)

Virilio, Paul. *War and Cinema: The Logistics of Perception*, trans. Patrick Camiller (1984; London, Verso, 1989)

Virilio, Paul. *The Vision Machine*, trans. Julie Rose (Bloomington and London, Indiana University Press and the British Film Institute, 1994)

'The War and Nervous Breakdown' (leader), *The Lancet*, 23 January 1915, 189–90

'War Paintings by Wyndham Lewis', *The Nation*, 8 February 1919, 546–7

'The War and Nervous Breakdown' (leader), *The Lancet*, 23 January 1915, 189–90

'The War in Relation to Insanity', *The Lancet*, 25 September 1915, 732

'War on Tap', *Nation and Athenaeum*, 7 October 1922, 7–8

'War Shock in the Civilian', *The Lancet*, 4 March 1916, 522

Ward, Mrs Humphry. *Towards the Goal* (London, John Murray, 1917)

Ward, Stephen R. *The War Generation: Veterans of the First World War* (Port Washington NY, Kennikat Press, 1975)

Watson, James G. *William Faulkner: Letters and Fictions* (Austin, University of Texas Press, 1987)

Waugh, Evelyn. *Decline and Fall* (1928; Harmondsworth, Penguin, 1977)

Waugh, Evelyn. *Vile Bodies* (1930; London, Penguin, [1991])

Waugh, Patricia. *Feminine Fictions: Revisiting the Postmodern* (London, Routledge, 1989)

West, Rebecca. *The Return of the Soldier* (1918; London, Virago, 1980)

Wharton, Edith. *A Son at the Front* (London, Macmillan, 1923)

'Wholesale Murder in Armenia: Exterminating a Race', *The Times*, 30 September 1915, 5

Wiesenfarth, Joseph. 'The Art of Fiction and the Art of War: Henry James, H. G. Wells, and Ford Madox Ford', *Connotations*, 1, 1 (1991), 55–73

William Foster and Co. *The Tank: Its Birth and Development* (1920; Hinckley, T.E.E. Publishing, 1977)

Williams, Gordon. '"Remember the *Llandovery Castle*": Cases of Atrocity Propaganda in the First World War', in Jeremy Hawthorn, ed., *Propaganda, Persuasion and Polemic* (London, Edward Armold, 1987)

Williams, Linda Ruth. *Sex in the Head: Visions of Femininity and Film in D. H. Lawrence* (Hemel Hempstead, Harvester Wheatsheaf, 1993)

Williamson, Henry. *The Patriot's Progress* (1930; rev. edn London, Sphere, 1991)

Wilson, Angus. *The Strange Ride of Rudyard Kipling: His Life and Works* (London, Secker and Warburg, 1977)

Wilson, Trevor. *The Myriad Faces of War: Britain and the Great War, 1914–1918* (Cambridge, Polity, 1986)

Wiltshire, Harold. 'A Contribution to the Etiology of Shell Shock', *The Lancet*, 17 June 1916, 1207–12

Winter, Denis. *Death's Men: Soldiers of the Great War* (London, Allen Lane, 1978)

Winter, J. M. *The Great War and the British People* (Basingstoke, Macmillan, 1986)

Winter, J. M. *The Experience of World War I* (Oxford, Equinox, 1988)

Winter, J. M. *Sites of Memory, Sites of Mourning: The Great War in European Cultural History* (Cambridge University Press, 1995)

*The Wipers Times*, compiled and introd. Patrick Beaver (London: Papermac, 1988)

Wittenberg, Judith Bryant. *Faulkner: The Transfiguration of Biography* (Lincoln, University of Nebraska Press, 1979)

'Wittenberg', review of *The Horrors of Wittenberg*, *Times Literary Supplement*, 8 June 1916, 266

Wolfsohn, Julian M. 'The Predisposing Factors of War Psycho-Neuroses', *The Lancet*, 2 February 1918, 177–80

*Women: A Cultural Review*, 1, 2, special issue on Melanie Klein (1990)

Woods, Roger. 'The Conservative Revolution and the First World War: Literature as Evidence in Historical Explanation', *Modern Language Review*, 85 (January 1990), 77–91

Woolf, Leonard. *Beginning Again: An Autobiography of the Years 1911–1918* (London, The Hogarth Press, 1964)

Woolf, Leonard. *Downhill All the Way: An Autobiography of the Years 1919–1939* (London, Hogarth, 1967)

Woolf, Virginia. *Jacob's Room* (1922; Oxford University Press, 1992)

Woolf, Virginia. *Mrs Dalloway* (1925; Oxford University Press, 1992)

Woolf, Virginia. *To the Lighthouse* (1927; Oxford University Press, 1992)

Woolf, Virginia. *The Years* (1937; Oxford University Press, 1992)

Woolf, Virginia. *Three Guineas* (1938; Oxford University Press, 1992)

Woolf, Virginia. *The Diary of Virginia Woolf*, vol. 1, 1915–19, ed. Anne Olivier Bell (1977; Harmondsworth, Penguin, 1979)

Woolf, Virginia. *The Pargiters*, ed. Mitchell Leaska (London, Hogarth, 1978)

Woolf, Virginia. *The Diary of Virginia Woolf*, vol. 2, 1920–24, ed. Anne Olivier Bell

(1978; Harmondsworth, Penguin, 1981)

Woolf, Virginia. *The Diary of Virginia Woolf*, vol. 3, 1925–30, ed. Anne Olivier Bell (1980; Harmondsworth, Penguin, 1982)

Woolf, Virginia. *The Essays of Virginia Woolf*, vol. 2, 1912–18, ed. Andrew McNeillie (London, Hogarth, 1987)

Worthen, John. *D. H. Lawrence and the Idea of the Novel* (Basingstoke, Macmillan, 1979)

Worthen, John. *D. H. Lawrence: A Literary Life* (Basingstoke, Macmillan, 1989)

Wright, D. G. 'The Great War, Government Propaganda and English "Men of Letters" 1914–1916', *Literature and History*, 7 (1978)

Wright, Elizabeth. *Psychoanalytic Criticism* (London, Methuen, 1984)

Wright, Elizabeth, ed. *Feminism and Psychoanalysis: A Critical Dictionary* (Oxford, Blackwell, 1992)

'Zeppelin Raids', *The Times*, 23 September 1915, 7

'The Zeppelin Threat: Surgical First Aid for the Metropolis', *The Lancet*, 22 May 1915, 1104

Zilboorg, Caroline. 'Richard Aldington in Transition: His Pieces for the *Sphere* in 1919', *Twentieth Century Literature*, 34, 4 (winter 1988), 489–506

Zilboorg, Caroline. 'H.D. and R.A.: Early Love and the Exclusion of Ezra Pound', *H.D. Newsletter*, 3, 1 (1990), 26–34

Zizek, Slavoj. *The Sublime Object of Ideology* (London, Verso, 1989)

Zizek, Slavoj. *Looking Awry: An Introduction to Jacques Lacan through Popular Culture* (Cambridge MA, MIT Press, 1991)

Zwerdling, Alex. *Virginia Woolf and the Real World* (Berkeley, University of California Press, 1986)

# INDEX

'n.' refers to a note on the page indicated.